Farm Income in India

Farm Income in India

Myths and Realities

A. NARAYANAMOORTHY

OXFORD
UNIVERSITY PRESS

OXFORD
UNIVERSITY PRESS

Oxford University Press is a department of the University of Oxford. It furthers the University's objective of excellence in research, scholarship, and education by publishing worldwide. Oxford is a registered trademark of Oxford University Press in the UK and in certain other countries.

Published in India by
Oxford University Press
22 Workspace, 2nd Floor, 1/22 Asaf Ali Road, New Delhi 110002, India

First Edition published in 2021

ISBN-13 (print edition): 978-0-19-012613-1
ISBN-10 (print edition): 0-19-012613-2

ISBN-13 (eBook): 978-0-19-099158-6
ISBN-10 (eBook): 0-19-099158-5

Typeset in Adobe Garamond Pro 11/13
by Tranistics Data Technologies, Kolkata 700 091
Printed in India by Rakmo Press, New Delhi 110 020

To
My father
Narayanasamy Annasamy
from whom I learned the real economics of farming

Contents

PART III PROFITABILITY AND FARM INCOME

PART IV FOOD SECURITY, PROCUREMENT, AND FARM INCOME

PART V INPUT USE, INFRASTRUCTURE, AND FARM INCOME

Tables and Figures

Tables

Figures

Abbreviations

ACP	agrarian crisis period
ADM	average distance to market
AEZ	agro-ecological zones
AIMTO	area irrigated more than once
APMC	Agricultural Produce Marketing Committee
APMT	absolute procurement
ASMTO	area sown more than once
CACP	Commission for Agricultural Costs and Prices
CCS	Cost of Cultivation Survey
CGR	compound growth rate
CI	cropping intensity
CIFA	Confederation of Indian Farmers Association
COC	cost of cultivation
CPIAL	Consumer Price Index for Agricultural Labourers
CRIDA	Central Research Institute for Dry Land Agriculture
CV	coefficient of variation
CWC	Central Water Commission
DA	dearness allowance
DMI	drip method of irrigation
ESCAP	Economic and Social Commission for Asia and the Pacific
FGA	foodgrains area

FCI	Food Corporation of India
FIRMs	Farmers' Involved Regulated Markets
FRP	fair and remunerative price
GCA	gross cropped area
GDP	gross domestic product
GIA	gross irrigated area
GM	genetically modified
GOAP	Government of Andhra Pradesh
GoI	Government of India
GRP	Green Revolution period
GVO	gross value of output
ha	hectare
HAHP	high area high productivity
HALP	high area low productivity
HPS	high productivity states
HYVs	high yielding varieties
kg	kilogramme
LAMP	low area with medium productivity
LPS	low productivity states
MAHP	medium area with high productivity
MGNREGA	Mahatma Gandhi National Rural Employment Guarantee Act
MGNREGS	Mahatma Gandhi National Rural Employment Guarantee Scheme
mha	million hectares
MIS	Market Intervention Scheme
mm	millimetre
MoA	Ministry of Agriculture
MoRD	Ministry of Rural Development
MSP	minimum support price
mt	million tonnes
NCAER	National Council of Applied Economic Research
NCF	National Commission on Farmers
NCIWRD	National Commission on Integrated Water Resources Development
NIA	net irrigated area
NITI	National Institution for Transforming India
NSA	net sown area

NSAPAM	net sown area per agriculture market
NSS	National Sample Survey
NSSO	National Sample Survey Office
NWM	number of wholesale markets
OLS	ordinary least squares
PMT	procurement
PPMT	percentage of procurement
qtl	quintal (100 kg)
R&D	research and development
RBI	Reserve Bank of India
SANAP	states with the above national average in procurement
SAS	Situation Assessment Survey
SBNAP	states with the below national average in procurement
SHANLI	states having above national level irrigation
SHBNLI	states having below national level irrigation
SRI	System of Rice Intensification
SSI	Sustainable Sugarcane Initiative
TE	triennium ending
TFL	total fallow land
VAO	value of agriculture output
VOP	value of output
WPI	Wholesale Price Index
WTO	World Trade Organization
WWF	World Wide Fund

Foreword

Agricultural growth has a crucial role in the process of economic development, particularly in terms of its direct effect on rural economy and indirect spillover effects on urban economy. Very few countries in the world have achieved sustained gross domestic product (GDP) growth without agricultural growth in the early phase of their development. The virtuous cycle between agriculture and non-farm enterprises plays a strategic role in providing employment opportunities in rural areas. East Asian countries such as the Republic of Korea, Malaysia, Taiwan, and People's Republic China have experienced the transfer of labour from agriculture to manufacturing, which contributed to rapid reduction in poverty; whereas the structural changes in India did not conform to this pattern. The cycle between agriculture and non-farm enterprises, which plays a strategic role, is missing in India; the share of agriculture in GDP is sharply falling but the share of agricultural workers among the total workers in the country remains high.

What is the history of India's agriculture growth? Prior to Independence, agricultural production was virtually stagnant for several decades. The per capita agricultural output declined by 0.72 per cent per annum during 1911–41, and foodgrain output, a major source of food security, declined by 1.14 per cent per annum. The national government formed after Independence accorded high priority to agriculture by undertaking several measures.

The main policy thrust prior to the mid-1960s was on agrarian reforms as well as modernizing agriculture through large-scale investment in irrigation and power, creation of other infrastructure such as credit institutions, regulated markets, roads and extension, as well as research institutions. Community development schemes, national extension services, and cooperatives were promoted. These reforms and programmes could reverse the declining trend of agricultural growth and achieve productivity-led growth.

The good performance of agriculture witnessed during this early phase of planning could not be sustained. During the mid-1960s, when the population was rapidly growing, India experienced drought in successive years, in addition to two wars, which led to a food crisis. There was severe imbalance between the demand for and supply of food. This crisis prompted the government to give an overriding priority to the goal of achieving self-sufficiency in foodgrains by launching the Green Revolution. Public investment in irrigation and agricultural research was stepped up. India achieved near self-sufficiency in foodgrain production and experienced an improvement in food security. The 1980s were considered to be the best years of Indian agriculture when labour productivity and total factor productivity were at their peak. Consequently, the dependency on imports declined in the Green Revolution period. In the 1980s, production of cotton, chillies, and livestock products also recorded high growth. The acceleration in the growth of high-value agricultural products came, however, more from area shift from coarse cereals rather than from productivity improvement. There has also been a significant reduction in poverty, especially since the 1980s.

The early phase of the post-reform period (1990s) witnessed a decline in the overall growth rate of agriculture and allied sectors. It further slowed down in the 2000s and beyond. What is worse, foodgrain production recorded a very low growth rate between 2011–12 and 2016–17. This is undoubtedly leading to a worse form of agrarian crisis.

Understandably, the issue of farm income or farm profitability received more attention, especially after the late 1990s, because agrarian distress was contributing to farmers' suicides. The distress is attributed to the decline in the profitability of traditional agriculture. In order to increase farm income, many suggestions have been made by different committees and researchers. While some have suggested that the increased supply of institutional credit (mainly to marginal and small farmers and also tenant farmers) will help in improving the farm income, others have proposed that increased productivity of crops supported by remunerative prices will enhance farm income.

The author of the present volume, Professor A. Narayanamoorthy, an eminent agricultural economist and a prolific writer on contemporary issues, attempts to track Indian agriculture over the past five decades and addresses pertinent issues relating to farm income, such as what has been the state of farm income in India over the years? Are there significant differences in the level of farm income between irrigated and un-irrigated crops? Has the introduction of the Mahatma Gandhi National Rural Employment Guarantee Scheme (MGNREGS) affected farm income? What is the impact of irrigation development on farm profitability? Is there any relationship between rural infrastructure development and farm income? What are the determinants of farm income? Other than minimum support price (MSP), what other measures are needed to increase farm income? How does procurement policy influence farm income? What is the role of agricultural markets in determining farm income?

Professor A. Narayanamoorthy has not only made a valiant effort to cover a wide range of issues on farm income but also provided many useful policy prescriptions to policymakers to double farm income by 2022–3. I have no doubt that this volume will be very useful for researchers, policymakers, students, and other common readers who are concerned about Indian agriculture and farm income.

R. Radhakrishna
Chairman, Centre for Economic Social Studies, Hyderabad
Former Chairman, National Statistical Commission, Government of India, New Delhi
Former Director, Indira Gandhi Institute of Development Research, Mumbai
Former Vice Chancellor, Andhra University, Visakhapatnam
March 2020

Preface

Indian agriculture has made rapid strides in terms of production and productivity of different agricultural commodities, especially after the introduction of the Green Revolution, thanks to farmers' effort. But farmers have been passing through a painful phase during the last two decades. Farmers' suicides, indebtedness, crop failures, un-remunerative prices for crops, and poor returns over the cost of cultivation are the foremost features of India's agriculture today. Farmers committing suicide was never heard of before the mid-1990s, but it has become a widespread and regular phenomenon today in many states in India. Over 300,000 farmers have committed suicide in India since the mid-1990s and the proportion is alarmingly high in states such as Maharashtra, Andhra Pradesh, and Karnataka. Why is this happening in India? The root cause for all these problems is poor returns from farming. In the absence of reliable information on farm income in India, many myths are making the rounds, which should be addressed.

What is the trend in farm income in India? Is farm income increasing or decreasing in India over the years? If it is declining, is it happening uniformly in both irrigated and un-irrigated regions? Are the returns from irrigated crops better than un-irrigated crops? Does increased productivity in any way guarantee increased farm income? Has the agricultural price policy benefitted paddy farmers in India? What does the cost of cultivation survey data reveal about farm profitability? Commercial crops such as sugarcane reportedly provide large incomes for farmers compared to other crops because of assured marketing and guaranteed price. But, of late, even sugarcane farmers have started agitating stating that their income has also been squeezed over the years because of increased cost of production. Is sugarcane still profitable to farmers in India? It is fiercely debated that the introduction of the Mahatma Gandhi National Rural Employment Guarantee Scheme (MGNREGS) has increased the wage rate substantially, leading to increased cost of cultivation and squeezed farm income. Is it correct to say that the employment scheme has affected farm profitability? What is the real nexus between public procurement of foodgrain and farm income in India? To what extent does rural infrastructure development in different Indian districts help in increasing farm income? These are some of the issues confronting farm income today for which I will try to provide plausible responses in this volume.

My research towards farm income is not natural but rather inadvertent. My major area of research is economics of irrigation water, including micro-irrigation. When the issue of farmer suicides started surfacing for the first time in Maharashtra during the late 1990s, I noticed some flawed narratives about them which were against my understanding of Indian farmers. While some wrote that farmers are not brave, others attributed farmer suicides to behavioural and social factors. It is common understanding that Indian farmers are very brave, mentally strong, and they are capable of facing any kind of eventuality. My hunch was that inadequate farm income from crop cultivation could be the main reason for taking such an extreme step. Utilizing data from cost of cultivation surveys published by the Commission of Agricultural Costs and Prices and the Situation Assessment Survey of farmers published by the National Sample Survey Office, I wrote three articles which were published in the *Economic and Political Weekly*, wherein I demonstrated that reduced farm income could be the main reason for increased indebtedness and farmer suicides. I have received very good feedback from my academic colleagues on these articles, which encouraged me to probe further on the issue of farm income.

While working on different chapters included in this volume, I have benefitted immensely from different scholars and reviewers in terms of methodological inputs and comments. First of all, I would like to profusely thank Professor R. S. Deshpande, former Director, Institute for Social and Economic Change, Bangalore, for providing methodical comments at various stages of writing this book and also helping in all my academic endeavours since November 1994. I would also like to thank Professor V. M. Rao (who passed away recently), Professor R. Maria Saleth, Professor S. Neelakantan, Professor C. Ramasamy, Professor K. Palanisami, Professor S. Iyyampillai, and Professor N. Chandrasekhara Rao for reading and offering constructive comments on my writings on farm income at different times. My tenure (1994–2008) at the Gokhale Institute of Politics and Economics (GIPE), Pune, helped to refine my understanding of various issues of farm income while working on different projects at the Agro-Economic Research Centre. Particularly, I owe a lot to Professor V. S. Chitre, former director of GIPE, for his support and encouragement for my research endeavour throughout the period.

The chapter on farm profitability in Andhra Pradesh included in this volume is a shortened version of the detailed paper that I wrote for the Commission on Inclusive and Sustainable Agriculture Development of Andhra Pradesh constituted by the Government of Andhra Pradesh under the Chairmanship of Professor R. Radhakrishna. I am grateful to him, Professor Y. K. Alagh, and Professor D. Narasimha Reddy for their comments on this paper while presenting it to the commission's seminar at different times.

The National Bank for Agriculture and Rural Development (NABARD), Mumbai, awarded me the prestigious NABARD Chair Professor position (2011–16) with generous funding through which I was able to probe some of the issues connected with farm income using macro-level data. I am grateful to NABARD for providing uninterrupted financial support for the research. At the time of presenting some of the chapters included in this volume at different conferences and seminars, I received many constructive comments from the participants. Particularly, I must record my sincere thanks to the participants of the annual conferences of the Indian Society of Agricultural Economics and the Indian Society of Agricultural Marketing for their comments.

I do not know what would have happened to my academic career if I had not completed my doctoral research under the guidance of the great Professor Venkatesh B. Athreya, who taught me the nuances of research in agriculture and rural economics, which is helping me even today. Although he may not fully agree with me on several points that I have made in this volume, it is my duty to thank him profusely for providing meticulous training during my early days of research. My students P. Alli, R. Suresh, Susanto Kumar Beero, and P. Jothi have helped me in compiling and processing the macro-level data that I have used for preparing different chapters for this volume. I am thankful to all of them.

Although I have reworked and put together all the chapters in a coherent manner after joining as Member (Official) with the Commission for Agricultural Costs and Prices, New Delhi, I wrote most of the chapters when I was working as Professor and Head of the Department of Economics and Rural Development, Alagappa University, Karaikudi, Tamil Nadu. While thanking all my colleagues, I would like to register my sincere thanks to our former vice chancellor Professor S. Subbiah and the present vice chancellor Professor N. Rajendran for their continuous support and encouragements for my academic endeavour. I am also thankful to the Alagappa University for providing research assistance from the RUSA Phase 2.0 Scheme for updating the data used in different chapters in the volume.

Professor R. Radhakrishna, an eminent economist, policymaker, and an academic administrator, wrote the foreword for this book without second thought in response to my request. I am grateful to him for it. The comments that I received from the two anonymous reviewers on the earlier version of the manuscript helped in many ways to improve the overall presentation of the manuscript. I would like to thank both the reviewers for making very constructive comments on the manuscript. Besides the reviewers, Dhiraj Pandey of Oxford University Press has not only provided many useful suggestions at different points of time but also suggested reducing the size of the manuscript without compromising on the academic merit of the work. I profusely thank him for providing useful suggestions. My sincere thanks to Binita Roy of Oxford University Press for patiently sending queries and also responding to all my queries in the course of bringing out this volume.

I must also thank my wonderful wife and my son for allowing me undisturbed time when I was writing different chapters for this volume. Finally, the views expressed in this volume are my own and should not be attributed to anyone mentioned here or the institutions with which I am affiliated.

A. Narayanamoorthy
September 2020

1

Introduction

After the introduction of the Green Revolution, India's agricultural sector has not only undergone rapid transformation in technology adoption in different areas but also witnessed spectacular achievements in production and productivity of different agricultural commodities. Amidst a fourfold increase in its population, India has now emerged from being a net importer of foodgrains to a net exporter of different agricultural commodities. Between 1965–6 and 2016–17, rice production increased from 30.59 million tonnes (mt) to 110.15 mt, while wheat production increased from 10.40 mt to 98.38 mt, and total foodgrain production increased from 72.35 mt to 275.68 mt (GoI, 2018). Apart from foodgrains, spectacular achievements have also been made in the production of non-foodgrain crops. While the production of oilseeds increased from just 6.40 mt to 32.10 mt, cotton production increased from 4.85 million bales (one bale is equivalent to 170 kg) to 33.09 million bales, and sugarcane production increased from 123.99 mt to 306.72 mt during this period. Of late, revolutionary progress has also been made in the production of horticultural crops, which has already started contributing to overall agricultural growth in a big way. Today, India's agricultural sector ranks as one of the biggest sectors in the world in the production of foodgrains, fruits and vegetables, and milk. Some estimates suggest that India's gross production of agricultural commodities is more than one billion tonnes today.

But has this high production benefitted the farmers in terms of increased income? Although this question was asked some 20 years ago when farmers for the first time started committing suicide in certain parts of India, the issue continues to occupy centre stage in the discourse on farm income as farmers in most parts of India are reeling under severe crisis even today. Farmers from agriculturally well-developed states such as Punjab, Andhra Pradesh, and Tamil Nadu are also committing suicide citing increased indebtedness that piled up due to poor income from farming (see Deshpande and Arora, 2010). Frequent massive protests by farmers cultivating both foodgrain and non-foodgrain crops in recent years are also reinforcing the fact that something is terribly wrong with the farming sector. Because of inadequate income from farming, farmers are unable to repay the loans that they have taken for agricultural purposes, which not only leads to increased indebtedness but at times forces them to commit suicide as well (Deshpande, 2002; Deshpande and Prabhu, 2005). Professor Radhakrishna's committee on agricultural indebtedness appointed by the Ministry of Finance to study the reasons for farm indebtedness clearly underlined that inadequate income from crop cultivation was the root cause for widespread indebtedness in India (GoI, 2007).

Issues with Farm Income

The issues pertaining to farm income are many, and they are also growing. While many new issues have emerged in the recent past, the old issues continue, albeit with a changed face. Why are the farmers not able to get increased income despite significant increase in production and productivity of different crops? Although over two-thirds of the population still directly rely on the agricultural sector for their livelihood, the issues relating to farm income somehow did not receive adequate attention in policy circles till the late 1990s. Food security has been the prime agenda of successive governments and, therefore, increased thrust has been given to augment production of foodgrains and other commodities. Farmers seem to have been treated as mere agents of agricultural production over the years. Their economic well-being never received due attention until the early 2000s, when farmer suicides and indebtedness became a widespread phenomenon in different parts of the country. Researchers and policymakers began to take serious note of this agrarian catastrophe only when there was repeated resurfacing of the distress across the country. The issue of farm income came into the limelight after the release of the report of the National Commission on Farmers, headed by noted agriculture scientist M. S. Swaminathan. The report not only underlined the pathetic plight of farmers but also suggested the fixing of minimum support price (MSP) for mandated crops over and above 50 per cent of gross cost of production to increase farm income (NCF, 2006). Serious deliberations on the issue of farm income and crop profitability have taken place as well in recent policy debates on the agricultural sector. For instance, the recently released NITI Aayog (2015) report 'Raising Agricultural Productivity and Making Farming Remunerative to Farmers' has suggested many pointers with increased focus on market infrastructure to augment farm income.

Researchers keep asking whether the income of Indian farmers has increased or if farmers are getting any profit from crop cultivation. This is because of the fact that comprehensive studies directly focusing on farm income at the macro level in India were not available till the publication of the farmers' situation assessment survey (SAS) data for the period 2002–3 (NSSO, 2005). Now, we have one more round of SAS data for the year 2012–13 (NSSO, 2014), which can be compared with its earlier round to see whether farm income has increased. Increased farm income is essential not only to improve the welfare of the farm households but also to accelerate growth in the agricultural sector. So, there is a need to understand various issues confronting farm income so that appropriate policy intervention can be introduced to augment it. What is the trend in farm income in India? Is farm income increasing or decreasing over the years? If it is declining or increasing, is it happening uniformly in both irrigated and un-irrigated regions? It is a known fact that irrigated crops provide better yield than un-irrigated crops (Dhawan, 1988; NSSO, 2018). Can the increased productivity in any way guarantee increased farm income?

Among the various crops cultivated in India, paddy is one that has received relatively good state support in terms of MSP and procurement policy over the years (see Rao and Dev, 2010). Because of this reason, it is argued that paddy farmers are able to realize better income from its cultivation. Has the agricultural price policy really benefitted the paddy farmers in India? Some reported that farm profitability in real terms has declined over the years. Is this true? The Commission for Agricultural Costs and Prices (CACP) has been publishing cost of cultivation survey (CCS) data for different crops since 1970–1.[1] What does the CCS data reveal on farm profitability for different crops? Sugarcane crop reportedly gives better income to its farmers than other crops because of assured marketing channel from sugar industries with guaranteed price. But, of late, even sugarcane farmers have come under distress stating that their income has also lowered over the years because of increased cost of production (Narayanamoorthy and Alli, 2013). What happened to the cash-rich sugarcane crop? Is sugarcane still profitable to farmers in India?

Many new issues are emerging on the agricultural front now, which had never been experienced earlier. For instance, farmers voluntarily declaring crop holiday were unheard of in the history of Indian agriculture. Andhra Pradesh is one of the agriculturally well-endowed states where farmers have recently taken an unprecedented step by declaring crop holiday (for paddy) in a large tract of fertile area. A committee was also formed to study the problems of farmers in crop-holiday affected *mandals*[2] of the east Godavari district of Andhra Pradesh under the chairmanship of Mohan Kanda (GOAP, 2011). What has forced the paddy farmers to declare crop holiday? Is the farm income from crop cultivation in Andhra Pradesh low when compared to other states? What is the trend in farm profitability among the major crops cultivated in Andhra Pradesh over the years?

The Mahatma Gandhi National Rural Employment Guarantee Scheme (MGNREGS) was introduced during 2006 with the aim of providing assured employment and wage rate for rural labourers. It has been fiercely debated that the introduction of MGNREGS

[1] More details about crops that are covered under the COC scheme can be found on www.cacp.dacnet.nic.in.

[2] *Mandals* are administrative divisions of a district, which are known differently in different parts of the country, for example, *tehsil*, *taluka*, community development block, and revenue circle.

has increased wage rate substantially, leading to increased cost of cultivation (COC) and lowered farm income (Narayanamoorthy and Bhattarai, 2013). Gulati, Jain, and Satija surmise that 'MGNREGA has "pushed" up the average wage of casual workers, distorted the rural labour markets by diverting them to non-farm rural jobs, thus creating an artificial labour shortage and raising the cost of production of agricultural commodities' (2013: 9). Not many studies have analysed the impact of the employment guarantee scheme on farm income. Is it correct to say that the employment scheme affected farm profitability? If so, which are the crops (foodgrains or non-foodgrains) and states (irrigated or un-irrigated) that were affected by the employment scheme? In the context of agrarian distress, it was argued sometime back that the poor growth in agriculture was due to 'technology fatigue' (see Narayanamoorthy, 2007). However, Dr M. S. Swaminathan argues that the root cause of agrarian distress lies in economics, not technology.[3] When there is a perpetual 'policy fatigue', is it correct to argue that 'technology fatigue' is responsible for declining agricultural growth and farm income?

Improved, transparent, and widely covered market facilities are very important for realizing increased income from farming. But in the entire discourse on the issue of farm income, market infrastructure was not given as much importance as MSP, which allegedly benefits only about 4 per cent of farmer households even in the case of paddy (NSSO, 2014). Besides assured prices, market infrastructures and access to it also play a pivotal role in helping farmers realize increased farm income. It is found that wherever state-managed procurement infrastructures are readily available for farmers, it helps them to reap better profits from their crops (Singh et al., 2015). What is the real nexus between public procurement of foodgrains and farm income in India? How does access to the agricultural market help the farmers to reap increased profit across districts in India? These are some of the important issues relating to agricultural markets that require detailed answers.

Similar to market infrastructure, other rural infrastructure such as roads, electricity, irrigation development, and so on are the important

3 For details, see https://www.newsclick.in/agrarian-crisis-roots-economy-MS-Swaminathan-interview, last accessed 7 July 2020.

drivers of farm income.[4] With the changing nature of agriculture, substantial improvement has taken place in rural infrastructure both in terms of quantity and quality. To what extent the development of rural infrastructure in different Indian districts help increase farm income is an important question which needs to be addressed using econometric analysis with strong coverage of data.

Improved adoption of inputs such as quality seeds, fertilizers, irrigation, and machinery is essential to increase crop productivity as well as profitability. Costs of these inputs have registered substantial increase since the late 1990s, which is also borne out from the analysis of data on COC of different crops (see Narayanamoorthy, 2013). Given the skyrocketing of inputs costs, it will be very difficult to achieve the optimum level of income from crop cultivation without increasing the efficiency of various inputs. In this context, there is a need to study whether the inputs are used efficiently in crop cultivation with the help of econometric analysis. It is also equally important to study which inputs are effectively helping farmers generate better output in different crops.

Income from crop cultivation on a regular basis is essential for farmers to repay their debts and to make further investments in farming. Are farmers getting steady income from different crops on a year on year basis? Is there any perceptible change in income received from different crops and different regions after the onset of agrarian crisis? Solid answers to these questions are important for policymaking which need to be studied using spatial and temporal data. Although researchers have attempted to deliberate the issue of farm income for some specific crops or at a state level, a comprehensive attempt covering all the major issues delineated in the preceding paragraphs in a single volume on the Indian context seems to be missing.

About This Volume

This volume has 12 chapters in all, including the introductory chapter, all of which in one way or the other deal with the issues

[4] An excellent exposition on how rural infrastructure can influence rural poverty and agricultural growth can be seen in Fan, Hazell, and Thorat (1999; 2000).

confronting farm income in India. Owing to poor remuneration from crop cultivation that leads to increased indebtedness, widespread suicides of farmers have been reported in different parts of the country. Many researchers have come out with contested findings on farm income by making use of different sets of data. Besides the issues pertaining to the estimate, many myths on farm income have not been adequately addressed with the help of reliable data. Chapter 2, 'Farm Income in India: Trends, Dimensions, and Myths', tries to unravel the myths surrounding the issue of farm income. Utilizing two sets of data—namely CCS published by CACP and SAS of farmers published by National Sample Survey Office (NSSO)—the chapter presents a detailed analysis of the condition of farm income across states in India.

It is believed that irrigated crops generate more profit than the same crops cultivated in rainfed or less irrigated conditions. This belief is based on the fact that irrigated crops show significantly higher productivity than un-irrigated crops. Can the higher productivity guarantee higher profit for irrigated crops? How far does this perception hold true at a time when farmers across regions have been groaning under the pressure of rising costs of cultivation and inadequate remuneration from crop cultivation? Utilizing the COC data published by CACP, an attempt is made in Chapter 3, 'Farm Income: Irrigated versus Un-irrigated Crops', to understand the economics of seven important crops—namely jowar, bajra, maize, tur, gram, groundnut, and cotton—grown in two distinct conditions, that is, irrigated and rainfed, in different states in India.

Markets for agricultural produce in India are mostly unorganized and distorted, where farmers are often unscrupulously exploited. Besides, since the elasticity of demand for agricultural commodities, particularly foodgrains, is less than unit in most cases, increased production during the period of bumper harvest brings down the prices of agricultural commodities sharply, which severely harms farmers. Keeping this in view, the support price scheme has been implemented on a regular basis for paddy and other crops since 1965 in India. However, the support price provided to paddy has come under severe scrutiny and attack for various reasons in recent years. Farmers have been demanding higher support price for paddy citing the fact that the support price is not even adequate to cover the

COC. On the other hand, some economists argue that increasing paddy price is 'dirty economics and dirtier politics'. Utilizing time series data from CCS, Chapter 4, 'Has Agricultural Price Policy Benefitted Paddy Farmers?', attempts to provide answers to the following questions: Has the support price scheme helped paddy-cultivating farmers in terms of increasing their income? What is the trend in support price of paddy vis-à-vis other crops? Has the trend in support price of paddy changed in the recent years given the increased COC? What is the level of procurement of paddy at the national level and across the states in India? Is it correct to say that the support price is not remunerative to paddy farmers belonging to high and low productivity states?

The important relationship between agricultural development and investment in infrastructure has long been recognized all over the world. A plethora of studies also confirm that rural infrastructure is a sine qua non for significantly improving agricultural production and the failure to access such services is the greatest impediment to the growth of agricultural productivity. Recent literature indicates that in addition to factors such as human capital, credit markets, extension services, and technological research, the presence of reliable infrastructure such as roads and market sites increase the efficiency of both marketing and production by bringing down transaction costs and ensuring more competitive pricing conditions in marketing than would occur in their absence. How does agriculture market access help farmers reap higher income from farming? Chapter 5, 'Agricultural Market Access and Farm Income Nexus', tries to make a departure from most of the earlier studies by taking data from 235 districts as the unit of analysis and attempts to find an empirical basis for the perceived nexus between market access, agriculture infrastructure, and value of agricultural output (VAO) from the Indian perspective.

It is argued that the MGNREGS introduced during 2006 has increased farm wage rate substantially, which has resulted in a sharp reduction in farm profitability. Is there any substance in this argument? Chapter 6, 'Has MGNREGS Affected Farm Profitability?', makes a specific attempt to study this issue utilizing CCS data available for different crops published by the CACP. It covers five different crops, namely paddy, gram, groundnut, sugarcane, and cotton, for the analysis. As the productivity of a crop often determines its profitability, two states for each crop, one each from the category of high area with high productivity (HAHP) and high area with low productivity (HALP), have been considered for the analysis.

Sugarcane has traditionally been considered to be a profitable crop; but recently its growers are coming out in large numbers, agitating against the rising COC and poor remuneration of the crop, which is unprecedented (Narayanamoorthy and Alli, 2013). Several studies have shown that in recent years farm income has been plummeting due to soaring price of farm inputs, with sugarcane crop being no exception. While sugarcane farmers demand a better price for their produce, the fair and remunerative price (FRP) or state-advised price periodically announced by the government reportedly fails to take into account the ever increasing cost of farm inputs. Why is a unanimously distressed voice heard from the country's sugarcane fields today? Is it a justifiable claim by the farmers that sugarcane crop is no more remunerative? Do the high productive states have an edge over the low and medium productive states with regard to the profitability of sugarcane crop? Chapter 7, 'Is Sugarcane Cultivation Profitable to Farmers?', attempts to answer these questions utilizing the CCS data pertaining to six important sugarcane cultivating states.

Farmers in general and from Andhra Pradesh (undivided) in particular are passing through a painful phase with widespread indebtedness and high proportion of farmer suicides during the last two decades. What is the cause of this crisis? Is it because of low remuneration from crop cultivation? If low remuneration is the problem, is it caused by increased COC or due to reduced income from crop cultivation? Although a large number of studies have attempted to find out the possible reasons for this unprecedented crisis, the issue of profit from crop cultivation covering longer period of data in different crops has not been studied in detail. Taking data from CCS pertaining to eight important crops, namely paddy (rice), jowar, maize, arhar, moong, groundnut, sugarcane and cotton, Chapter 8, 'Farm Profitability in Andhra Pradesh: A Temporal Analysis', attempts to reveal whether farmers are able to reap any steady profit from these crop cultivations both in terms of cost A2 and cost C2.

Although India's foodgrain production has increased significantly from 50.82 mt in 1950–1 to over 278 mt in 2016–17, foodgrain demand has been continuously rising due to increase in consumers' income, population growth, and other reasons. A projection made by the National Commission on Integrated Water Resources Development (NCIWRD) indicates that the total demand for foodgrains would be about 316 mt by 2025 and 441 mt by 2050. Given the severe agrarian crisis we have been experiencing over the last 15 years or so, there are apprehensions now about whether production of foodgrains can be increased to meet the projected level of demand. On the one hand, the area allotted for foodgrain crops has been declining persistently in relation to gross cropped area (GCA); but on the other hand, the growth rate in production and productivity of various foodgrain crops has decelerated sharply during the last decade. Adding to this problem, the paddy-cultivating farmers from the state of Andhra Pradesh, which is the rice bowl of India, declared for themselves a crop holiday for the kharif season 2011–12 in an area of about 400,000 acres. The crop holiday, something that was unheard of in the history of Indian agriculture, was declared by farmers who belonged neither to the rainfed areas nor the drought-prone regions but were from the districts of a highly irrigated region in Andhra Pradesh. The farmers leading the crop holiday campaign urged their peers in Punjab, Tamil Nadu, and Karnataka to go on crop holiday so as to protest against the poor remuneration from paddy cultivation. Since the contribution of irrigated agriculture to the total production of foodgrains is large, this move can potentially harm the production of foodgrains that may lead to food security problems as well. Why did the farmers suddenly declare crop holiday? Will the crop holiday affect the production of foodgrains? What are the implications of crop holidays on foodgrain production? Do we have any other threats to foodgrain production besides crop holidays? Utilizing the available secondary data pertaining to crop holiday and other related parameters, Chapter 9, 'Crop Holiday and India's New Food Security Worries', attempts to answers these questions as well as to highlight India's emerging food security concerns in the context of dwindling farm income.

Procurement of foodgrains by state agencies with pre-announced MSPs helps the farmers in many ways to increase their income from farm enterprise. Although studies are available on the role of MSPs on farm income of different crops, not many studies are available on public procurement of paddy and wheat with its farm income covering different states over a time. Is the increased procurement of paddy/wheat helping farmers realize higher income from these crops? A detailed analysis is needed to answer this question. With the use of state-level data from 1970–1 to 2015–16, Chapter 10, 'Procurement of Foodgrains and Farm Income Nexus', attempts to study the impact of public procurement of paddy and wheat on farm income.

Infrastructure such as irrigation, road, electricity, and others are essential for agricultural development in any region. Not many studies are available on the impact of these infrastructure on agricultural output. Whether the impact of infrastructural factors on agricultural output is increasing over time is an important issue, which seems to have not been adequately studied so far using data from different time points. Despite the fact that infrastructure development cannot make an impact instantaneously on agricultural output, most of the available studies have analysed the impact of infrastructure factors on agricultural output without using them as lagged variables. Keeping this in view, with the help of econometric analysis, Chapter 11, 'Rural Infrastructure and Agricultural Output Nexus', presents the relationship between infrastructure development and agricultural output (measured in terms of INR/hectare) by using data from 256 districts from 3 time points.

It is assumed that the poor efficiency in input use is one of the reasons for reduced farm income. Input use efficiency in crop cultivation and farm income are closely related. The issue of how efficiently farmers are using various farm inputs in crop cultivation has been an important topic of research over the years. Many studies from India seem to suggest that farm inputs are mostly used sub-optimally. There is also no conclusive evidence to show that the inputs are used more efficiently in high productivity states than in low productivity states for different crops. Not many studies are available on input use efficiency covering different crops and states using temporal and spatial data. Chapter 12, 'Are Inputs Used Efficiently in Crop Cultivation?', attempts to bring forth the efficiency of different inputs used for cultivating six different crops, namely paddy, wheat, gram, groundnut, cotton, and sugarcane, with the help of econometric analysis.

On the whole, utilizing massive data and econometric analysis, this book covers a wide range of topical issues confronting farm income in India. While analysing the issues associated with the COC/cost of production and MSPs, the volume also provides detailed discussions on the importance of market infrastructures and state-supported procurement systems for augmenting farm income. In the absence of a detailed book focusing on farm income in India, it is expected that this volume will serve as a one-stop repository for all those who are interested in understanding the myths and realities of farm income.

Bibliography

Deshpande, R. S. 2002. 'Suicide by Farmers in Karnataka: Agrarian Distress and Possible Alleviatory Steps'. *Economic and Political Weekly*, vol. 37, no. 26, pp. 2601–10.

Deshpande, R. S., and S. Arora (eds). 2010. *Agrarian Crisis and Farmer Suicides*. Sage Publications, New Delhi.

Deshpande, R. S., and N. Prabhu. 2005. 'Farmers' Distress: Proof beyond Question'. *Economic and Political Weekly*, vol. 40, nos 44–5, pp. 4663–5.

Dhawan, B. D. 1988. *Irrigation in India's Agricultural Development: Productivity, Stability, Equity*. Sage Publications, New Delhi.

Fan, S., P. Hazell, and S. K. Thorat. 1999. *Linkages between Government Spending, Growth, and Poverty in Rural India*. Research Report No. 110. International Food Policy Research Institute, Washington, D.C., U. S. A.

———. 2000. 'Government Spending, Growth and Poverty in Rural India'. *American Journal of Agricultural Economics*, vol. 82, no. 4, pp. 1038–51.

GoAP (Government of Andhra Pradesh). 2011. *Report of State Level Committee to Study the Problems of Farmers in Crop Holiday Affected Mandals of East Godavari District of Andhra Pradesh* (Chairman: Mohan Kanda).

GoI (Government of India). 2007. *Report of the Expert Group on Agricultural Indebtedness* (Chairman: R. Radhakrishna). Ministry of Finance, Government of India, New Delhi.

———. 2018. *Agricultural Statistics at a Glance 2017*. Directorate of Economics and Statistics, Ministry of Agriculture and Farmers Welfare, Government of India, New Delhi.

Gulati, A., S. Jain, and N. Satija. 2013. *Rising Farm Wages in India—The 'Pull' and 'Push' Factors*. Discussion Paper No. 5. Commission for Agricultural

Costs and Prices, Department of Agriculture and Cooperation, Ministry of Agriculture, Government of India, New Delhi.

Narayanamoorthy, A. 2007. 'Deceleration in Agricultural Growth: Technology Fatigue or Policy Fatigue'. *Economic and Political Weekly*, vol. 42, no. 25, pp. 2375–9.

———. 2013. 'Profitability in Crops Cultivation in India: Some Evidence from Cost of Cultivation Survey Data'. *Indian Journal of Agricultural Economics*, vol. 68, no. 1 (January–March), pp. 104–21.

———. 2018. 'India's Drip Irrigation Policy'. *Geography and You*, vol. 18, no. 11 (December 1–15), pp. 32–8.

Narayanamoorthy, A., and P. Alli. 2013. 'Sugarcane Leaves Farmers Crushed'. *The Hindu Business Line*, 16 April, p. 9.

Narayanamoorthy, A., and M. Bhattarai. 2013. 'Rural Employment Scheme and Agricultural Wage Rate Nexus: An Analysis across States'. *Agricultural Economics Research Review*, vol. 26, pp. 149–63.

NCF (National Commission on Farmers). 2006. *Serving Farmers and Saving Farming, Report V Excerpts*. Ministry of Agriculture, Government of India, New Delhi.

NITI Aayog. 2015. *Raising Agricultural Productivity and Making Farming Remunerative to Farmers*. Government of India, New Delhi.

———. 2016. *Evaluation Report of Efficacy of Minimum Support Prices (MSP) on Farmers*. Development Monitoring and Evaluation Office, New Delhi.

NSSO (National Sample Survey Office). 2005. *Situation Assessment Survey of Farmers: Income, Expenditure and Productive Assets of Farmer Households*, 59th Round. Ministry of Statistics and Programme Implementation, Government of India, New Delhi.

———. 2014. *Key Indicators of Situations of Agricultural Households in India*, 70th Round. Ministry of Statistics and Programme Implementation, Government of India, New Delhi.

———. 2018. *Consolidated Results of Crop Estimation Survey on Principal Crops: 2015–16*. NSSO Field Operation Division. Ministry of Statistics and Programme Implementation, Government of India, Faridabad, Haryana.

Rao, N. Chandrasekhara, and S. Mahendra Dev. 2010. 'Agricultural Price Policy, Farm Profitability and Food Security'. *Economic and Political Weekly*, vol. 45, nos 26 and 27 (June), pp. 174–82.

Singh, R., U. S. Mehta, G. Shukla, and N. K. Singh. 2015. *Minimum Support Price and Farmers' Income*. CUTS International, Jaipur, India.

PART I

MACRO ANALYSIS OF FARM INCOME

2

Farm Income in India

Trends, Dimensions, and Myths

The main purpose of this chapter is to bring out the state of farm income in India and also to unravel some of the myths associated with it. The focus of Indian agriculture has been changing ever since the introduction of the planning era (see Deshpande et al., 2004). Because of severe shortage in foodgrain production, increased attention was given to augment productivity and production of foodgrains starting from the late 1960s till the 1980s. Sustaining the growth of the farm sector from the impact of the World Trade Organization (WTO) regime was the main focus during the 1990s.[1] As a result of a production-centred approach, the gross production of foodgrains and other agricultural commodities has increased significantly over the years; foodgrain production increased from just 51 mt in 1950–1 to about 264 mt in 2014–15. A similar trend is noticed in many non-foodgrain crops as well (see GoI, 2016). Today, India is not only a self-sufficient country in foodgrains but also an exporter of

1 The World Trade Organisation (WTO) is an intergovernmental organization which regulates international trade between countries. The WTO regime officially commenced on 1 January 1995 signed by 125 countries, and it is continuing till date.

foodgrains to many countries (see Bhattacharya, 2004; Deshpande et al., 2004).

Although over two-thirds of the population relies on the agricultural sector for their livelihood, farm income–related issues have somehow not received adequate attention in the policy circles till the late 1990s (see Deshpande et al., 2004; Sen and Bhatia, 2004). Farmers were treated as mere agents of agricultural production over the years. Their economic well-being never received due attention until the late 1990s when farmer suicides and indebtedness became widespread phenomena. Scholars and policymakers began to take serious note of this agrarian catastrophe only when the distress resurfaced again in the recent years in the farm heartlands of the country (see Sainath, 2010). Serious deliberations on the issue of farm income and crop profitability have occupied the centre stage in recent policy debates on the agricultural sector, especially since the early 2000s. Experts across various quarters keep questioning whether the income of Indian farmers has increased or if the farmers are getting any profits from crop cultivation. As a major step towards understanding and studying the nature and causes of widespread farmer suicides and to find out whether reduced income is the major reason for increased indebtedness among farm households, the Union Government appointed the Expert Group on Agricultural Indebtedness under the chairmanship of R. Radhakrishna (GoI, 2007). Following this, many researchers also conducted detailed field-level studies in this direction and have reported that decline in productivity, supply constraints in institutional credit, market irregularities, and so on are the major reasons for the sudden spurt in farmer suicides and indebtedness (see Deshpande, 2002; Deshpande and Prabhu, 2005; Vaidyanathan, 2006; Narayanamoorthy, 2006a; 2007).

Comprehensive studies directly focusing on farm income at the macro level in India were not available till the publication of the SAS data (NSSO, 2005a; 2005b). Because of the absence of data on farm income, most studies have used data from terms of trade computations between agriculture and other sectors to judge its performance (see Kahlon and Tyagi, 1980; Gulati and Rao, 1994; Misra and Hazell, 1996). The CCS published by the CACP is another data source that was used to understand the trends in farm income

(Sen and Bhatia, 2004). In many ways CCS data are different from SAS data. While CCS data provide crop-wise cost and income details per hectare, SAS provides annual income from crop cultivation per household. A large number of scholars have studied the trends in farm income using CCS data over the years. For instance, with the help of CCS data from 1981–2 to 1999–2000, Sen and Bhatia (2004) concluded that farm business income per farmer was miniscule and inadequate to pay even for the essentials (as cited by Chand, Saxena, and Rana, 2015).

Assured prices appear to help farmers to efficiently allocate scarce resources among different crops (see Schultz, 1964; Deshpande, 1996; Rao, 2001). Studies have analysed the effectiveness of MSP in raising farm income using CCS data. Gulati (2012) argued that hikes in MSP are necessary to get positive returns and also to propel agricultural gross domestic product (GDP). But Bhalla (2012) counter-argued that increasing MSP of paddy is 'dirty economics and dirtier politics'. With the focus on the impact of MSP on farm income, Rao and Dev (2010) have studied the profitability of paddy and wheat in detail using CCS data from 1981–2 to 2007–8 and found that the value of output (VOP) has been more than the costs in both paddy and wheat throughout the period of analysis at the all-India level. Similarly, utilizing data from CCS for the period 1975–6 to 2006–7 by covering six important crops, Narayanamoorthy (2013) found an insignificant increase in profitability of foodgrain crops at constant prices mainly because of substantial increase in COC (cost C2). The National Commission on Farmers (NCF) that looked into various aspects of farming in detail has also underlined that the returns from crop cultivation are very poor and inadequate (NCF, 2006). After the publication of SAS data, quite a few studies have been carried out specifically focusing on farm income. For instance, Narayanamoorthy (2006a) analysed the level of farm income using SAS data across the major states and found that the annual average income from crop cultivation for the country as a whole was only INR 11,628 per household. That is, the per day income of the farmers' household was just about INR 32 during 2002–3, which was much lower than the average agricultural wage rate that prevailed at that time in the country. The pitiable condition of farm households has also been clearly narrated using SAS data by the Expert Group on Agricultural Indebtedness under the chairmanship of Professor R. Radhakrishna (GoI, 2007).

But, Chand, Saxena, and Rana (2015) have questioned the validity of the estimates that were made based on CCS data. Their contentions are as follows:

> The cost of cultivation data is representative of crops or crop complexes in major growing states, but it does not cover the entire country or the entire agriculture sector. Even the productivity of sample crops reported in COC data show significant difference from state averages. COC data also does not cover horticultural crops and several minor crops that constituted 38% of the total value of the crop sector in 2011–12. Further, the importance of horticultural crops has been rising, and their productivity in India is more than four times that of other crops. Their exclusion makes a significant difference to the level and growth in farm business income. Also, the data on income from the livestock sector is not appropriately captured in the cost of cultivation schedules, which do not intend to do so. Because of these reasons, farm business income derived from the COC data is not an adequate measure of actual farm business income in the country or a state. At best, these can be used as indicators of income from selected crops. (140)

Keeping in view the limitations of the existing estimates on farm income, Chand, Saxena, and Rana (2015) made an entirely new attempt to estimate the level of farm income for the country as a whole taking data from National Income Accounting from 1983–4 to 2011–12. They estimated farm income by deducting GDP of agriculture and allied sectors from capital consumption and wage bill for hired labour employed in agriculture. As per this estimate, the real farm income earned by Indian farmers (at 2004–5 prices) increased from INR 211,000 crore in 1983–4 to INR 625,536 crore in 2011–12. That is, per cultivator income increased from INR 16,103 to INR 42,781 during this period. Interestingly, the annual growth rate of per cultivator farm income increased at a rate of 7.29 per cent during 2004–5 to 2011–12, which is more or less equivalent to the overall growth of the economy during this period. While these estimates appear to be systematic, one needs to look at them carefully to ascertain whether the estimate based on macro-level data can reflect the reality on farm income. This question arises due to three important reasons. First, the transaction cost involved in farming activities is huge (my field survey experience suggests that it will be around 20 per cent of cost A2),[2] which never gets included in the macro-level cost.[3] Second, the wholesale cost of inputs at the macro level used in the estimate would be much lower than the retail price of inputs. For instance, the retail price of fertilizer sold in the district headquarters is lower than the price of fertilizer prevailing in the retail shop located in a village or block. Third, the managerial cost (CACP considers 10 per cent of C2 cost as managerial cost) is another big cost which may not have been included in the macro-level cost used by Chand, Saxena, and Rana (2015). If we include these costs in the estimate, then there is a possibility that the farm income estimated by them would exhibit a declining trend.

Besides the issues concerning the estimate on farm income, many puzzles and myths pertaining to the income of farmers need to be answered to better understand the reality. First of all, given the contesting estimates from different scholars, we must find what the actual level of income is that farmers get from crop cultivation. What is the variation in the level of farm income across the states in India? Has the farm income increased over the years? If yes, has it increased consistently in all regions and crops? There is a myth that the income reaped by farmers belonging to irrigated regions is higher than its counterpart, the less irrigated regions: is this true? Is there any difference in profitability of crops cultivated under irrigated and less irrigated conditions? There is another myth which has emerged in the context of alleviating the agrarian crisis, which is that farm income can be increased by augmenting productivity of crops. In this context the question comes up as to whether farmers of high

[2] Cost A2 is one among the nine cost concepts used by the CACP for fixing MSPs for crops. Cost A2 includes all actual expenses in cash and kind incurred in production by the owner plus rent paid for leased-in land.

[3] Detailed studies on transaction cost involved in crop cultivation are seldom available in the Indian context. A study on transaction costs in agriculture from planting decision to selling at wholesale market carried out in Sri Lanka estimated a 15 per cent of transaction cost in the total cost of production among the small-holder farmers (see De Silva, Ratanadiwakara, and Soya, 2008).

productivity states (HPS) are reaping higher profits than farmers from less productivity states in different crops. Is it true that farmers are unable to reap profits consistently across years? We seem to have inadequate answers to these questions in the available literature. Unless these questions are adequately answered one may not be able to say anything clearly about the state of farm income in India. In this chapter, therefore, while making an effort to answer these questions, an attempt has been made to bring out the real state of farm income in India mainly using data available from two important sources, namely SAS and CCS.

The chapter is organized into five sections. Section two presents an analysis of farm income for the period between 2002–3 and 2012–13 using SAS data, which has income details by source for farmer households. The level of farm income per farm household across the states is analysed in section three. Utilizing CCS data for different states covering the period from 1971–2 to 2013–14, a detailed analysis on trends in farm income by crops is provided in section four. The last section presents a few agenda points for increasing farm income in the future.

Has Farm Income Increased?

In the absence of comprehensive farm income–related data, various scholars have employed different methodologies/data sources to estimate farm income. Divergent views are available in the existing studies on farm income, which has also been underlined earlier. While estimates of the existing studies have provided useful information, we have actual data on farm income that is fairly comparable[4] for

[4] It is necessary to mention here that the definition of farmer households followed in the 70th round of the NSSO is a bit different from that of the 59th round of the NSSO (SAS data). The major differences in definitions are summarized as follows (NSSO, 2014):

(*a*) Possession of land was an essential condition for defining a person as farmer (farmer household) in the 59th round, but an agricultural household as defined in the NSS 70th round may or may not possess land. (*b*) In the 59th round, farmers who had insignificant farming

two time points, 2002–3 and 2012–13, from SAS published by the NSSO (2005b; 2014), which can reveal the reality about the state of farm income. SAS provides data on annual income for farmer households by the various sources, that is, wages, cultivation, farming of animals, and non-farm business income. Using this data, the actual level of farm income reaped by Indian farmers can be easily judged.

The concept of farm income has been used differently by different scholars. While questioning the validity of the income estimated through CCS data, Chand, Saxena, and Rana (2015) argued that farm income should include the income from the livestock sector as well. While their argument is probably correct in a broader context, we must recognize the questions raised in the debate on farm income during the last decade or so. Farmers have been questioning the income realized from crop cultivation and not the income from other sources. Farmers in various parts of India are demanding higher income from crop cultivation but not from livestock or other sectors. The NCF has also primarily referred to farm income as the income received from crop cultivation. Therefore, in order to understand the ground reality of farm income, it is necessary to consider the income from crop cultivation, which is an issue discussed intensively today.

It is essential to look into the changes in the income from crop cultivation vis-à-vis other sources between the two time periods mentioned earlier utilizing SAS data which is presented at constant value (at 1986–7 prices) in Table 2.1. It is clear that the annual income per farm household from cultivation has increased from INR 3,645 in 2002–3 to INR 5,502 (at constant prices of 1986–7) in 2012–13, an increase of about 3.81 per cent per annum. But, the question which needs to be answered here is whether the income from crop cultivation increased at a faster rate as compared to other sources of

activities, such as kitchen garden, were excluded from the survey coverage. In order to eliminate households pursuing agricultural activities of insignificant nature in the 70th round, households with at least one member self-employed in agriculture either in principal status or subsidiary status and having total value of produce during last 365 days of more than INR 3,000 were only considered for inclusion in the survey coverage.

Table 2.1 Average Annual Income per Farmer Household by Source across Major States during 2002–3 and 2012–13 (INR/ha at 1986–7 prices)

State	2002–3				
	Wages	Cultivation	Farming of Animals	Non-farm Business	Total
1. Andhra Pradesh	2,419	2,795	350	583	6,147
2. Assam	3,660	6,741	530	959	11,891
3. Chhattisgarh	2,667	3,051	–11	380	6,087
4. Gujarat	3,480	4,379	1,712	527	10,097
5. Jammu and Kashmir	7,749	9,126	1,437	2,332	20,645
6. Jharkhand	3,476	3,205	324	779	7,783
7. Karnataka	3,954	4,762	493	632	9,841
8. Kerala	7,572	4,213	579	2,697	15,062
9. Madhya Pradesh	2,107	3,747	–854	380	5,379
10. Maharashtra	3,006	4,751	542	967	9,265
11. Odisha	2,155	1,264	60	515	3,995
12. Rajasthan	3,502	1,350	19	764	5,635
Average of SHBNLI	**3,812**	**4,115**	**432**	**960**	**9,319**
	(40.91)	**(44.16)**	**(4.63)**	**(10.30)**	**(100)**
13. Bihar	1,870	3,182	997	760	6,809
14. Haryana	4,770	5,620	–888	1,339	10,841
15. Punjab	5,500	10,616	888	1,655	18,658
16. Tamil Nadu	4,157	2,479	414	745	7,794
17. Uttar Pradesh	2,103	3,145	199	696	6,143
18. West Bengal	3,337	2,772	290	1,422	7,821
Average of SHANLI	**3,623**	**4,636**	**317**	**1,103**	**9,678**
	(37.43)	**(47.90)**	**(3.27)**	**(11.40)**	**(100)**
All India	**3,081**	**3,645**	**342**	**888**	**7,956**
	(38.72)	**(45.82)**	**(4.30)**	**(11.16)**	**(100)**

Table 2.1 *(Cont'd)*

State	2012–13				
	Wages	Cultivation	Farming of Animals	Non-farm Business	Total
1. Andhra Pradesh	4,432	3,611	1,920	714	10,677
2. Assam	2,554	7,520	1,427	455	11,955
3. Chhattisgarh	3,300	5,977	–34	2	9,245
4. Gujarat	4,791	5,238	3,446	679	14,154
5. Jammu and Kashmir	13,100	5,470	1,430	2,648	22,648
6. Jharkhand	3,284	2,591	2,130	425	8,430
7. Karnataka	4,780	8,804	1,071	1,116	15,771
8. Kerala	9,382	6,305	1,027	4,516	21,229
9. Madhya Pradesh	2,379	7,171	1,307	230	11,089
10. Maharashtra	3,850	6,886	963	1,489	13,189
11. Odisha	3,064	2,513	2,346	963	8,886
12. Rajasthan	4,525	5,604	1,727	1,268	13,125
Average of SHBNLI	**4,953**	**5,641**	**1,563**	**1,209**	**13,367**
	(37.06)	**(42.20)**	**(11.70)**	**(9.04)**	**(100)**
13. Bihar	2,363	3,063	498	429	6,354
14. Haryana	6,234	14,048	4,723	770	25,775
15. Punjab	8,534	19,396	2,961	1,357	32,248
16. Tamil Nadu	5,182	3,423	1,964	1,895	12,464
17. Uttar Pradesh	2,054	5,098	970	671	8,791
18. West Bengal	3,796	1,748	402	1,161	7,107
Average of SHANLI	**4,694**	**7,796**	**1,920**	**1,047**	**15,457**
	(30.37)	**(50.44)**	**(12.42)**	**(6.77)**	**(100)**
All India	**3,698**	**5,502**	**1,363**	**914**	**11,475**
	(32.23)	**(47.95)**	**(11.87)**	**(7.97)**	**(100)**

(Cont'd)

Table 2.1 *(Cont'd)*

State	Compound Growth Rate (per cent/annum)				
	Wages	Cultivation	Farming of Animals	Non-farm Business	Total
1. Andhra Pradesh	5.66	2.36	16.74	1.86	5.15
2. Assam	–3.22	1.00	9.41	–6.55	0.05
3. Chhattisgarh	1.95	6.30	00	–38.57	3.87
4. Gujarat	2.95	1.64	6.57	2.33	3.12
5. Jammu and Kashmir	4.89	–4.55	–0.04	1.16	0.85
6. Jharkhand	–0.52	–1.91	18.69	–5.36	0.73
7. Karnataka	1.74	5.74	7.32	5.31	4.38
8. Kerala	1.97	3.73	5.34	4.80	3.17
9. Madhya Pradesh	1.11	6.08	00	–4.45	6.80
10. Maharashtra	2.28	3.43	5.36	4.01	3.26
11. Odisha	3.25	6.44	39.52	5.84	7.54
12. Rajasthan	2.36	13.81	50.81	4.72	7.99
Average of SHBNLI	**2.41**	**2.91**	**12.41**	**2.12**	**3.33**
13. Bihar	2.15	–0.35	–6.11	–5.07	–0.63
14. Haryana	2.46	8.69	00	–4.91	8.19
15. Punjab	4.08	5.63	11.57	–1.79	5.10
16. Tamil Nadu	2.02	2.98	15.21	8.86	4.36
17. Uttar Pradesh	–0.22	4.49	15.46	–0.33	3.31
18. West Bengal	1.18	–4.11	3.02	–1.83	–0.87
Average of SHANLI	**2.38**	**4.84**	**17.80**	**–0.47**	**4.35**
All India	**1.67**	**3.81**	**13.38**	**0.27**	**3.39**

Sources: NSSO (2005a; 2014).

Notes: SHANLI: States having above national level of irrigation coverage in 2002–3; SHBNLI: States having below national level of irrigation coverage in 2002–3; figures in brackets are percentages of total income.

income of farmer households. The answer is very clear; the increase in income from crop cultivation was not very significant as compared to the income realized through farming of animals. This means that farmers who are relying purely on cultivation income not only earn less but the growth of their income has also been very low in India during the last one decade or so.

The other puzzle which refuses to be solved in the debates is whether farm income of irrigated regions is higher than that of less irrigated regions. It is an established fact that productivity of any crop cultivated in an irrigated region is higher than that in less irrigated or un-irrigated regions (see Vaidyanathan et al., 1994). Temporal and spatial data on crop productivity published by the Union Ministry of Agriculture (MoA) reinforces this fact. But, unfortunately, farmers belonging to the irrigated regions have also committed suicides citing poor returns from crop cultivation in the recent years. Farmers in Andhra Pradesh belonging to highly irrigated regions have even declared crop holiday specifically because of poor income from farming. Given these unpleasant developments, there is a need to validate whether farmers from irrigated regions reap higher profit than their counterparts from less irrigated regions.

Data available for all the major states for two time points from SAS provides an opportunity to look into this issue. Statistics provided in Table 2.1 show that the average income from cultivation for the states having above national level irrigation (SHANLI) is not substantially different from that of the states having below national level irrigation (SHBNLI) at both time points, namely 2002–3 and 2012–13. During 2002–3, the average annual income of SHANLI was INR 4,636 per household, whereas the same was INR 4,115 in SHBNLI category, a difference of only about INR 521. A similar trend was also observed during 2012–13. Interestingly, quite a few states belonging to SHBNLI category were able to earn higher income from cultivation than states falling under SHANLI category. This was not unexpected due to the fact that although gross income from crops cultivated under irrigated condition is higher because of higher productivity, increased COC might have counterbalanced the net returns from crop cultivation (see Narayanamoorthy, 2013).

Farm Income across States

Although the issue of farm income has been discussed by researchers and policymakers extensively for over a decade in India, the performance of various states in terms of farm income has not been adequately covered, possibly because of data constraints. What is happening at the country level might not be the same across different states due to variations in cropping patterns, irrigation coverage, adoption of modern technologies, procurement policies, market arrangements, and such other factors. It has always been believed that states with more area under commercial crops can generate higher farm income than states with larger area under foodgrain crops. But this question could not be answered convincingly due to data constraints so far. Now, the data available from SAS reports for two time points permit us to study this issue.

The annual income from cultivation per farmer household varies substantially across the states in India, as expected. During 2002–3, it varied from INR 10,616 per household in Punjab to INR 1,264 in Orissa at 1986–7 prices. Similarly, the same income varied from INR 19,396 per household in Punjab to INR 1,748 in West Bengal during 2012–13. Besides substantial variation in farm income among the states, it is found that farm income is very low in most states where predominantly paddy is cultivated during both time points. For instance, during 2012–13, the average cultivation income for the country as a whole was INR 5,502 per household. But it was much lower than this in states such as Andhra Pradesh, Odisha, Bihar, Tamil Nadu, Uttar Pradesh, and West Bengal where traditionally paddy has been cultivated predominantly; these states together accounted for 53 to 56 per cent of India's total paddy area during 2002–3 and 2012–13 (GoI, 2016). This, in a way, supports the issue of rising dissent of paddy farmers who have been arguing for over a decade now that the income from its cultivation dwindled substantially. It is true for other crops as well.

Besides low income from cultivation, its growth is also not very appreciable among the major states between 2002–3 and 2012–13. The average growth of cultivation income for the whole of India is estimated to be about 3.81 per cent per annum between the two periods, but it was less than that of India's average growth rate in 11 out of 18 states reported in Table 2.1. In states such as Chhattisgarh, Karnataka, Madhya Pradesh, Haryana, Punjab, and Uttar Pradesh, cultivation income grew at a faster rate than the rate of national-level average. To our surprise, the growth rate of income from cultivation was negative in states such as Jammu and Kashmir, Jharkhand,

Bihar, and West Bengal. This poor growth in income from cultivation might have affected the livelihood conditions of the farmers living in these states. On the whole, the analysis based on the data available from SAS clearly shows that the income from cultivation per farmer household was very low and its growth rate was also nowhere near the growth rate estimated by Chand, Saxena, and Rana (2015).[5]

Myths on Farm Income—Results of CCS Data

Before the publication of SAS data, information on farm income was available only from CACP, which has been publishing data for different crops since 1970–1 on operation-wise cost, productivity, and income collected through a national-level scheme called Comprehensive Scheme for Studying Cost of Cultivation of Principal Crops.[6] As the data on each aspect of crop cultivation has been collected directly from the farmers on a regular basis, CCS data has been considered as an important source of information on cost and income. The fixing of MSP every year for various crops by the Union Government is also primarily undertaken using CCS data (see Sen and Bhatia, 2004). Therefore, it is necessary to study using CCS data whether farmers

[5] As per the study of Chand, Saxena, and Rana (2015), farm income per cultivator grew at a rate of 1.96 per cent per annum during 1993–4 to 2004–5, but it registered growth of 7.29 per cent per annum during 2004–5 to 2011–12, which is not borne out from the estimate of SAS data. The other dimensions of growth (per cent/annum) in farm income estimated by Chand, Saxena, and Rana (2015) are presented here for ready reference:

Period	Total	Per Cultivator	Per Holding	Per Hectare of Net Sown Area (NSA)
1983–4 to 1993–4	3.67	2.74	1.85	3.73
1993–4 to 2004–5	3.30	1.96	2.10	3.38
2004–5 to 2011–12	5.36	7.29	3.94	5.31

[6] The details of methodology used for collecting data under the scheme of CCS can be found on the website of CACP (www.cacp.dacnet.nic.in).

are able to generate any profit from the cultivation of different crops over the years to understand the state of income in crop cultivation.

An important issue that evaded analysts' attention is the level of profitability of crops cultivated under irrigated and less irrigated conditions. Many in academia and policy circles have believed all along that the crops cultivated under irrigated conditions generate significantly higher income than their less irrigated counterparts. They believe that since the productivity of crops is higher in irrigated areas as compared to the same cultivated in less irrigated areas, the profitability would also be higher. However, profitability of any crop is not determined by its productivity alone. Factors such as COC of the crop, market price of the produce, and marketing facility from government agencies play an important role in deciding the profit. There is a possibility that because of increased supply (production) of agricultural output in irrigated regions, the unit price of the crop can be lower than that in less irrigated regions where reduced supply is common.

With the use of CCS data from 1970–1 to 2013–14, an analysis is attempted here to verify whether any significant difference exists in farm profitability between irrigated and less irrigated regions. Jowar, bajra, maize, gram, groundnut, and cotton are mostly cultivated both in irrigated conditions and in very less irrigated conditions in different states; therefore, these crops have been considered for the analysis. Profitability in crop cultivation has been calculated both in relation to cost A2 and C2. Against the expectation of many, CCS data does not show any bright picture in favour of crops cultivated with higher coverage of irrigation in terms of profitability. Between TE 1973–4 and TE 2013–14, the profit computed in relation to cost C2 is pathetically poor in both the regions except in the case of cotton crop, where the profitability of irrigated Gujarat was very high as compared to its neighbouring state of Maharashtra (see Table 2.2).

In relation to cost A2 too, except for cotton crop, the profitability of crops cultivated under higher irrigation coverage is not consistently very high as compared to the same crops cultivated in less irrigated conditions at all time points. Even the quantum of profit realized in relation to cost was not very high in irrigated states, which is evident from the low ratio of VOP to cost A2 and C2. In fact, in crops such as gram and groundnut, farmers from the less

Table 2.2 Profitability in Different Crops Cultivated in Irrigated and Less Irrigated States (INR/ha at 1986–7 prices)

Crops	States	Category of States	Profit in Relation with Cost A2					Profit in Relation with Cost C2				
			TE 1973–7	TE 1983–8	TE 1993–4	TE 2003–4	TE 2013–14	TE 1973–4	TE 1983–4	TE 1993–4	TE 2003–4	TE 2013–14
Jowar	Karnataka	IRS	1,027	784	568	–96	124	389	103	91	–838	–176
	Madhya Pradesh	LRS	NA	514	446	102	569	NA	–203	–614	–1,119	–673
Bajra	Gujarat	IRS	625	1,023	1,247	445	1,914	–212	–106	–51	–988	–248
	Rajasthan	LRS	443	389	378	594	563	17	–123	–376	–796	–1,181
Maize	Andhra Pradesh	IRS	NA	NA	NA	1,471	4,152	NA	NA	NA	–810	646
	Rajasthan	LRS	1,189	866	546	333	1,538	204	–520	–1,019	–2,039	–1,831
Gram	Madhya Pradesh	IRS	NA	1,588	1,869	2,547	3,343	NA	626	396	734	1,161
	Uttar Pradesh	LRS	NA	1,855	NA	3,161	2,341	NA	406	NA	1,049	148
Groundnut	Tamil Nadu	IRS	1,279	1,726	NA	1,121	3,373	13	43	NA	–2,244	–212
	Gujarat	LRS	1,157	1,131	1,584	3,594	2,657	234	–184	–37	1,298	–81
Cotton	Gujarat	IRS	NA	2,459	3,452	3,789	6,502	NA	676	1,332	1,264	2,637
	Maharashtra	LRS	NA	991	NA	1,533	3,963	NA	125	NA	–501	236

Source: Computed using data from CACP (various years).

Notes: IRS: Irrigated state; LRS: Less irrigated state.

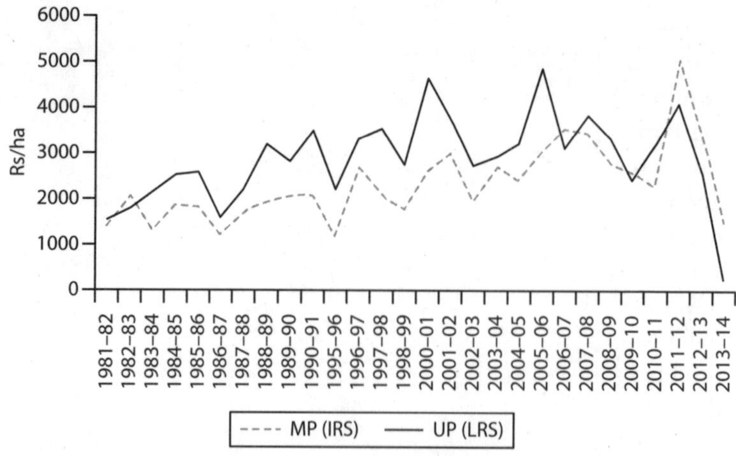

Figure 2.1 Trends in Profitability from Gram in Irrigated and Less Irrigated States
Source: CACP (various years).
Notes: MP: Madhya Pradesh; UP: Uttar Pradesh; IRS: Irrigated states; LRS: Less Irrigated States

irrigated states have reaped higher profit in quite a few years than their counterparts in irrigated areas (see Figure 2.1). How does this happen? One of the important reasons for this unusual tendency is the increased COC in irrigated areas. With increased irrigation coverage, farmers are encouraged to adopt modern yield-increasing inputs for crop cultivation, which result in increased COC. But this seems to have not happened in the case of less irrigated crops, possibly because of the risk in getting expected yield and income. Therefore, it is not always correct to conclude that the farmers in irrigated regions reap higher profits than their counterparts in less irrigated areas.[7]

Another myth which needs to be studied and answered in the context of farm profitability is: can we increase farm income by increasing the productivity of crops? It is often believed that increased productivity would help farmers reap higher profit. An occasional paper by the NITI Aayog (2015) titled 'Raising Agricultural

[7] A detailed analysis using CCS data on profitability in different crops cultivated under irrigated and less irrigated areas can be found in Narayanamoorthy, Alli, and Suresh (2015).

Productivity and Making Farming Remunerative for Farmers' has also stressed this point elaborately to generate more income from farming. Although increased productivity is necessary for augmenting farm income, many fail to understand that rising productivity alone would not help in increasing farm income since it depends upon many other factors. Access to a well-structured market is a key requirement for raising farm income. If procurement arrangements are not made adequately at appropriate times, any amount of increase in productivity would not benefit farmers. Similarly, if the increase in COC is higher than that of the income realized through increased productivity, then farmers would not benefit from increased productivity. Therefore, it is necessary to study whether productivity of crops plays any significant role in deciding farm profitability.

An analysis carried out with the help of CCS data does not clearly show that the increased productivity would help the farmers reap higher profits. To clarify this issue further, an attempt has been made to find to what extent the profitability of HPS is different from the low productivity states (LPS) for six important crops: paddy, wheat, tur, groundnut, sugarcane, and cotton. The results generated from 1971–2 to 2013–14 prove that the profitability of HPS is not significantly different from that of LPS in most crops presented in Table 2.3.

Those states in the HPS category have neither managed to reap profit in a consistent manner nor been able to generate significantly higher profit than those in the LPS category in all the time points considered for the analysis (see Table 2.4).

A question arises here: why are HPS not able to reap higher profits? We have the answer to this question from CCS data itself. The COC in HPS in all the crops is not only substantially higher than that of the crops cultivated in LPS but it also increased at a faster rate.[8] Although the VOP of the crops from LPS is substantially higher, the increased COC has reduced the profitability. In fact, because of increased investments made by the farmers in agriculture, cost C2 has increased much faster in recent years than in the 1980s

[8] Due to brevity of space, data on COC (A2 and C2) is not presented in the tables. A detailed analysis on COC increase can be found in Narayanamoorthy (2013).

Table 2.3 Profitability in Crop Cultivation among High and Low Productivity States (INR/ha at 1986–7 prices)

Crops	State	Category of States	Profit in Relation with Cost A2				Profit in Relation with Cost C2			
			TE 1983–4	TE 1993–4	TE 2003–4	TE 2013–14	TE 1983–4	TE 1993–4	TE 2003–4	TE 2013–14
Paddy	Andhra Pradesh	HPS	1,904	NA	4,110	5,134	–112	NA	91	723
	Odisha	LPS	1,326	NA	1,186	1,566	–2,436	NA	–1,327	–1,615
Wheat	Punjab	HPS	2,283	3,016	4,327	5,976	414	588	1,102	2,109
	Madhya Pradesh	LPS	1,380	1,516	1,849	4,207	180	–186	–252	1,189
Gram	Madhya Pradesh	HPS	1,588	1,869	2,547	3,343	626	396	734	1,161
	Haryana	LPS	809	1,851	1,326	2,935	–165	524	–296	522
Tur	Uttar Pradesh	HPS	NA	4,456	3,212	2,977	NA	2,269	534	–915
	Madhya Pradesh	LPS	NA	1,747	2,057	3,243	NA	625	248	1,044
Groundnut	Gujarat	HPS	1,131	1,584	3,594	2,657	–184	–37	1,298	–81
	Karnataka	LPS	1,604	NA	558	1,502	561	NA	–536	–569
Sugarcane	Tamil Nadu	HPS	11,768	NA	11,821	18,505	7,708	NA	4,481	11,093
	Maharashtra	LPS	7,951	6,833	3,999	18,663	3,544	2,633	–2,348	9,566
Cotton	Gujarat	HPS	NA	2,459	3,452	3,789	NA	676	1,332	1,264
	Maharashtra	LPS	991	NA	1,533	3,963	125	NA	–501	236

Source: Computed using data from CACP (various years).

Notes: HPS: High productivity state; LPS: Low productivity state.

Table 2.4 Number of Years Profit (ratio > 1 to cost) Reaped or Loss (ratio < 1 to cost) Incurred by Farmers in Various Crops from 1970–1 to 2013–14

Crop Name	State	Ratio > 1.00 (VOP to Cost A2)			Ratio > 1.00 (VOP to Cost C2)		
		1970–1 to 1994–5	1995–6 to 2013–14	1970–1 to 2013–14	1970–1 to 1994–5	1995–6 to 2013–14	1970–1 to 2013–14
Paddy	Punjab	14/14	18/18	32/32	13/14	18/18	31/32
	West Bengal	16/16	20/20	36/36	09/16	00/20	09/36
Wheat	Punjab	23/23	20/20	43/43	17/23	19/20	36/43
	Madhya Pradesh	19/19	20/20	39/39	11/19	15/20	26/39
Gram	Madhya Pradesh	16/16	20/20	36/36	15/16	18/20	33/36
	Haryana	15/15	17/17	32/32	10/15	10/17	20/32
Tur	Uttar Pradesh	09/09	18/18	27/27	09/09	16/18	25/27
	Madhya Pradesh	10/10	20/20	30/30	10/10	19/20	29/30
Groundnut	Gujarat	16/16	19/20	35/36	11/16	12/20	23/36
	Karnataka	12/12	17/17	29/29	9/12	01/17	10/29
Rapeseed and Mustard	Rajasthan	11/11	20/20	31/31	11/11	20/20	31/31
	Assam	11/11	20/20	31/31	11/11	02/20	13/31
Sugarcane	Tamil Nadu	04/04	17/17	21/21	04/04	17/17	21/21
	Maharashtra	15/15	20/20	35/35	15/15	14/20	29/35
Cotton	Punjab	19/19	20/20	39/39	17/19	13/20	30/39
	Maharashtra	09/09	18/18	27/27	07/09	10/18	17/27

Source: Computed using data from CACP (various years).

Notes: Numerators are number of years profit reaped; denominators are total number of years for which data was available.

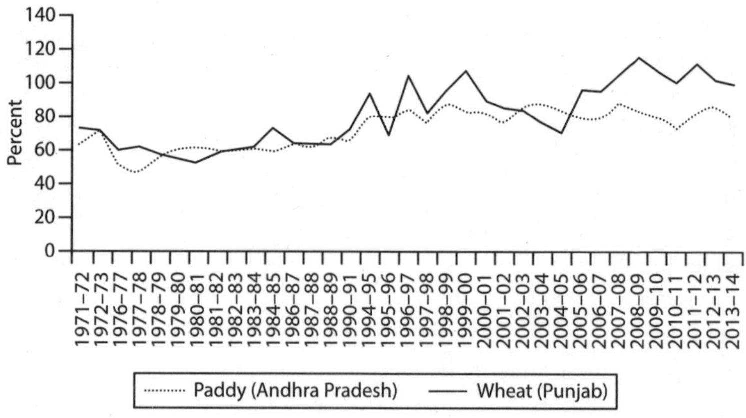

Figure 2.2 Percentage Difference between Cost A2 and C2 in Paddy and Wheat
Source: CACP (various years).

and 1990s (see Figure 2.2). In addition to low profitability, the year-on-year fluctuations in profitability are also found to be very high in HPS, which might be hurting the farmers.

Fully knowing the ground reality of the farm sector, the recent report by NITI Aayog on remunerative farming heavily stressed upon the productivity of crops for raising farm income. It surmises the following:

> To increase productivity, progress is required along three dimensions: (i) Quality and judicious use of inputs such as water, seeds, fertilizer and pesticides; (ii) judicious and safe exploitation of modern technology including genetically modified (GM) seeds; and (iii) shift into high value commodities such as fruits, vegetables, flowers, fisheries, animal husbandry and poultry. In the longer run, productivity enhancement requires research toward discovery of robust seed varieties and other inputs, appropriate crops and input usage for a given soil type and effective extension practices. (NITI Aayog, 2015)

Increase in productivity is surely not the solution and if we allow the market to have low prices during high productivity/production years. Therefore, this strategy alone would not help farmers get sufficient income from farming. Raising productivity might help the consumers and the country to further strengthen food security with reduced food inflation. But the farmers at large would not benefit through increased productivity unless simultaneous efforts are made to control COC and improve the procurement arrangements through state agencies, which are missing in the listed strategies. Farmers have been arguing in recent years that increased COC, especially the wage cost, has seriously affected the income from crop cultivation, which is also supported by CCS data. More fundamentally, it is not simply high productivity but better prices that dictate income trends. Increase in COC was also cited as the main reason for declaring paddy crop holiday in about 400,000 acres of fertile area of Andhra Pradesh. Therefore, measures are urgently needed to cut down COC wherever possible while formulating policies for promoting productivity of crops.

Future Agenda

It is clear from the analysis of SAS and CCS data that the income realized by farmers from different crop cultivation is very low. Although the income from crop cultivation alone (at 1986–7 prices) has increased from INR 3,645 in 2002–3 to INR 5,502 in 2012–13 per farmer household as per SAS data at the national level, it was found to be far less than the national-level average in many states of India. In fact, the income realized from cultivation by the farmer household at current prices works out to be only about INR 101 per day during 2012–13. Can a farmer household satisfy the family's consumption needs and other expenditures with this meagre income? Similar to SAS data, data from CCS from 1971–2 to 2013–14 too reinforce the fact that the income from crop cultivation is very poor across different crops and states in India. The poor income from crop cultivation is not only seen with the crops cultivated under rainfed/less irrigated conditions but also among crops that are cultivated under increased coverage of irrigation. Against common notions, CCS data of different crops show no significant and consistent difference in profitability between HPS and LPS. Farmers were unable to realize increased income consistently in any of the crops considered for the analysis.

Farmers have suffered losses or realized low income due to both increased COC and insignificant increase in VOP due to market failure. Productivity and production increase can in no way be a solution as the simple law of market economics defeats the logic.

Larger the arrival in the markets lower is the price of the product, and hence the increase in production will be eroded by consequent fall in prices. This needs to be comprehended. The reduced margin of profit from crop cultivation would not provide any incentive to farmers to continue to engage in agriculture in an intensive manner (see Swaminathan, 2008). As per SAS data (NSSO, 2005b), about 40 per cent of farmers are reportedly willing to quit agriculture because of poor remuneration from farming. The income from crop cultivation is not even enough to meet the annual cultivation expenditure in many states, which is also proved by SAS data. No single programme can help increase the income of farmers on a continuous basis. Farmers need sustained support in the form of increased returns from their crop cultivation. Therefore, along with price incentives, concerted efforts need to be taken to strengthen the non-price incentives such as the procurement system and market infrastructure, public investment in agriculture, irrigation infrastructure, and institutional credit.

Although the awareness about the MSP is very low among farmers, it plays a key role in deciding the market price of agricultural commodities (NITI Aayog, 2016). It is alleged that MSPs are not fixed in consonance with COC in most cases. The analysis of CCS data also seems to support this point. Therefore, as a first step towards increasing farm income, MSP should be fixed keeping in view the market trends in produce as also input prices. The NCF (2006) suggested the MSP for crops to be at 50 per cent more than the actual cost of production (cost C3). Prices fixed based on cost A2 do not cover the entire COC. Due to the changing nature of agriculture, cost of fixed investment, rent, and supervisory cost has increased substantially over the years. For instance, in Punjab, the difference between cost A2 and C2 was only about 60 per cent during TE 1982–3, but this difference increased to about 105 per cent in TE 2013–14 for wheat crop. Similar situations are seen for paddy in Andhra Pradesh and sugarcane in Maharashtra. The cost A2 does not include these important items, which cannot be justified by economic logic. Therefore, MSP should be fixed based on cost C2, after working out real COC based on credible data. In addition to this, in order to protect farmers from inflationary pressure, MSPs for various crops can also be fixed by linking with the Wholesale Price Index (WPI) of produce as also the inputs, as followed for salaried classes by way of dearness allowance (DA).

Mere announcement of MSPs will not help farmers, but along with MSPs, there is also a need to strengthen the procurement infrastructure. Even in paddy and wheat, except for a few states such as Andhra Pradesh, Punjab, and Haryana, the procurement levels by state agencies has all along been very poor (see Narayanamoorthy and Suresh, 2012). At the country level, the ratio of procurement of paddy and wheat to its total production was only about 30 per cent and about 32 per cent respectively during 2014–15. Farm income, especially from paddy crop, is found to be very low or negative in all those states (for example, West Bengal and Odisha) where procurement level is pathetically low. Procurement arrangements are also very poor in non-foodgrain crops such as oilseeds and pulses, which is clearly evident from SAS data as well. This has allowed private market agents to scrupulously exploit farmers and then consumers. Studies carried out across 236 districts in India show that density of market to cropped area and average distance to market play a significant role in deciding the per hectare VOP realized by farmers (see Narayanamoorthy, Alli, and Beero, 2013). Therefore, procurement as well as state-managed market infrastructures must be strengthened.

The Agricultural Produce Marketing Committee (APMC) Act of 2003 (Rules in 2007) should be implemented on a war footing. As rightly mentioned in the 16th Report of Committee on Agriculture, 'Pricing on Agricultural Produce', APMC

> advocates inter alia provision for private markets and E-markets, contract farming, direct purchase of agricultural produce from farmers by processors/bulk retailers/wholesalers/exporters nearer to the production centre, direct sale of produce by farmers to the consumers, etc. Such multiple options will enable the farmer to sell the produce for optimum returns without being compelled to make distress sale in local mandis. (GoI, 2014)

The role of farmers in deciding the price should be promoted by directly involving them in the market activities extensively. Farmer-managed markets in states such as Tamil Nadu and Andhra Pradesh have proved to be beneficial to them (see Kallummal and Srinivasan, 2007). Therefore, producers' markets on the lines of rythu bazaars (farmers' markets) should be encouraged across every part of the country to improve the farm income and to eliminate middlemen as underlined in the National Agricultural Policy of 2000 (GoI, 2000).

In order to protect farmers from distress sales during the glut periods, the price behaviour of sensitive commodities needs to be monitored closely for making swift interventions through the Market Intervention Scheme (MIS), as suggested by the Expert Group Committee on Indebtedness led by R. Radhakrishna. While regulating the output markets, it is also necessary to simultaneously regulate the input markets effectively to improve the pathetic income level of the farmer households. Use of spurious inputs is also partly responsible for crop failures and increased use of pesticides in crops such as cotton.

Besides price incentives, policymakers should also focus on the non-price incentives to increase the productivity of crops and also to reduce COC. Increased capital formation from public account is essential to reduce the transaction cost for private farmers. Except in the recent years, fixed capital formation by the public sector in agriculture has been continuously declining both in absolute terms and also in relation to the agricultural GDP. Efforts should be made to increase public investment so that COC can be reduced. The other important non-price incentive needed for the farmer is the assured supply of institutional credit. Non-availability of institutional credit often forces farmers to rely on non-institutional sources of credit to meet their credit requirements for crop cultivation that ultimately increases COC. Therefore, farmer-friendly policies need to be framed to provide adequate credit in time to increase farm income.

One of the reasons for increased COC and reduced income from crop cultivation is the increased reliance on groundwater irrigation in recent years. Not only has the fixed cost requirement for establishing groundwater irrigation structures increased over the years, but the recurring cost has also increased. CCS data clearly show an increasing trend in the cost on account of irrigation in most crops, especially in the recent years. This is because of stagnation in the expansion of public sector–managed surface irrigation facilities such as canals and tanks since the mid-1990s. Surface irrigation is a low-cost source of irrigation that can reduce the private cost of the farmers substantially. Therefore, adequate allocation of funds required for completing ongoing irrigation projects with better monitoring by state agencies needs to be focused upon.

Increased COC (not only cost A2 but C2 as well) has been the major issue encountered by farmers in recent years, which needs to be controlled by all means. Even if MSP is announced in consonance with COC (cost C2) for crops, it would not guarantee better income for farmers unless procurement infrastructures are strengthened sufficiently. Therefore, along with remunerative MSPs for different crops, the government should also strengthen farmer-friendly market infrastructure along with other non-price incentives such as adequate credit and improved surface irrigation facility. There is no doubt that the income of farmers can be increased adequately if procurement arrangements and other non-price (technology, credit, and irrigation) incentives are packaged and sequenced appropriately along with revision of MSP in consonance with COC.

Bibliography

Bhalla, S. S. 2012. 'Price of Paddy Populism'. *The Financial Express*, 10 May.

Bhattacharyya, B. 2004. *State of the Indian Farmer: Agricultural Exports*. Academic Foundation, New Delhi.

CACP (Commission for Agricultural Costs and Prices). Various years. *Report of the Commission for Agricultural Costs and Prices*. Ministry of Agriculture, Government of India, New Delhi.

Chand, R., R. Saxena, and S. Rana. 2015. 'Estimates and Analysis of Farm Income in India: 1983–84 to 2011–12'. *Economic and Political Weekly*, vol. 40, no. 22, pp. 139–45.

Darling, M. L. 1925. *The Punjab Peasant in Prosperity and Debt*. Oxford University Press, Delhi.

Deshpande, R. S. 1996. 'Demand and Supply of Agricultural Commodities: A Review'. *Indian Journal of Agricultural Economics*, vol. 51, nos 1–2 (January–June), pp. 270–87.

———. 2002. 'Suicide by Farmers in Karnataka: Agrarian Distress and Possible Alleviatory Steps'. *Economic and Political Weekly*, vol. 37, no. 26, pp. 2601–10.

Deshpande, R. S., M. J. Bhende, P. Thippiah, and M. Vivekananda. 2004. *State of the Indian Farmer: Crops and Cultivation*. Academic Foundation, New Delhi.

Deshpande, R. S., and N. Prabhu. 2005. 'Farmers' Distress: Proof beyond Question'. *Economic and Political Weekly*, vol. 40, nos 44–5, pp. 4663–5.

De Silva, H., D. Ratanadiwakara, and S. Soya. 2008. 'Transaction Costs in Agriculture: From the Planting Decision to Selling at Wholesale Market'. LIRNEasia, Colombo, Sri Lanka.

The Hindu Business Line. 2010. 'Fix MSP for Crops 50% over Actual Cost of Cultivation'. 16 December.

Rao, N. Chandrasekhara, and S. Mahendra Dev. 2010. 'Agricultural Price Policy, Farm Profitability and Food Security'. *Economic and Political Weekly*, vol. 45, nos 26 and 27 (June), pp. 174–82.

GoI (Government of India). 2000. *National Agricultural Policy: 2000*. Ministry of Agriculture, Government of India, New Delhi.

———. 2007. *Report of the Expert Group on Agricultural Indebtedness* (Chairman: R. Radhakrishna). Ministry of Finance, Government of India, New Delhi.

———. 2014. *Pricing of Agricultural Produce*, Sixteenth Report of the Committee on Agriculture (2013–14). Lok Sabha Secretariat Government of India, New Delhi.

———. 2016. *Agricultural Statistics at a Glance*. Directorate of Economics and Statistics, Ministry of Agriculture, Government of India, New Delhi.

Gulati, A. 2012. 'Hike MSPs or Free Up Agriculture'. *The Financial Express*, 15 June.

Gulati, A., and C. H. H. Rao. 1994. 'Indian Agriculture: Emerging Perspectives and Policy Issues'. *Economic and Political Weekly*, vol. 29, no. 53, pp. 158–69.

Kahlon, A. S., and D. S. Tyagi. 1980. 'Inter-Sectoral Terms of Trade'. *Economic and Political Weekly*, vol. 15, no. 52, pp. 173–84.

Kallummal, M., and K. S. Srinivasan. 2007. *The Dynamics of Farmers Market: A Case of 'Uzhavar Sandhai' of Tamil Nadu*. Make Trade Fair Campaign, CENTAD, New Delhi.

Misra, V. N., and P. B. R. Hazell. 1996. 'Terms of Trade, Rural Poverty, Technology and Investment: The Indian Experience, 1952–53 to 1990–91'. *Economic and Political Weekly*, vol. 31, no. 13, pp. 158–69.

Narayanamoorthy, A. 2006a. 'Relief Package for Farmers: Can It Stop Suicides?'. *Economic and Political Weekly*, vol. 41, no. 31, August 5, pp. 3353–5.

———. 2006b. 'State of India's Farmers'. *Economic and Political Weekly*, vol. 41, no. 6 (11 February), pp. 471–3.

———. 2007. 'Deceleration in Agricultural Growth: Technology Fatigue or Policy Fatigue'. *Economic and Political Weekly*, vol. 42, no. 25 (23 June), pp. 2375–9.

———. 2011. 'Development and Composition of Irrigation in India: Temporal Trends and Regional Patterns'. *Irrigation and Drainage*, vol. 60, no. 4, pp. 431–45.

———. 2013. 'Profitability in Crops Cultivation in India: Some Evidence from Cost of Cultivation Survey Data'. *Indian Journal of Agricultural Economics*, vol. 68, no.1 (January–March), pp. 104–21.

Narayanamoorthy, A., P. Alli, and S. K. Beero. 2013. 'Agricultural Market Access, Infrastructure and Value of Output Nexus: A District-Level Study'. *Indian Journal of Agricultural Marketing*, vol. 27, no. 3 (September–December), pp. 75–93.

Narayanamoorthy, A., P. Alli, and R. Suresh. 2015. 'How Profitable Is Cultivation of Rainfed Crops? Some Insights from Cost of Cultivation Studies'. *Agricultural Economics Research Review*, vol. 27, no. 2 (July–December), pp. 233–41.

Narayanamoorthy, A., and R. Suresh. 2012. 'Agricultural Price Policy in India: Has It Benefitted Paddy Farmers?'. *Indian Journal of Agricultural Marketing*, vol. 26, no. 3 (September–December), pp. 87–106.

NCF (National Commission on Farmers). 2006. *Serving Farmers and Saving Farming, Report V Excerpts.* Ministry of Agriculture, Government of India, New Delhi. Available at www.krishakayog.gov.in.

NITI Aayog. 2015. *Raising Agricultural Productivity and Making Farming Remunerative to Farmers.* Government of India, New Delhi.

———. 2016. *Evaluation Report of Efficacy of Minimum Support Prices (MSP) on Farmers.* Development Monitoring and Evaluation Office, New Delhi.

NSSO (National Sample Survey Office). 2005a. *Situation Assessment Survey of Farmers: Income, Expenditure and Productive Assets of Farmer Households.* Report No. 497. Ministry of Statistics and Programme Implementation, Government of India, New Delhi.

———. 2005b. *Situation Assessment Survey of Farmers: Some Aspects of Farming.* 59th Round (January–December 2003). Ministry of Statistics and Programme Implementation, Government of India, New Delhi.

———. 2014. *Key Indicators of Situations of Agricultural Households in IndiaI,* 70th Round (May). Ministry of Statistics and Programme Implementation, Government of India, New Delhi.

Rao, V. M. 2001. 'The Making of Agricultural Price Policy: A Review of CACP Reports'. *Journal of Indian School of Political Economy*, vol. 13, no. 1, pp. 1–28.

Sainath, P. 2010. 'Farm Suicides—a 12 Year Saga'. *The Hindu*, 25 January.

Schultz, T. W. 1964. *Transforming Traditional Agriculture.* Yale University Press, New Haven, U. S. A.

Sen, Abhijit, and M. S. Bhatia. 2004. *State of the Indian Farmer: Cost of Cultivation and Farm Income in India.* Academic Foundation, New Delhi.

Swaminathan, M. S. 2008. 'Ending the Debt Trap and Attaining Food Security'. *The Hindu*, 3 March, p. 12.

Vaidyanathan, A. 2006. 'Farmers' Suicides and the Agrarian Crisis'. *Economic and Political Weekly*, vol. 4, no. 38 (23 September), pp. 4009–13.

Vaidyanathan, A., Asha Krishna Kumar, A. Rajagopal, and D. Varatharajan. 1994. 'Impact of Irrigation on Productivity of Land'. *Journal of Indian School of Political Economy*, vol. 6, no. 4 (October–December), pp. 601–45.

3

Farm Income

Irrigated versus Un-irrigated Crops

The major focus of this chapter is to study and understand the economics of identical crops which are cultivated under irrigated and less irrigated or rainfed regions in India. Until recently, the country's policymakers and academicians held on to the conventional wisdom that farmers in irrigated regions reap more profits than the rainfed farmers. However, recent evidence shows that farmers are unable to recover even the COC from the cultivation of irrigated crops such as paddy and sugarcane due to substantial increase in COC (Narayanamoorthy, 2006; 2012; 2013).[1] If this is so, what might be the condition of rainfed or less irrigated crops where the instability

[1] The farmers of fertile and irrigated East Godavari and West Godavari districts of Andhra Pradesh, in an unprecedented manner, went on a crop holiday, refusing to cultivate paddy in about four lakh acres of land during the kharif season in 2011, citing poor remuneration. Sugarcane farmers across the country have been relentlessly agitating for a right price for their produce and a commensurate share of profits earned by the mill owners. The agitation took a serious turn with the death of a sugarcane farmer in a police firing in Sangli district of Maharashtra in 2012 (see Narayanamoorthy and Alli, 2013).

of output is very significant? From which part of India's farmlands is the farmers' cry of distress predominantly heard? Is it from the resource-poor and drought-prone rainfed regions or from the regions bestowed with most fertile lands supported by well-marked irrigation systems?

Agricultural research has traditionally focused primarily on maximizing agricultural production and yield. A plethora of studies have focused time and again on the technical aspects of farming, issues related to the problem of instability of yield and output, low resource use, and so on. Research studies have reported that productivity gains in irrigated agriculture trickles down through enhanced farm income and prevents farmers from getting into a debt trap (Lipton et al., 2002). Another study revealed that farmers' gross income from irrigated farming not only turned out to be much less unstable than rainfed farming but is also found to have risen across the country by the late 1970s (Dhawan 1985; 1987). All these studies implied that higher income generation from the farm by itself indicates the profitability of the crop. Without having compared the income generated from farms with the cost involved in the cultivation of the crop, how can higher income indicate its remunerativeness? Similar to all other enterprises, farming is also an enterprise that entirely rests on profits. Farmers' decision to cultivate crops in the following season rests entirely on the premise that income from the farm is substantially higher than the cost involved in cultivating the crops. After paying off the borrowed loan, the surplus income that remains at a farmer's disposal is what concerns him the most, irrespective of whether he is an irrigated crop grower or un-irrigated crop grower.

It has been argued that irrigated agriculture yielded immense benefits to developing societies (Hussain and Hanjra, 2004). This proposition is questionable on the ground that despite most of the increase in the agricultural output over the years having taken place under irrigated conditions (Kerr, 1996), the country continues to be plagued by the suicide spree of farmers, acute farm indebtedness, and frequent farmers' agitations demanding a right price for their produce (see GoI, 2007). What makes the farmers lament the non-remunerativeness of irrigated crops in spite of a favourable bias in terms of research and infrastructural investments (Kerr, 1996)?

Touted as the by-passed areas of the country, rainfed areas are highly diverse, ranging from resource rich areas[2] with good agricultural potential to resource poor areas with much more restricted potential. Despite the paucity and uncertainty of rainfall, depressing yields, and unstable income, rainfed agriculture accounts for about 83 per cent of pulses, about 70 per cent of oilseeds, and about 65 per cent of cotton (CRIDA, 2011). Various field-level studies that primarily focused on the yield potential of rainfed crops reported that high yielding varieties (HYVs) contribute to a substantial increase in the gross income per hectare (Kanitkar, 1960; Rastogi and Annamalai, 1981; Rastogi and Reddy, 1982; Rangaswamy, 1982). When HYVs generally come at a higher price and are found to be the villain in escalating COC, such empirical findings need to be reassessed with regard to the ground reality. First, when the resource poor rainfed farmers continue to remain in the grip of dwindling farm income, newly introduced HYVs are beyond their reach. Second, farmers of rainfed regions prefer raising mostly traditional low yielding varieties because of their ability to withstand low rainfall better than HYVs (Kahlon and Sandhu, 1971). If the use of HYVs is not practically feasible in rainfed farms, in a scenario of scanty rainfall, perpetual drought, and rising COC, how remunerative are rainfed crops? How true is the commonly held belief that it is only the rainfed crops that continue to remain in a state of perpetual stagnation? In the wake of distressed voices echoing from across the diverse agro-climatic regions of the country, it will be meaningful to compare the profitability of a rainfed crop in one pocket of the scanty zone, say a completely un-irrigated or less irrigated area, with another pocket which is endowed with modest irrigation coverage. Probably, our study will be the first of its kind in trying to analyse the profitability of rainfed crops that are cultivated under irrigated and rainfed conditions utilizing a longer data period. With an attempt to answer some of the most pertinent questions with regard to the profitability of

[2] According to Kerr (1996) the resource rich rainfed areas are potentially highly productive and have already experienced widespread adoption of improved seeds, while the resource poor rainfed areas are those where productivity growth has lagged behind and there is widespread poverty and degradation of natural resources.

irrigated and un-irrigated crops and the number of times the farmers were able to reap profits, secondary level data from CCS on seven important rainfed crops covering a period from 1971–2 to 2009–10 is utilized for the purpose. The major objectives of the study are (i) to study the economics of similar crops cultivated under irrigated and less irrigated regions over the period; (ii) to study the trends in profitability of crops cultivated under irrigated and un-irrigated conditions; (iii) to find out whether the profitability of irrigated and un-irrigated crops has changed during the agrarian crisis period (ACP); and (iv) to find out how many times farmers cultivating these crops were able to reap profits during the period of analysis.

Data and Method

This study has been entirely carried out using secondary data covering the period from 1971–2 to 2009–10. As the study mainly focuses on the economics of crop cultivation under irrigated and less irrigated conditions over a long period of time, the data needed for this study has been compiled from various publications of the CACP, which has been publishing data on COC for different crops originally generated from the scheme on comprehensive survey on COC.[3] A total of seven major rainfed crops—jowar, bajra, maize, tur, gram, groundnut, and cotton—cultivated under irrigated and less irrigated (or rainfed) conditions in major growing states have been considered for studying the profitability. One of the objectives of this chapter is to find out whether the profitability of these crops cultivated under irrigated conditions is in any way better than that of the crops cultivated in less irrigated conditions. For this purpose, we have selected two states for each crop, one with better irrigation facility and another with very less irrigation coverage (see Table 3.1). The CACP has been using nine different cost concepts (A1, A2, A2+FL, B1, B2, C1, C2, C2*, and C3) for measuring the economics of various crop cultivation.[4] For this study, cost C2 has been considered for computing the

[3] For details, see www.cacp.dacnet.nic.in.

[4] The following are the cost concepts the CACP has been using:

Cost A1 = all actual expenses in cash and kind incurred in production by owner

Table 3.1 Crops and States Selected for the Study on Irrigated vs Un-irrigated Crops

Crops	States Selected for Study	Category of State Selected	Area (in mha) under Cultivation in 2009–10	% of Irrigation Coverage of the Selected Crop in 2009–10
Jowar	Maharashtra	Irrigated	4.17	9.53
	Madhya Pradesh	Rainfed	0.44	0.22
Bajra	Gujarat	Irrigated	0.67	22.17
	Rajasthan	Rainfed	5.16	4.51
Maize	Andhra Pradesh	Irrigated	0.78	44.18
	Rajasthan	Rainfed	1.09	1.00
Arhar	Uttar Pradesh	Irrigated	0.31	14.42
	Maharashtra	Rainfed	1.09	1.60
Gram	Madhya Pradesh	Irrigated	3.08	47.86
	Uttar Pradesh	Rainfed	0.61	16.66
Groundnut	Tamil Nadu	Irrigated	0.41	37.79
	Gujarat	Rainfed	1.82	11.03
Cotton	Gujarat	Irrigated	2.46	56.65
	Maharashtra	Rainfed	3.49	2.63

Source: GoI (2011)
Notes: mha: million hectares.

Cost A2 = Cost A1 + rent paid for leased-in land

Cost A2+ FL = Cost A2 + imputed value of family labour

Cost B1 = Cost A1 + interest on value of owned capital assets (excluding land)

Cost B2 = Cost B1 + rental value of owned land (net of land revenue) and rent paid for leased-in land

Cost C1 = Cost B1 + imputed value of family labour

Cost C2 = Cost B2 + imputed value of family labour

Cost C2* = Cost C2 estimated by taking into account statutory minimum or actual wage, whichever is higher

Cost C3 = Cost C2* + 10 per cent of cost C2* on account of managerial functions performed by farmer

profitability of irrigated and less irrigated crops as it covers all the variable and fixed costs needed for crop cultivation. In order to study whether the profitability of crops cultivated under irrigated and rainfed conditions is increased or not, all the cost- and income-related data of the selected crops have been converted into constant prices using CPIAL deflator at 1986–7 prices. Profits of various irrigated and rainfed crops are computed by deducting the cost C2 from VOP.

Economics of Irrigated and Rainfed Crop Cultivation

The need to analyse the profitability of the crops cultivated under irrigated and un-irrigated conditions comes in the wake of farmers agitating against the non-remunerativeness of various high value crops such as sugarcane, paddy, and cotton. It is observed that the COC of traditional crops as well as commercial crops is moving at a faster pace than the VOP (Narayanamoorthy, 2007). While innumerable reasons are being cited for this disturbing situation, a question that continues to remain at hand is, why is farm income not remunerative despite a slew of policy initiatives? A general perception is that the irrigated crop growers reap relatively higher profits than the rainfed crop growers, but this needs to be investigated empirically because of the fast-changing agricultural environment in the recent years. Besides analysing the trends in profitability of crops cultivated under irrigated and un-irrigated conditions, we will also be looking at how many times (number of years) farmers of the different crops were able to reap profit during the entire period of analysis from 1970–1 to 2009–10. The agrarian crisis that started from the early 1990s (along with initiation of economic reforms) has arguably reduced the profitability of both foodgrain and non-foodgrain crops (Kalamkar and Narayanamoorthy, 2003; Narayanamoorthy, 2013). Therefore, an attempt has also been made to find out whether any difference exists in the profitability of crops cultivated under irrigated and un-irrigated conditions before and after 1995–6.

Economics of Jowar Cultivation

Jowar, an important foodgrain crop cultivated predominantly under rainfed conditions, occupies about 5 per cent of the total area under foodgrain cultivation as of today (GoI, 2012). The area under jowar has witnessed a drastic decline from 15.57 mha in 1950–1 to 7.38 mha in 2010–11, a decline of about 111 per cent. Maharashtra, Karnataka, and Madhya Pradesh are the three leading producers, which together accounted for 78 per cent of total area and 79 per cent of total production of jowar in 2010–11. Of these three states, while Maharashtra and Karnataka accounted for about 55 per cent and 16 per cent of area respectively, Madhya Pradesh accounted for only about 5 per cent of area in 2010–11. Maharashtra, which accounts for about 55 per cent of area of jowar, cultivated this crop with irrigation coverage of about 10 per cent, while Madhya Pradesh had irrigation coverage of merely 0.20 per cent in 2009–10. Therefore, Maharashtra has been considered as an irrigated state and Madhya Pradesh has been selected as a less irrigated (rainfed) state to study the profitability of jowar. It is astounding to see that Maharashtra, which was the largest producer of jowar in the country, was unable to make any appreciable profits during the eight time points presented in Table 3.2. The farmers were able to reap profits in only two out of eight time points. It is found that the cost C2 has risen at a faster pace as compared to VOP, giving absolutely no chance to the farmers to reap even marginal profits. In fact, it is during the ACP that the loss has been very significant and rampant. The COC involved in cultivating the jowar crop in Madhya Pradesh is observed to have risen consistently showing no signs of slowing down in any of the time points considered in the analysis. The farmers of the rainfed areas of Madhya Pradesh have been suffering an absolute loss in all seven time points considered for the analysis. It is quite evident that jowar cultivation in Madhya Pradesh is a loss-making proposition pushing farmers to the brink of immiseration.

As mentioned earlier, besides studying the absolute profit level of irrigated and less irrigated or rainfed crops, an attempt has also been made to study as to how many times farmers are able to reap profits in cultivating jowar during the entire period of analysis (1971–2 to 2009–10). Our analysis shows that of the total 28 years for which we have got data for Maharashtra,[5] farmers were able to reap profit

[5] We have covered the period from 1971–2 to 2009–10 (a total 39 years) for the study. However, the data on cost and income pertaining to the

Table 3.2 Profitability in Jowar Cultivation from Irrigated and Less Irrigated States (in INR/ha at 1986–7 prices)

Year	Cost C2		Value of Output (VOP)		Profit	
	Maharashtra (IR State)	Madhya Pradesh (RF State)	Maharashtra (IR State)	Madhya Pradesh (RF State)	Maharashtra (IR State)	Madhya Pradesh (RF State)
1973–4	1,415	DNA	1,478	DNA	63	DNA
1978–9	1,302	1,293	1,306	1,258	4	–35
1984–5	1,744	1,419	1,441	1,018	–302	–401
1989–90	2,276	1,971	2,122	1,342	–155	–629
1994–5	2,219	2,194	1,947	2,069	–272	–125
1999–2000	3,634	2,061	2,723	1,349	–911	–712
2004–5	3,031	2,308	2,038	1,583	–994	–725
2009–10	3,983	2,513	2,467	1,755	–1,515	–758

Sources: Computed using data from CACP (various years).

Notes: DNA: data not available; IR: irrigated; RF: rainfed; due to non-availability of data for some specified years, data from the nearest point is used for the analysis.

for barely 6 years (21.42 per cent). That is, of the total 28 years the irrigated farmers of Maharashtra have incurred losses in 22 years, the loss having occurred more number of times during the ACP. Such a huge loss in case of an irrigated crop is indeed a big surprise. In case of Madhya Pradesh, where the crop is cultivated predominantly under un-irrigated condition, it is found that out of 31 years, the rainfed farmers have incurred losses in almost 30 years. What is clear from the analysis of jowar crop is that neither the irrigated nor the rainfed farmer is reaping any appreciable profits.

Economics of Bajra Cultivation

Bajra, the poor man's staple food, is a rapidly growing warm weather crop, which occupies about 8 per cent of the total area of foodgrains (GoI, 2012). Unlike jowar, the area under bajra has seen a gradual increase from 9.02 mha in 1950–1 to 9.61 mha in 2010–11 (GoI, 2012). Rajasthan, Uttar Pradesh, and Gujarat are the three leading producers of bajra, and they together accounted for 76 per cent of the total area and 70 per cent of the total production of bajra in 2010–11. While Rajasthan and Uttar Pradesh accounted for about 57 per cent and 10 per cent of area respectively, Gujarat accounteed for 9 per cent of area in 2010–11. Of the three states, we have selected Rajasthan, which has lower irrigation coverage (4.51 per cent) and Gujarat, which has higher irrigation coverage (22.17 per cent) to study the profitability of bajra. Our analysis on profitability shows that out of the eight time points, the irrigated bajra crop could yield profit in only once (Table 3.3). It is observed that the cost C2 almost doubled from INR 2,749/ha in 1994–5 to INR 4,047/ha in 2009–10, eventually making bajra cultivation a costly venture under irrigated condition. The bajra crop grown under rainfed condition in Rajasthan is also seen to have made profit in only one out of the eight time points. A complete loss in seven out of eight time

selected seven crops were not available from CACP's publications consistently for all the years for any of the states selected. Only those years for which data were available was considered for the analysis. Therefore, the total number of years (data time points) considered for the analysis would vary considerably from one crop to another.

Table 3.3 Profitability in Bajra Cultivated in Irrigated and Less Irrigated States (in INR/ha at 1986–7 prices)

Year	Cost C2		Value of Output (VOP)		Profit	
	Gujarat (IR State)	Rajasthan (RF State)	Gujarat (IR State)	Rajasthan (RF State)	Gujarat (IR State)	Rajasthan (RF State)
1973–4	1,767	603	1,832	885	65	283
1978–9	2,620	1,012	2,095	634	–525	–378
1984–5	2,599	805	2,280	731	–319	–74
1989–90	DNA	1,035	DNA	576	DNA	–459
1994–5	2,749	1,276	2,521	972	–228	–303
1999–2000	3,588	1,732	3,432	1,098	–157	–634
2004–5	3,619	2,108	2,906	1,412	–713	–696
2009–10	4,047	2,143	3,978	1,401	– 69	–741

Sources: Computed using data from CACP (various years).

Notes: DNA: data not available; IR: irrigated; RF: rainfed; due to non-availability of data for some specified years, data from the nearest point is used for the analysis.

points explains the un-viability of the crop in both irrigated and less irrigated states.

This picture gets darker while looking at the entire period of analysis. Of the total 26 years (Table 3.4) for which the data is available, the irrigated bajra cultivators of Gujarat were able to make profits in only 6 years (23.07 per cent). It meant that these farmers had to bear a huge loss in 20 out of 26 years (76.92 per cent), with much of the loss having occurred during the ACP. The rainfed cultivators on the other hand were in an equally pitiable situation with profits being observed in only 3 out of 32 years (9.32 per cent). A loss in 29 out of 32 years (90.62 per cent) is bound to put the bajra farmers of the rainfed areas in a dire situation. The area of this highly nutritious crop may come down in the future if its cultivation remains non-remunerative under both irrigated and un-irrigated conditions.

Economics of Maize Cultivation

This 'crop of the future' is grown in different production environments in India. The area under maize has seen a big jump from 3.16 mha in 1950–1 to 8.55 mha in 2010–11 (GoI, 2012). This crop accounts for about 7 per cent of the total area under foodgrains. Karnataka, Andhra Pradesh, Maharashtra, and Rajasthan are the leading producers of maize, which together accounted for about 47 per cent of the total area and about 60 per cent of its total production in the country. Considering the area under cultivation and data availability, we have selected Andhra Pradesh (where this crop is cultivated with 44.2 per cent of irrigation coverage) as irrigated state and Rajasthan (irrigation coverage of this crop was only 1.02 per cent in 2009–10) as less irrigated state for studying profitability of maize. Our analysis shows that out of the eight time points, with data available only for four time points, the maize crop incurs losses in four. It is evident from Table 3.5 that the upward movement of cost C2 keeps pace with the VOP, thereby blocking all possible ways for maize cultivators to earn any decent returns. The farmers cultivating maize under rainfed conditions in Rajasthan are found to have reaped profits in only one out of eight time points. That is, farmers are subjected to loss in six out of eight time points. It is observed that the cost C2 has risen extensively to the extent that the farmers' loss

Table 3.4 Number of Years When Profit Was Reaped or Loss Was Incurred by Jowar and Bajra Farmers from 1971–2 to 2009–10

Crops	States	Category of State	Pre–agrarian Crisis Period (1971–2 to 1994–5)		Agrarian Crisis Period (1995–6 to 2009–10)		Entire Period of Analysis (1971–2 to 2009–10)	
			Ratio of VOP to Cost C2		Ratio of VOP to Cost C2		Ratio of VOP to Cost C2	
			> 1.00	< 1.00	> 1.00	< 1.00	> 1.00	< 1.00
Jowar	Maharashtra	IR	6/14	8/14	0/14	14/14	6/28	22/28
			(42.85)	(57.14)	(0.00)	(100.00)	(21.42)	(78.57)
	Madhya Pradesh	RF	1/16	15/16	0/15	15/15	1/31	30/31
			(6.25)	(93.75)	(0.00)	(100.00)	(3.22)	(96.77)
Bajra	Gujarat	IR	5/14	9/14	1/12	11/12	6/26	20/26
			(35.71)	(64.28)	(8.33)	(91.66)	(23.07)	(76.92)
	Rajasthan	RF	3/18	15/18	0/14	14/14	3/32	29/32
			(16.66)	(83.33)	(0.00)	(100.00)	(9.37)	(90.62)

Sources: Computed using data from CACP (various years).

Notes: VOP: value of output; IR: irrigated; RF: rainfed; bracketed figures are percentage of total number of years.

Table 3.5 Profitability in Maize Crop Cultivated in Irrigated and Less Irrigated States (in INR/ha at 1986–7 prices)

Year	Cost C2		Value of Output (VOP)		Profit	
	Andhra Pradesh (IR State)	Rajasthan (RF State)	Andhra Pradesh (IR State)	Rajasthan (RF State)	Andhra Pradesh (IR State)	Rajasthan (RF State)
1973–4	DNA	1,353	DNA	1,450	DNA	96
1978–9	DNA	DNA	DNA	DNA	DNA	DNA
1984–5	DNA	2,752	DNA	1,819	DNA	–933
1989–90	DNA	2,732	DNA	1,898	DNA	–834
1994–5	4,164	3,584	3,127	2,706	–1,037	–878
1999–2000	4,101	3,803	3,120	2,000	–981	–1,802
2004–5	5,611	3,586	4,519	1,969	–1,092	–1,617
2009–10	7,517	4,712	7,311	3,115	–207	–1,597

Sources: Computed using data from CACP (various years).

Notes: DNA: data not available; IR: irrigated; RF: rainfed; due to non-availability of data for some specified years, data from the nearest point is used for the analysis.

is found to be massive and damaging. Similar to crops such as jowar and bajra, this crop also fails to bring any appreciable returns for farmers even in Andhra Pradesh, where this crop is cultivated with higher irrigation coverage.

The position of profitability from maize cultivation did not change dramatically when one considers the entire period of analysis from 1971–2 to 2009–10. The irrigated maize cultivators of Andhra Pradesh are found to have been in the grip of massive losses in 14 (93.33 per cent) out of 15 years for which COC data was available from CACP sources (Table 3.6). As expected, the loss incurred by the farmers is found to have been more in the number of years during the ACP. Under rainfed conditions too, maize farmers were able to get marginal profits in 4 (13.79 per cent) out of 29 years, and in the remaining 25 years (86.20 per cent) farmers have incurred losses in relation to cost C2. Clearly, the analysis based on CCS data shows that there are no significant differences in the profitability of maize crop cultivated between high irrigated and less irrigated conditions.

Economics of Tur Cultivation

After studying the profitability of cereal crops, we will now turn our focus on the pulse crops which are mostly cultivated under rainfed conditions. An important pulse crop of India is arhar (tur), which accounts for about 3 per cent of the total foodgrains area. Its cultivated area has increased gradually from 2.18 mha in 1950–1 to 4.37 mha in 2010–11 possibly because of increased demand for the crop. Maharashtra, Karnataka, and Uttar Pradesh are the three leading producers of tur, which together accounted for about 58 per cent of the total area and about 64 per cent of its production in 2010–11 (GoI, 2012). While Maharashtra and Karnataka accounted for 29.75 per cent and 20.37 per cent of area respectively, Uttar Pradesh accounted for 7.78 per cent of area in 2010–11. Of these three states, it is Maharashtra which cultivates this crop with lowest irrigation coverage of 1.60 per cent and Uttar Pradesh cultivates it with the irrigation coverage of 14.30 per cent as per the data of 2009–10. Therefore, Uttar Pradesh is considered as irrigated state and Maharashtra as rainfed state in order to study the economics of irrigated and un-irrigated tur crop.

Table 3.6 Number of Years When Profit Was Reaped or Loss Was Incurred by Maize Farmers from 1971–2 to 2009–10

Crop	State	Category of State	Pre–agrarian Crisis Period (1971–2 to 1994–5)		Agrarian Crisis Period (1995–6 to 2009–10)		Entire Period of Analysis (1971–2 to 2009–10)	
			Ratio VOP to C2		Ratio VOP to C2		Ratio VOP to C2	
			> 1.00	< 1.00	> 1.00	< 1.00	> 1.00	< 1.00
Maize	Andhra Pradesh	IR	0/1 (0.00)	1/1 (100.00)	1/14 (7.14)	13/14 (92.85)	1/15 (6.66)	14/15 (93.33)
	Rajasthan	RF	4/14 (28.57)	10/14 (71.42)	0/15 (0.00)	15/15 (100.00)	4/29 (13.79)	25/29 (86.20)

Sources: Computed using data from CACP (various years).
Notes: VOP: value of output; DNA: data not available; IR: irrigated; RF: rainfed; due to non-availability of data for some specified years, data from the nearest point is used for the analysis.

Our analysis shows that unlike the three cereal crops (jowar, bajra, and maize) studied in preceding sections, the irrigated tur has not entirely disappointed farmers in terms of profitability. Out of eight time points, irrigated tur cultivators were able to reap profits in six time points in Uttar Pradesh (see Table 3.7). Although farmers have not incurred any losses in any of the time points, yet the profit over cost C2 is found to have declined in each of the time points considered for the analysis. Similar to irrigated tur, the rainfed tur of Maharashtra has indeed proven to be remunerative to the farmers, which was not expected by us. The crop has yielded profits to farmers in four out of four time points. While the amount of loss is found to have increased during the ACP in case of the three cereal crops (jowar, bajra, and maize) analysed earlier, farmers were able to get appreciable returns in case of the rainfed tur crop during the ACP. While looking at the entire period of analysis, the irrigated tur crop, which was observed to have benefitted farmers, has indeed profited them in all the 23 years (100.00 per cent). Equally, the farmers were able to reap profits in 13 out of 14 (92.85) years in case of the rainfed tur crop too (see Table 3.9). As mentioned previously, it is in the ACP that both the irrigated and rainfed tur farmers were able to reap a decent profit. Although the results are perplexing to us, steep increase in MSP for tur in the recent years, which has been hiked from INR 1,200 per quintal in 2000–1 to INR 4,400 per quintal in 2012–13, could be one of the main reasons for reaping profit from its cultivation (see Narayanamoorthy, 2012).

Economics of Gram Cultivation

Another important pulse crop considered for analysis is gram, which is an important rabi crop accounting for about 7 per cent of the total foodgrains area. The area under gram has steadily increased from 7.57 mha in 1950–1 to 9.19 mha in 2010–11 (GoI, 2012). Madhya Pradesh, Rajasthan, Maharashtra, and Uttar Pradesh are the leading producers of gram, which together accounted for about 75 per cent of area and about 74 per cent of production of gram in 2010–11. Of these four states, Madhya Pradesh, which accounted for about 34 per cent of area, had the highest irrigation coverage of 49 per cent, while Uttar Pradesh, which accounted for about 6 per cent of

Table 3.7 Profitability in Tur Crop Cultivated in Irrigated and Less Irrigated States (in INR/ha at 1986–7 prices)

Year	Cost C2		Value of Output (VOP)		Profit	
	Uttar Pradesh (IR State)	Maharashtra (RF State)	Uttar Pradesh (IR State)	Maharashtra (RF State)	Uttar Pradesh (IR State)	Maharashtra (RF State)
1973–4	DNA	DNA	DNA	DNA	DNA	DNA
1978–9	DNA	DNA	DNA	DNA	DNA	DNA
1984–5	3,417	DNA	4,834	DNA	1,417	DNA
1989–90	3,524	DNA	4,916	DNA	1,393	DNA
1994–5	3,842	2,438	5,776	4,207	1,934	1,769
1999–2000	4,143	2,788	5,205	4,312	1,062	1,524
2004–5	4,787	4,290	5,564	5,021	777	731
2009–10	4,609	7,857	4,745	11,939	136	4,081

Sources: Computed using data from CACP (various years).

Notes: DNA: data not available; IR: irrigated; RF: rainfed; due to non-availability of data for some specified years, data from the nearest point is used for the analysis.

area, cultivated gram only with 17 per cent of irrigation coverage in 2009–10. Therefore, Madhya Pradesh as irrigated state and Uttar Pradesh as rainfed state have been selected for studying the profitability of gram crop.

The analysis reveals that the irrigated gram crop is found to be profitable in seven out of eight time points, which is indeed a remarkable trend (see Table 3.8). However, the profit over cost C2 is found to have fluctuated every alternate year, which is a matter of serious concern as it explains the instability of the income from the gram crop cultivation. Similar to the irrigated state, the rainfed gram cultivated in Uttar Pradesh is also found to be profitable to the farmers in six out of eight time points. But the profit over cost C2 from the rainfed gram crop is observed to be unsteady throughout the period considered for the analysis. The variation is observed to be very marked from INR 1,195/ha during 2004–5 to INR 295/ha in 2009–10. The analysis carried out by taking the entire period also shows that the irrigated gram crop is profitable to farmers in 30 out of 32 years (93.75 per cent), with much of the profits being reaped during the ACP (see Table 3.9). As far as the rainfed gram crop is concerned, farmers have reaped profits in 23 out of 24 years (95.83 per cent). Though there are variations in the quantum of profit reaped by the farmers cultivating gram under irrigated and rainfed conditions, we do not see any significant difference in the number of years of profits from gram cultivation between irrigated and rainfed states.

Profitability of Groundnut Cultivation

Most oilseed crops are also predominantly cultivated under rainfed conditions in India. Therefore, one of the important oilseed crops, namely groundnut, has been considered for studying the profitability. The total area under nine oilseed crops has increased tremendously from 10.73 mha in 1950–1 to 27.22 mha in 2010–11, an increase of about 154 per cent. Of the nine major oilseed crops, groundnut is the most significant one, which accounted for about 22 per cent of the total area under oilseeds in 2010–11 (GoI, 2012). The area under groundnut has increased moderately from 4.49 mha in 1950–1 to 5.86 mha in 2010–11. Gujarat, Andhra Pradesh, Tamil Nadu, and Karnataka are the major producers of groundnut, which together

Table 3.8 Profitability in Gram Crop Cultivated in Irrigated and Less Irrigated States (in INR/ha at 1986–7 prices)

Year	Cost C2		Value of Output (VOP)		Profit	
	Madhya Pradesh (IR State)	Uttar Pradesh (RF State)	Madhya Pradesh (IR State)	Uttar Pradesh (RF State)	Madhya Pradesh (IR State)	Uttar Pradesh (RF State)
1973–4	DNA	DNA	DNA	DNA	DNA	DNA
1978–9	1,829	DNA	2,538	DNA	709	DNA
1984–5	2,280	3,128	2,948	3,919	668	792
1989–90	2,276	3,525	3,530	4,724	611	1,199
1994–5	3,389	3,191	3,924	3,510	535	319
1999–2000	3,015	3,944	3,677	6,301	663	2,357
2004–5	3,265	3,564	4,009	4,759	745	1,195
2009–10	3,600	3,842	4,327	4,136	727	295

Sources: Computed using data from CACP (various years).

Notes: DNA: data not available; IR: irrigated; RF: rainfed; due to non-availability of data for some specified years, data from the nearest point is used for the analysis.

Table 3.9 Number of Years When Profit Was Reaped or Loss Was Incurred by Tur and Gram Farmers from 1971–2 to 2009–10

Crops	States	Category of State	Pre–agrarian Crisis Period (1971–2 to 1994–5)		Agrarian Crisis Period (1995–6 to 2009–10)		Entire Period of Analysis (1971–2 to 2009–10)	
			Ratio of VOP to C2		Ratio of VOP to C2		Ratio of VOP to C2	
			> 1.00	< 1.00	> 1.00	< 1.00	> 1.00	< 1.00
Tur	Uttar Pradesh	IR	9/9 (100.00)	0/9 (0.00)	14/14 (100.00)	0/14 (0.00)	23/23 (100.00)	0/23 (0.00)
	Maharashtra	RF	DNA	DNA	13/14 (92.85)	1/14 (7.14)	13/14 (92.85)	1/14 (7.14)
Gram	Madhya Pradesh	IR	10/17 (94.11)	1/17 (5.88)	14/15 (93.33)	1/15 (6.66)	30/32 (93.75)	2/32 (6.25)
	Uttar Pradesh	RF	10/10 (100.00)	0/9 (0.00)	13/14 (92.85)	1/14 (7.14)	23/24 (95.83)	1/24 (4.16)

Sources: Computed using data from CACP (various years).

Notes: VOP: value of output; DNA: data not available; IR: irrigated; RF: rainfed; due to non-availability of data for some specified years, data from the nearest point is used for the analysis.

accounted for about 80 per cent of area and about 78 per cent of its production in 2010–11. Of these states, we have selected Gujarat as the rainfed state as it cultivated groundnut with irrigation coverage of only 11 per cent and Tamil Nadu as irrigated state because it cultivated this crop with irrigation coverage of 38 per cent in 2009–10. The data on cost and income presented in Table 3.10 shows that out of eight time points, the irrigated groundnut crop turned out to be profitable to farmers in only two time points. With cost C2 rising drastically, the amount of loss is found to have varied excessively from INR 629/ha in 1978–9 to INR 971/ha in 2009–10. Under rainfed conditions, groundnut cultivators were able to make profit in four out of eight time points. A relatively large rise in cost C2 under rainfed conditions than under irrigated conditions appears to have affected the profitability of groundnut in rainfed areas.

The plight of groundnut farmers is found to be more or less the same for both irrigated and rainfed states as much of the losses occurred during the ACP. Out of 23 years the irrigated groundnut crop yielded profits to farmers in only 7 years (30.43 per cent), with losses having generally occurred during the ACP (Table 3.11). Meanwhile, the rainfed groundnut farmers earned profit in 20 out of 32 years (62.5 per cent). It seems that rainfed groundnut farmers are relatively better off than their irrigated counterparts in reaping profit in more number of years, although groundnut crop is not wholly a profitable crop in either irrigated or rainfed conditions.

Economics of Cotton Cultivation

One of the traditional and important commercial crops of our country is cotton, which is predominantly cultivated under rainfed conditions. Its area under cultivation has increased tremendously, particularly after the introduction of Bt varieties, from 5.88 mha in 1950–1 to 11.24 mha in 2010–11 (GoI, 2012). Gujarat, Andhra Pradesh, Maharashtra, and Punjab are the major producers of cotton, which together accounted for about 80 per cent of total area as well as production of cotton in 2010–11. Maharashtra and Gujarat, which are the two largest cotton cultivating states in the country, are chosen for the study. While Maharashtra has been considered as the rainfed state because its coverage of irrigation in cotton cultivation

Table 3.10 Profitability in Groundnut Crop Cultivated in Irrigated and Less Irrigated States (in INR/ha at 1986–7 prices)

Year	Cost C2		Value of Output (VOP)		Profit	
	Tamil Nadu (IR State)	Gujarat (RF State)	Tamil Nadu (IR State)	Gujarat (RF State)	Tamil Nadu (IR State)	Gujarat (RF State)
1973–4	4,077	2,932	4,501	3,088	425	156
1978–9	3,799	3,155	3,171	3,059	–629	–96
1984–5	4,081	3,938	4,126	4,020	45	81
1989–90	DNA	3,696	DNA	4,006	DNA	310
1994–5	6,274	4,693	5,606	5,393	–668	701
1999–2000	7,088	3,973	6,536	3,056	–552	–917
2004–5	7,433	5,073	8,090	5,054	656	–18
2009–10	6,455	6,053	5,483	5,383	–971	–671

Sources: Computed using data from CACP (various years).

Notes: DNA: data not available; IR: irrigated; RF: rainfed; due to non-availability of data for some specified years, data from the nearest point is used for the analysis.

Table 3.11 Number of Years When Profit Was Reaped or Loss Was Incurred by Groundnut Farmers from 1971–2 to 2009–10

Crop	States	Category of State	Pre–agrarian Crisis Period (1971–2 to 1994–5)		Agrarian Crisis Period (1995–6 to 2009–10)		Entire Period of Analysis (1971–2 to 2009–10)	
			Ratio VOP to C2		Ratio VOP to C2		Ratio VOP to C2	
			> 1.00	< 1.00	> 1.00	< 1.00	> 1.00	< 1.00
Groundnut	Tamil Nadu	IR	4/9 (44.44)	5/9 (55.55)	3/14 (21.42)	11/14 (78.57)	7/23 (30.43)	16/23 (69.56)
	Gujarat	RF	12/17 (70.58)	5/17 (29.41)	8/15 (53.33)	7/15 (46.66)	20/32 (62.5)	12/32 (37.5)

Sources: Computed using data from CACP (various years).
Notes: VOP: value of output; DNA: data not available; IR: irrigated; RF: rainfed; due to non-availability of data for some specified years, data from the nearest point is used for the analysis.

was only 3 per cent, Gujarat has been considered as the irrigated state as its coverage of irrigation was about 57 per cent in 2009–10.

Of the eight time points taken up for study, it is observed that the irrigated cotton crop is profitable in all eight times to the farmers (see Table 3.12). Although the cost C2 has almost doubled from INR 4,742/ha in 1989–90 to INR 8,245/ha in 2009–10 in the irrigated state, yet the profit over cost C2 increased substantially because of increased VOP. In Maharashtra, the rainfed cotton crop was profitable to farmers in seven out of eight time points. However, with the cost C2 rising abnormally, the cotton farmers of Maharashtra struggled to get a steady profit over cost C2 fluctuating every alternate year. This could be one of the reasons for the rainfed cotton farmers of Maharashtra to go on a suicide spree. Apart from reaping relatively better profit, the farmers belonging to the highly irrigated state of Gujarat have reaped profit more number of times as compared to their counterparts in Maharashtra (see Table 3.13). Out of 28 years, the better irrigated cotton farmers have reaped profits in 24 years (85.71 per cent), while the rainfed cotton farmers of Maharashtra have acquired profits only in 15 out of 23 years (65.21 per cent). Our analysis seems to suggest that the irrigated cotton crop growers are relatively better off compared to the rainfed cotton growers in terms of reaping profit from its cultivation.

***

The analysis of seven important rainfed crops grown under irrigated and rainfed conditions shows that farmers have either reaped miniscule profits or suffered massive losses in cultivating most of the investigated crops. More specifically, jowar, bajra, and maize crops were profitable neither under irrigated condition nor under rainfed condition. Our analysis also suggests that most of the losses were incurred in the selected cereal crops during the ACP, which is between 1995–6 and 2009–10. It is indeed tur and gram that have yielded appreciable profits to the farmers both in the irrigated and rainfed regions. Even the profitability of the rainfed tur and gram crops is found to be at par with that of the irrigated ones. A most surprising result that emerges out of the analysis of tur and gram is that much of the profits have been generated during the ACP period. Although the

Table 3.12 Profitability in Cotton Cultivated in Irrigated and Less Irrigated States (in INR/ha at 1986–7 prices)

Year	Cost C2		Value of Output (VOP)		Profit	
	Gujarat (IR State	Maharashtra (RF State)	Gujarat (IR State)	Maharashtra (RF State)	Gujarat (IR State)	Maharashtra (RF State)
1973–4	2,265	1,775	2,581	2,122	316	347
1978–9	8,504	1,656	9,540	2,030	1,036	374
1984–5	5,117	2,106	6,453	2,719	1,336	614
1989–90	4,742	2,970	5,689	3,511	947	541
1994–5	4,605	4,569	6,674	7,229	2,069	2,666
1999–2000	4,775	4,984	4,838	5,178	63	194
2004–5	6,937	6,229	8,858	5,487	1,920	–742
2009–10	8,245	6,983	11,745	7,749	3,501	767

Sources: Computed using data from CACP (various years).

Notes: DNA: data not available; IR: irrigated; RF: rainfed; due to non-availability of data for some specified years, data from the nearest point is used for the analysis.

Table 3.13 Number of Years When Profit Was Reaped or Loss Was Incurred by Cotton Farmers from 1971–2 to 2009–10

Crop	State	Category of State	Pre–agrarian Crisis Period (1971–2 to 1994–5)		Agrarian Crisis Period (1995–6 to 2009–10)		Entire Period of Analysis (1971–2 to 2009–10)	
			Ratio VOP to C2		Ratio VOP to C2		Ratio VOP to C2	
			> 1.00	< 1.00	> 1.00	< 1.00	> 1.00	< 1.00
Cotton	Gujarat	IR	12/14 (85.71)	2/14 (14.28)	12/14 (85.71)	2/14 (14.28)	24/28 (85.71)	4/28 (14.28)
	Maharashtra	RF	8/10 (80.00)	2/10 (20.00)	7/13 (53.84)	6/13 (46.15)	15/23 (65.21)	8/23 (34.78)

Sources: Computed using data from CACP (various years).

Notes: VOP: value of output; DNA: data not available; IR: irrigated; RF: rainfed; due to non-availability of data for some specified years, data from the nearest point is used for the analysis.

groundnut and cotton crops have helped the farmers to reap profits both in the irrigated and rainfed regions, the profit is found to be very insignificant. It is the soaring COC that has been playing havoc with these farmers in reaping any appreciable profits. The empirical results of the profitability analysis of these crops selected for the study have not completely supported the long-held common view that irrigated crops are more profitable than rainfed crops. Continued losses or meager earnings from crop cultivation would definitely discourage farmers from engaging in farming (Swaminathan, 2008). This is also reflected from the recently conducted SAS where 40 per cent of the farmers have reported their desire to quit farming citing poor remuneration as the reason (NSSO, 2005). A steady flow of remunerative income from crops will definitely encourage farmers to go in for cultivation in the following seasons. Therefore, well thought out strategies are needed to cut down COC and to improve VOP so as to increase the profitability of crops not only in irrigated regions but also in un-irrigated/rainfed regions.

The country's farming community has been in the grip of an acute crisis in both irrigated and rainfed regions, which is the result of the lack of profitability from the crops. A viable solution to cut off the vicious tentacles of this crisis is to provide incentives to farmers in the form of higher profitability, irrespective of whether it is to a farmer from an irrigated or rainfed region. The unabated farmer suicides reported from various parts of the country in recent years also suggest that one-time support, such as farm loan waiver[6] or enhancement of farm credit in every union budget, will in no way resurrect the dwindling status of the farmers. For the farmers, the main issue is bridging the gap between ever-increasing costs of inputs (labour, fertilizers, pesticides, and seeds) and lower income from their produce. To mitigate the ongoing uproar in the area of farming a reasonable profit margin is the need of the hour. This can be achieved

[6] The Vyas Committee on Flow of Credit to Agriculture and Related Activities (2004) recommended that the share of small and marginal farmers in agricultural credit should be commensurate with their holdings and credit needs. However, the data published by RBI shows that about one half of the total farm credit today is in the nature of indirect finance which goes to input dealers, fertilizers, and so on (RBI, 2012).

only by fixing the prices of the crops in tune with the COC. The reality remains very clear that farmers are not able to derive sufficient income to pay for the costs they incur. It is high time that policymakers begin to work towards the prime concern of the farmers, which is from plough to plate.

Bibliography

Bapna, S. L., H. P. Binswanger, and J. B. Quizon. 1984. 'Systems of Output Supply and Factor Demand Equations for Semi-Arid Tropical India'. *Indian Journal of Agricultural Economics*, vol. 39, no. 2, pp. 179–202.

CACP (Commission for Agricultural Costs and Prices). Various years. *Report on Price Policy for Kharif and Rabi Crops Season.* Ministry of Agriculture, Government of India, New Delhi.

CRIDA (Central Research Institute for Dryland Agriculture). 2011. *Vision 2030*, pp. 1–32. Hyderabad.

Dhawan, B. D. 1985. 'Irrigation Impact on Farm Economy'. *Economic and Political Weekly*, vol. 20, no. 39, pp. A124–8.

———. 1987. 'How Stable Is Indian Irrigated Agriculture?'. *Economic and Political Weekly*, vol. 22, no. 39, pp. A93–6.

GoI. 2007. *Report of the Expert Group on Agricultural Indebtedness.* Ministry of Finance, Government of India, New Delhi.

———. 2011 and 2012. *Agricultural Statistics at a Glance.* Ministry of Agriculture, Government of India, New Delhi.

Hussain, I., and M. A. Hanjra. 2004. 'Irrigation and Poverty Alleviation: Review of the Empirical Evidence'. *Irrigation and Drainage*, vol. 53, no. 1, pp. 1–53.

Kahlon, S. S., and H. S. Sandhu. 1971. 'Economic Evaluation of Dry Farming in India'. *Indian Journal of Agricultural Economics*, vol. 26, no. 4, pp. 334–42.

Kalamkar, S. S., and A. Narayanamoorthy. 2003. 'Impact of Liberalisation on Domestic Agricultural Prices and Farm Income'. *Indian Journal of Agricultural Economics*, vol. 58, no. 3 (July–September), pp. 353–64.

Kanitkar, V. V. 1960. *Dry Farming in India.* Indian Council of Agricultural Research, New Delhi.

Kerr, J. M. 1996. *Sustainable Development of Rainfed Agriculture in India.* EPTD Discussion Paper no. 20. International Food Policy Research Institute, Washington, U. S. A.

Kiresur, V. R., R. K. Pandey, and Mruthyunjaya. 1995. 'Technological Change in Sorghum Production: An Economic Study of Dharwad

Farmers in Karnataka'. *Indian Journal of Agricultural Economics*, vol. 50, no. 2, pp. 185–92.

Lipton, M., L. Julie, B. Rachel, D. Z. Darshini, Q. Lubina, and W. Hugh. 2002. *The Impact of Irrigation on Poverty.* Poverty Research Unit, University of Sussex, U. K.

Narayanamoorthy, A. 2006. 'State of India's Farmers'. *Economic and Political Weekly*, vol. 41, no. 6 (11 February), pp. 471–3.

———. 2007. 'Deceleration in Agricultural Growth: Technology Fatigue or Policy Fatigue'. *Economic and Political Weekly*, vol. 42, no. 25 (23 June), pp. 2375–9.

———. 2010. 'Sorry State of Rainfed Agriculture'. *The Hindu*, 11 May, p. 18.

———. 2012. 'Is the MSP Hike Justified?'. *The Financial Express*, 3 July, p. 9.

———. 2013. 'Profitability in Crops Cultivation in India: Some Evidence from Cost of Cultivation Survey Data'. *Indian Journal of Agricultural Economics*, vol. 68, no. 1, pp. 104–21.

Narayanamoorthy, A., and P. Alli. 2013. 'Sugarcane Leaves Farmers Crushed'. *The Hindu Business Line*, 16 April, p. 9.

Narayanamoorthy, A., and R. Suresh. 2012. 'Agricultural Price Policy in India: Has It Benefitted the Paddy Farmers?'. *Indian Journal of Agricultural Marketing*, vol. 26, no. 3 (September–December), pp. 87–106.

NSSO (National Sample Survey office). 2005. *Situation Assessment Survey of Farmers: Some Aspects of Farming*, Report No. 496, 59th Round (January–December, 2003). Ministry of Statistics and Programme Implementation, Government of India, New Delhi.

Ranagaswamy, P. 1982. *Dry Farming Technology in India—A Study of Its Profitability in Selected Areas.* Agricade Publishing Academy, New Delhi.

Rastogi, B. K., and V. Annamalai. 1981. *A Study on the Adoption and Diffusion of Recommended Technologies in Dryland Areas.* All India Coordinated Research Project for Dryland Agriculture (AICRPDA), Hyderabad.

Rastogi, B. K., and Y. V. R. Reddy. 1982. *A Study on Farm Structures in Dry Farming Areas.* AICRPDA, Hyderabad.

RBI (Reserve Bank of India). 2012. *Handbook of Statistics on Indian Economy: 2011–12.* Mumbai.

Swaminathan, M. S. 2008. 'Ending the Debt Trap and Attaining Food Security'. *The Hindu*, 3 March.

The Vyas Committee. 2004. *Report of the Advisory Committee on Flow of Credit to Agriculture and Related Activities.* Submitted to the RBI, June.

PART II

PRICE POLICY AND FARM INCOME

4

Has Agricultural Price Policy Benefitted Paddy Farmers?

In view of the distorted and unregulated market conditions prevailing for agricultural produce in India, support prices are imperative for farmers to get assured income from their crop cultivation (Acharya, 1997; Sen and Bhatia, 2004). Besides, since the elasticity of demand for agricultural commodities, particularly for foodgrains, is less than unit in most cases, increased production during the period of bumper harvest brings down the prices of agricultural commodities sharply, which severely harms farmers. Assured and remunerative prices are not only the known instrument of organizing and integrating production activities of farmers but have also proven to be the most imperative factor for increasing the production of foodgrains and other agricultural commodities in India and elsewhere in the world (Schultz, 1964). Assured prices also help farmers efficiently allocate the scarce resources among different crops (see Acharya, 1997; Deshpande, 1996; Rao, 2001; Rao and Dev, 2010). Keeping this in view, the Agricultural Price Commission (renamed as Commission for Agricultural Costs and Prices since March [CACP] 1985) was set up in January 1965 specifically to advise the government on price policy of major agricultural commodities.[1] With the recommendations of the CACP, MSPs have been announced for different crops by the government every year for both the kharif and rabi seasons. Though the MSP scheme was initially implemented for paddy and wheat crops during the mid-1960s, it has been extended to most of the major crops in India due to pressure from farmers and other stakeholders.[2] Currently, the MSP scheme covers 23 crops that account for about 85 per cent of cropped area in the country.

Among the various crops cultivated in India, MSPs have been provided for paddy and wheat for more than 45 years now, starting from 1965–6. Although MSP has helped to achieve the record production in both paddy and wheat, it has come under severe scrutiny and attack for various reasons in recent years. One of the arguments heard in recent years is that the MSP, particularly for paddy, has not been announced in consonance with the cost of production, which has escalated steeply, particularly during the last one decade or so (see Narayanamoorthy, 2006a; 2007; 2012). Farmers from Andhra Pradesh, which is one of the largest producers of paddy in India, declared 'paddy crop holiday' on a large scale citing poor remuneration from its cultivation. Gulati (2012a) illustrated that COCs of different crops including paddy were high, especially during the last three years, and, therefore, the price hike was necessary to get positive returns over the costs and also to propel the agricultural GDP. On the other hand, Bhalla (2012) argues that the recommendation of the CACP on increasing the price of paddy and other crops for the 2012 kharif season is 'dirty economics and dirtier politics'. Many fail to recognize the fact that the MSP is only the floor price which will not benefit farmers unless the procurement infrastructure is established effectively to procure the paddy from them. How can the farmers sell their paddy at a price fixed by the government without proper

[1] The detailed functions and objectives of CACP, including the factors that are considered for arriving at MSPs for different crops, can be found at its website, www.cacp.dacnet.nic.in.

[2] Covering close to four decades of various price policy reports published by the CACP, Rao (2001) has provided a splendid exposition on the role played by price policy and the various obstacles faced by it in achieving the macro objectives of price policy.

procurement arrangements? Data available from various reports of CACP underlined that the market price of paddy has dipped below the MSP in different centres located in different states because of poor implementation of MSP scheme (see CACP, 2012).[3]

Paddy is an important crop which contributes to about 40 per cent of India's total foodgrain production (see MoA, 2012). Paddy also supports the livelihood of a large number of farmers besides helping to sustain the food security of the country. It is also one among the two crops where support price has been implemented since the mid-1960s. Therefore, a study on the price policy of paddy crop will be useful in ascertaining its effectiveness in increasing the income of farmers. Has the support price scheme helped paddy cultivating farmers in terms of increasing their income? What is the trend in support price offered to paddy crop vis-à-vis other crops? Has the trend in support price offered to paddy crop changed in recent years given the increased COC in paddy crop? What is the level of procurement of paddy at the national level and across the major producing states in India? Is it correct to say that the support price is not remunerative to paddy cultivating farmers belonging to different states? While making an attempt to answer some of these questions utilizing secondary-level data from 1965–6 to 2010–11,

[3] Not to our surprise, CACP reports on price policy of different years have underlined that the market price of paddy dipped in many centres located in different states. For the immediate reference of the readers, the following table lists a few states and its centres where the price of paddy dipped below MSP (INR 1,000 per quintal) during 2010–11 as reported in CACP (2012):

States	Centre's Name	Range in Market Prices from October 2010 to January 2011
Karnataka	Mysore	850–990
Maharashtra	Gondia	968–982
Odisha	Sambalpur	900–900
Uttar Pradesh	Shahjahanpur	865–975
	Attara	975–980
West Bengal	Sainthiya	955
	Indas	980

an attempt is made in this chapter to study the overall functioning as well as the effectiveness of the support price policy in benefitting farmers cultivating paddy crop in terms of increasing their income.

This chapter is organized in seven sections. Following the introductory section, data sources including its coverage have been presented in section two. As the present study focuses mainly on paddy crop, section three presents the overall trends in paddy cultivation covering both national- and state-level data. Section four explains the trends in MSP in paddy versus other crops from 1965–6 to 2012–13. Trends in procurement of paddy to its production by state agencies have been presented in section five. Utilizing the data on CCS, the profitability of paddy crop in HAHP and HALP states is analysed in section six. The last section presents the conclusion and policy pointers.

Data

This study has been carried out entirely using secondary data covering the period from 1950–1 to 2011–12. Although the main objective of the study is to ascertain the effectiveness of the support price scheme on the profitability of paddy cultivation, it also studies the overall state of paddy cultivation, trends in MSP for paddy vis-à-vis other crops, level of procurement of paddy, and so on. The data needed for this study has been compiled from various government sources. For studying the state of paddy cultivation in India, related data has been compiled mainly from two publications, namely *Agricultural Statistics at a Glance* and *Area and Production of Principal Crops*, both published by the MoA, Government of India. Data on MSPs for different crops have been compiled from the CACP's website (www.cacp.dacnet.nic.in), *Agricultural Statistics at a Glance*, and also from the *Handbook of Statistics on the Indian Economy* published by the Reserve Bank of India (RBI). In order to study the procurement status of paddy, data relating to procurement of paddy have been compiled from the *Bulletin on Food Statistics*, *Agricultural Statistics at a Glance*, and also from the RBI's *Handbook of Statistics of Indian Economy*. CACP has been publishing data on COC for different crops, which are generated from the scheme on comprehensive survey on COC. For studying the profitability in paddy crop, all cost- and income-related data on paddy cultivation have been compiled from the CACP's publication *Report on Price Policy for Kharif Crops* of different years and also from its website. A total of six states belonging to the category of HAHP (Andhra Pradesh, Punjab, and Tamil Nadu) and HALP (Odisha, Uttar Pradesh, and West Bengal) have been considered for studying the profitability. The methodology adopted for computing profitability in paddy cultivation is explained in the appropriate section of the chapter.

Status of Paddy Cultivation

As this chapter mainly focuses on the effectiveness of the price policy on paddy crop, it is useful to understand the overall state of paddy cultivation in terms of its area, production, and productivity over the years. Unlike wheat and some other crops, paddy has been cultivated in all parts of India in all three seasons, but its spread is not the same in the three seasons. The area under paddy at the national level has increased from 35.47 million hectare (mha) in 1965–6 to 42.56 mha in 2010–11, but its increase has not been very appreciable in recent years (see Table 4.1). The average area under paddy was 37.88 mha during the Green Revolution period (GRP) (1965–6 to 1979–80), which increased to 41.27 mha post GRP (1980–1 to 1994–5), and further to 43.52 mha during the ACP (1995–6 to 2010–11). But the pace of growth in area under paddy has slowed considerably, especially after the GRP. For instance, the area under paddy increased at a rate of 0.86 per cent during the GRP, whereas the same recorded negative growth of –0.11 per cent per annum during the ACP. As a result of deceleration in area, there has also been a deceleration in the rate of increase in production and productivity of paddy especially since after the GRP. In fact, the deceleration in production and productivity of paddy was very significant during the ACP over the GRP.

The state-wise scenario of paddy cultivation in terms of area is somewhat different from the national-level picture (see Table 4.2). The area under paddy has increased in absolute terms in almost all the states except in Tamil Nadu, where it reduced from 2.74 mha in 1970–3 to 1.89 mha in 2008–11. However, some substantial changes have taken place in the share of paddy area occupied by different

Table 4.1 Trends in Area, Yield, and Production of Paddy in India, 1950–1 to 2010–11

Period	Area (mha)	Production (mt)	Yield (kg/ha)	Irrigation Coverage (%)	Paddy Area to GCA (%)	Paddy Area to FGA (%)
Pre-GRP (1950–1 to 1964–5)	32.84	29.51	892	35.24	22.20	29.66
GRP (1965–6 to 1979–80)	37.88	41.76	1,098	38.88	22.90	30.81
Post-GRP (1980–1 to 1994–5)	41.27	65.45	1,580	44.82	22.96	32.81
ACP (1995–6 to 2010–11)	43.52	87.77	2,015	53.61	22.90	35.59
	Compound Growth Rate (per cent/annum)					
Pre-GRP	1.45	4.35	2.86	1.27	0.16	0.07
GRP	0.86	2.91	2.03	0.71	0.19	0.24
Post-GRP	0.52	3.50	2.96	1.34	−0.04	0.82
ACP	−0.11	1.17	1.28	1.08	−0.37	−0.14

Sources: Computed utilizing data from MoA (2012) and www.dacnet.nic.in.

Notes: ACP: Agrarian Crisis Period; GCA: gross cropped area; FGA: foodgrain area; GRP: Green Revolution Period; mha: million hectares; mt: million tonnes.

Table 4.2 Trends in Area under Paddy by Major Growing States in India, 1970–3 to 2008–11

State	Area (in million hectares)			State's Share (%) to Total Area			Compound Growth Rate in Area (per cent per annum)	
	1970–3	1990–3	2008–11	1970–3	1990–3	2008–11	1990–3 over 1970–3	2008–11 over 1990–3
West Bengal	5.01	5.74	5.50	13.40	13.55	12.67	0.66	–0.20
Punjab	0.44	2.05	2.79	1.17	4.85	6.42	7.63	1.47
Uttar Praesh	4.55	5.50	5.63	12.19	12.99	12.95	0.91	0.11
Andhra Pradesh	3.16	3.86	4.19	8.47	9.11	9.65	0.95	0.40
Odisha	4.54	4.47	4.35	12.17	10.54	10.01	–0.08	–0.13
Tamil Nadu	2.74	2.05	1.89	7.34	4.84	4.36	–1.37	–0.38
Assam	2.00	2.51	2.52	5.36	5.93	5.79	1.09	0.01
Bihar	5.13	5.00	6.88	13.75	11.81	15.84	–0.12	1.53
Others	9.76	11.18	9.69	26.14	26.38	22.31	0.65	–0.68
India	37.35	42.37	43.44	100.00	100.00	100.00	0.60	0.12

Sources: Computed utilizing data from MoA (2012) and www.dacnet.nic.in.

states since the early 1960s. Punjab, which is not a traditionally paddy-growing state, accounted for only 1 per cent of India's total paddy area during 1970–3, but it increased to about 6.40 per cent in 2008–11. On the other hand, the traditionally paddy-growing state Tamil Nadu has reduced its share of paddy area from 7.34 per cent during 1970–3 to 4.36 per cent during 2008–11. The share of paddy area occupied by Odisha too has declined from 12.17 per cent to 10.01 per cent during the same period. However, similar to the national-level trend, the pace of increase in area under paddy has decelerated in all the major paddy-growing states between 1990–3 and 2008–11 as compared to the period of 1970–3 to 1990–3. Since the contribution of paddy to the national food basket is still the largest,[4] any significant reduction in area under paddy cultivation will have serious implications on the food security of the country. Therefore, it is essential to find out why the pace of growth of area under paddy slowed down, particularly during the ACP. It is also equally important to probe as to why paddy area is declining in traditional paddy-growing states such as Odisha and Tamil Nadu.

Trends in MSP: Paddy versus Other Crops

One of the objectives of this chapter is to study the trends in MSP for paddy vis-à-vis other crops. Though MSPs announced by the government for different crops are only the floor prices, one way or the other it determines the profitability of crop cultivation. If the MSP for paddy crop is increased at a rate higher than its cost of production, it should theoretically help paddy-cultivating farmers. If the MSP is not announced in consonance with the rise in cost of production, it will certainly hurt paddy-growing farmers. There is also a feeling in some quarters that the support price for paddy has been increased substantially over the years, which is unwarranted

[4] In spite of significant increase in the production of wheat and coarse cereals since the introduction of the Green Revolution, paddy continues to occupy the major share in the total production of foodgrains. In fact, the share of paddy in the total production of foodgrains has increased from 39 per cent in 1970–1 to over 40 per cent in 2011–12.

(Bhalla, 2012). In this section, while studying the trends in MSP for paddy crop, an attempt is also made to study the trends in MSPs for other crops so as to understand the relative position of paddy crop. As mentioned earlier, data on MSPs for various crops from 1965–6 to 2012–13 published by the Directorate of Economics and Statistics, MoA, GoI, has been used for studying the trends.

Let us first look at the trends in MSP for paddy crop over the years. It is evident from Table 4.3 that the MSP for paddy at current prices has increased from INR 39.82 per quintal in 1965–6 to INR 1,250 per quintal in 2012–13, which is an increase of 7.44 per cent/annum. Has the MSP increased uniformly over the years? The increase in MSP is not the same across different time periods. While the increase in MSP for paddy was 6.24 per cent/annum during 1965–6 to 1985–6 (GRP), it increased at a rate of 8.82 per cent/annum from 1985–6 to 1995–6 (post GRP). Surprisingly, the annual compound growth rate of MSP for paddy crop decelerated to 7.16 per cent during the ACP (1995–6 to 2012–13) compared to the previous decade. One must find out why the growth of MSP for paddy crop decelerated during the ACP when the COC of paddy actually appears to have increased at a faster rate.

Is the support price for paddy higher than that of wheat? The support price provided to paddy crop is not higher than that of wheat crop since 1965–6. The support price provided to paddy (INR 39.82 per quintal) was only about 67 per cent of wheat price (INR 59.27 per quintal) during 1965–6. But the inter-crop price parity between paddy and wheat has reduced over the years, which was only around 3 per cent during 2012–13. While the reasons for the reduced disparity in support price between paddy and wheat cannot be explained only by economic factors, the growth rate in MSP for wheat crop is found to be lower than that of the support price provided to paddy crop across different time periods and also between 1965–6 and 2012–13. This means that although the support price for paddy is relatively lower than that of wheat crop, it is increased at a pace higher than the support price offered to wheat crop over the years.

Apart from the disparity in support price between paddy and wheat crops, there are also substantial variations in support prices between paddy and other crops. Despite a large increase in paddy price over the years, the rate of increase in support prices for other crops, particularly

Table 4.3 Trends in Minimum Support Price for Different Crops in India, 1965–6 to 2012–13

Crops	Minimum Support Price (INR/quintal in current prices)					Compound Growth Rate (per cent/annum)			
	1965–6	1985–6	1995–6	2005–6	2012–13	1985–6 over 1965–6	1995–6 over 1985–6	2012–13 over 1995–6	2012–13 over 2005–6
Paddy Common	39.82	142	360	570	1,250	6.24	8.82	7.16	11.87
Coarse Cereals	DNA	130	300	525	1,500	—	7.90	9.35	16.18
Wheat	59.27	162	380	640	1,285	4.90	8.06	7.00	10.47
Gram	DNA	260	700	1,425	2,800	—	9.42	8.01	10.13
Arhar (Tur)	DNA	300	800	1,400	3,850	—	9.33	9.12	15.55
Moong	DNA	300	800	1,520	4,400	—	9.33	9.93	16.40
Urad	DNA	300	800	1,520	4,300	—	9.33	9.79	16.02
Sugarcane	DNA	16.5	42.5	79.5	170	—	8.98	8.01	11.47
Cotton	DNA	535	1350	1,980	3,900	—	8.78	6.07	10.17
Jute	DNA	215	490	910	2,200	—	7.78	8.70	13.44
Groundnut	DNA	350	900	1,520	3,700	—	8.97	8.17	13.55
Soyabean Black	DNA	250	600	900	2,200	—	8.28	7.49	13.62
Soyabean Yellow	DNA	275	680	1,010	2,240	—	8.58	6.85	12.05
Sunflower Seed	DNA	335	950	1,500	3,700	—	9.94	7.85	13.77
Rapeseed/Mustard	DNA	400	860	1,700	2,500	—	7.21	6.11	5.66
Safflower	DNA	400	800	1,550	2,500	—	6.50	6.53	7.07

Sources: Computed using data from MoA (2011); RBI (2011); www.dacnet.nic.in; and www.cacp.dacnet.nic.in.

Note: DNA: data not available.

pulses and oilseeds, outpaced the growth in paddy price. This is found to be particularly true in the recent years. Between 1985–6 and 1995–6,[5] the support price of paddy increased at a rate of close to 9 per cent per annum, which is also almost the same in most of the crops reported in Table 4.3. But this has completely changed between 2005–6 and 2012–13; MSP for paddy increased at a rate of 11.87 per cent per annum, whereas the prices of most pulses increased at a rate of 15 to 17 per cent per annum and the prices of oilseeds increased at a rate of 12 to 14 per cent per annum. Over the last couple of decades, the domestic supply of pulses and oilseeds has not been adequate to meet the growing demands of these commodities. Therefore, in order to increase the production of pulses and oilseeds to meet the domestic shortages, the prices of these two commodities have been increased at an increased pace in the recent years. On the whole, the analysis of trends in support price for paddy crop suggests that although the support price for paddy has increased at a faster rate as compared to wheat price, the pace in increase of paddy price is less as compared to most pulses and oilseed crops, especially in the recent years.

Procurement of Paddy

The true implementation of MSP for paddy or any other crops relies heavily on the level of procurement of crops by state agencies. If adequate infrastructure arrangements are not made to procure the commodities from farmers in time, there is no guarantee that any amount of rise in MSP would help the farmers. Therefore, after studying the trends in MSP for paddy and other crops, we turned our focus on the procurement of paddy so as to understand its level of procurement over the years. Data pertaining to all India and major producing states covering the period from 1970–1 to 2010–11 are used for this analysis. Since wheat is another important crop where support price has been provided since the 1960s, its procurement has been considered to compare with the paddy crop.

5 The government started announcing MSPs for most pulses and oilseed crops only from the late 1970s, almost a decade after announcing MSP for paddy and wheat. Therefore, in this chapter, paddy price could not be compared with prices of oilseeds and pulses till the early part of the 1980s.

It can be seen from Table 4.4 that the procurement of paddy in absolute terms has increased from 3.46 mt in 1970–1 to 32.35 mt in 2010–11 at the all-India level, which is an increase of about 5.60 per cent per annum. The share of procurement of paddy to its total production has also increased substantially from 8.20 per cent to 34 per cent during the same period. However, the procurement of paddy has not increased consistently along with its production over the years. The share of procurement of paddy has sharply declined in many years over previous years. For instance, the procurement of paddy to the total production declined from 13.31 per cent in 1976–7 to 8.68 per cent in 1977–8. Similarly, the procurement of paddy has declined from 30.12 per cent in 2005–6 to 26.89 per cent in 2006–7.

Table 4.4 Procurement of Paddy and Wheat by Government Agencies in India, 1970–1 to 2010–11

Year	Paddy			Wheat		
	PDN (mt)	PMT (mt)	% of PMT to PDN	PDN (mt)	PMT (mt)	% of PMT to PDN
1970–1	42.22	3.46	8.20	23.83	5.09	21.36
1976–7	41.92	6.00	14.31	28.84	6.62	22.95
1980–1	53.63	6.20	11.56	36.31	6.59	18.15
1986–7	60.56	9.14	15.09	44.32	10.53	23.76
1990–1	74.29	12.80	17.23	55.14	11.07	20.08
1995–6	76.98	10.04	13.04	62.10	12.32	19.84
2000–1	84.98	21.18	24.92	69.68	16.70	23.97
2005–6	91.79	27.65	30.12	69.35	15.27	22.02
2010–11	95.33	32.35	33.94	85.93	22.07	25.68
From 1970–1 to 1990–1						
Average	53.32	6.66	12.04	37.17	6.95	18.41
CV	20.56	39.67	25.19	28.23	34.40	22.27
From 1991–2 to 2010–11						
Average	86.18	20.11	21.93	71.00	15.53	21.44
CV	9.42	36.74	37.95	12.18	41.83	33.71

Sources: Computed using data from GoI (various years); MoA (2011); RBI (2011); and www.fcamin.nic.in.

Notes: PDN: production; PMT: procurement; CV: coefficient of variation.

Apart from year on year fluctuations, we have also noticed wide fluctuations in the share of procurement of paddy to its total production, especially after the introduction of economic reforms, which is clearly evident from the coefficient of variation (CV) reported in Table 4.4. As the level of procurement by the government agencies always directly influences the market price of paddy, one should find out what happened to the market price of paddy in those years when procurement declined sharply.

Apart from looking at the absolute procurement level of paddy crop, an attempt is also made to know whether the procurement of paddy vastly differs from its counterpart, the wheat crop. Although the procurement of paddy was very low in the 1970s as compared to wheat crop, it has increased at a relatively faster rate during the last two decades. During 1970–1, the share of procurement of paddy to its total production was only about 8.20 per cent, whereas the same was recorded at 21.36 per cent for wheat crop. This position has entirely changed since 2000–1. Today, the procurement of paddy accounts for over one-third of its production, whereas it is about one-fourth for the production of wheat. Similar to paddy crop, the fluctuations in procurement of wheat have also increased after the introduction of economic reforms.

Although the procurement of paddy has increased at the national level over the years, we do not know whether the level of procurement of paddy is same across the states in India. State-specific procurement levels of paddy are more important than country-level procurement in determining the profitability of paddy cultivation. Therefore, an attempt is made to find the level of procurement of paddy by major producing states covering three recent time periods, namely 1991–2, 2000–1, and 2010–11. It is evident from Table 4.5 that the procurement of paddy has widely varied across the major states at all the three time points considered for the analysis. During the year 1991–2, the procurement of paddy to its total production was in the range of 50 to 65 per cent in states such as Punjab and Haryana, but it was only 5–8 per cent in Madhya Pradesh, Odisha, and Uttar Pradesh. Shockingly, the procurement of paddy was less than 1 per cent of total production in West Bengal during 1991–2. The scenario of procurement of paddy has changed substantially in almost all the states since 1991–2. The procurement in states such as

Table 4.5 Procurement of Paddy and Wheat in Major Producing States, 1991–2, 2000–1, and 2010–11

State	1991–2			2000–1			2010–11		
	PDN (mt)	PMT (mt)	PMT to PDN (%)	PDN (mt)	PMT (mt)	PMT to PDN (%)	PDN (mt)	PMT (mt)	PMT to PDN (%)
Paddy									
Punjab	6.53	4.25	65.08	9.15	6.96	76.07	10.83	8.63	79.69
Haryana	1.83	0.92	50.27	2.69	1.48	55.02	3.47	1.68	48.41
Uttar Pradesh	10.26	0.83	8.09	11.67	1.17	10.03	11.99	2.4	20.02
Andhra Pradesh	9.65	2.26	23.42	12.45	7.17	57.59	14.41	8.76	60.79
Madhya Pradesh	5.73	0.4	6.98	0.98	0.17	17.35	1.77	0.4	22.60
Odisha	5.27	0.27	5.12	4.61	0.91	19.74	6.82	2.42	35.48
Tamil Nadu	5.78	0.99	17.13	7.36	1.69	22.96	5.79	1.43	24.70
West Bengal	10.43	0.08	0.77	12.42	0.43	3.46	13.04	1.00	7.67
Others	18.81	0.25	1.33	23.64	1.2	5.08	27.85	5.63	20.22
India	74.29	10.25	13.80	84.97	21.18	24.93	95.97	32.35	33.71
Wheat									
Punjab	12.15	5.54	45.60	15.55	9.42	60.58	16.47	9.67	58.71
Uttar Pradesh	18.6	0.36	1.94	25.16	1.54	6.12	30.00	0.59	1.97
Haryana	6.44	1.83	28.42	9.66	4.49	46.48	11.63	6.11	52.54
Rajasthan	4.3	0.01	0.19	5.54	0.53	9.57	7.21	0.35	4.85
Madhya Pradesh	5.83	NA	0.00	4.86	0.35	7.20	7.62	2.6	34.12
Others	7.81	0.012	0.15	8.91	0.37	4.15	21.56	5.35	24.81
India	55.13	7.75	14.06	69.68	16.70	23.97	86.87	22.07	25.41

Sources: Computed using data from GoI (various years); MoA (2011); RBI (2011); and www.fcamin.nic.in.

Notes: PDN: production; PMT: procurement; mt: million tonnes.

Andhra Pradesh and Tamil Nadu varied only from 17 to 23 per cent of their paddy production during 1991–2, but increased to over 60 per cent in Andhra Pradesh and to over 24 per cent in Tamil Nadu during 2010–11. Considerable improvement is also noticed in the procurement level in states such as Madhya Pradesh, Odisha, and Uttar Pradesh during 2010–11, which were procuring less than 8 per cent of their production during 1991–2. Despite being the largest producer of paddy, the procurement level is only about 7 per cent of the production even today in West Bengal. Could this be due to poor availability of procurement infrastructure? Or is this due to poor awareness about the support price scheme?[6] While making an attempt to find the reasons for the poor procurement in West Bengal, one must also find out how Punjab, Haryana, and Andhra Pradesh are able to procure large chunks of their paddy production. Keeping in view these questions, let us now focus on the profitability of paddy cultivation, which is the central focus of this chapter.

Profitability in Paddy Cultivation

An important question that often arises in relation to the support price scheme on paddy is whether it has benefitted farmers in terms of increasing their income and profitability. The hike in MSP for the kharif season in 2012 to the tune of about 15 per cent over the previous year's price of paddy has now generated intensive debate among policymakers and economists (see Gulati, 2012a; Bhalla, 2012; and Alagh, 2012). On the other hand, citing poor remuneration from paddy cultivation, farmers from the fertile region of Andhra Pradesh even declared paddy crop holiday during kharif season of

[6] The SAS carried out at the initiation of the Ministry of Agriculture, Government of India, during 2003 on various aspects of farming, including the awareness of technical and institutional developments in agriculture, reveals that about 30 per cent of farmers households in West Bengal not only understood the price scheme of MSP but also knew where to sell their paddy crop if the market price goes below the MSP (see NSSO, 2005). This awareness percentage in West Bengal is relatively higher than the national average of 29 per cent. Therefore, one is not sure whether awareness about MSP could be the reason for poor procurement of paddy in West Bengal.

2011–12. Farmers from neighbouring states of Tamil Nadu and Karnataka are also demanding higher price for paddy citing steep increase in COC, especially in recent years. In view of this, there is a need to find out whether or not the price policy followed for paddy crop has helped farmers reap profit over the years, which is also the central focus of this chapter. In order to answer this question, cost- and income-related data on paddy crop have been used from the CCS published by the CACP covering the period from 1971–2 to 2009–10. The cultivation of paddy varies widely from one state to another in terms of area, irrigation coverage, productivity, level of procurement, and so on. Productivity is one among the important factors that often determines the profitability of paddy crop. Farmers belonging to HPS will be able reap higher profits than those from LPS. Therefore, we have considered six important states to find the difference in profitability between the two groups of states: three from HAHP states (Andhra Pradesh, Punjab, and Tamil Nadu) and another three from HALP states (Odisha, Uttar Pradesh, and West Bengal). As one of our objectives is to find whether the profitability in paddy cultivation is increasing over time, we have converted all the cost- and income-related data of paddy to constant terms using CPIAL deflator at 1986–7 prices.

Table 4.6 presents statistics on cost C2, VOP, and profit (at 1986–7 prices) for paddy cultivation for HAHP and HALP states, with five-year intervals from 1971–2 to 2009–10. It is clear from the table that there is no clear-cut upward movement in the profitability (VOP minus cost C2) of paddy cultivation in both HPS and LPS. We expected the profitability from paddy cultivation to be better in HAHP states such as Andhra Pradesh, Punjab, and Tamil Nadu as compared to HALP states such Odisha, Uttar Pradesh, and West Bengal. To our surprise, except Punjab, where farmers have been reaping profit since 1980–1, all other states from both low and high productivity groups have incurred losses in most time points considered for the analysis. Why are only Punjab farmers able to reap profit from paddy cultivation consistently since 1980–1? Our analysis reveals that the VOP from paddy cultivation has increased at a much faster rate as compared to cost C2, which has helped the farmers of Punjab to reap profit from paddy cultivation. Another important reason for Punjab farmers consistently reaping profit could be due to

Table 4.6 Profitability in Paddy Cultivation in HAHP and HALP States, 1971–2 to 2009–10 (in INR/ha at 1986–7 prices)

Year	HAHP States								
	Andhra Pradesh			Punjab			Tamil Nadu		
	C2 Cost	VOP	Profit	C2 Cost	VOP	Profit	C2 Cost	VOP	Profit
1971–2	4,308	4,581	272	DNA	DNA	DNA	4,717	4,590	–126
1975–6	3,690	3,161	–529	4,869	4,073	–797	3,929	5,268	1,339
1980–1	5,640	5,481	–159	7,927	9,529	1,602	6,410	7,015	604
1985–6	7,000	6,857	–143	6,956	8,083	1,126	DNA	DNA	DNA
1990–1	7,307	6,563	–744	7,182	8,017	835	DNA	DNA	DNA
1995–6	7,684	7,518	–166	6,635	7,468	833	DNA	DNA	DNA
2000–1	8,582	8,216	–366	7,313	9,877	2,563	9,152	8,716	–436
2005–6	8,288	8,455	167	8,501	10,525	2,024	9,290	7,305	–1,985
2009–10	10,566	11,964	1,398	9,873	13,766	3,893	9,154	10,261	1,107

(*Cont'd*)

Table 4.6 *(Cont'd)*

Year	HALP States								
	Odisha			Uttar Pradesh			West Bengal		
	C2 Cost	VOP	Profit	C2 Cost	VOP	Profit	C2 Cost	VOP	Profit
1971–2	2,445	2,743	297	DNA	DNA	DNA	3,665	4,144	479
1975–6	2,057	1,919	–137	2,951	2,681	–269	3,211	2,944	–266
1980–1	2,803	2,929	126	3,713	2,951	–761	4,072	3,515	–557
1985–6	3,320	3,120	–200	3,448	4,703	1,255	4,443	4,561	118
1990–1	3,832	3,771	–61	4,796	4,378	–418	6,908	6,886	–22
1995–6	4,206	4,302	96	4,829	5,794	964	5,220	4,953	–267
2000–1	4,949	4,077	–871	4,840	4,586	–254	6,240	4,232	–2,007
2005–6	5,320	4,124	–1,197	5,824	5,492	–332	7,128	5,672	–1,456
2009–10	5,486	5,346	–140	6,302	7,208	907	7,429	7,078	–351

Sources: Computed using data from CACP (various years).

Notes: VOP: value of output; DNA: data not available; HAHP: high area with high productivity; HALP: high area with low productivity. Due to non-availability of data for some specified years, data from the nearest point is used for the analysis.

increased share of procurement of paddy by state agencies as reported earlier. While the national average procurement of paddy was only about 33 per cent during 2010–11, it was as high as 80 per cent in the case of Punjab. This increased procurement must have helped the farmers of Punjab to get the MSP fixed by the government, whereas in other states the farmers would have got only lower price for paddy because of low procurement by the government. The experience of Punjab clearly reinforces our apriori notion that any increase in MSP will not benefit the farmers unless adequate arrangements are made to procure the paddy from the farmers.

Besides analysing the trends in profitability of paddy cultivation, we have looked at how many times (years) paddy cultivators were able to reap profit during the entire period of analysis from 1971–2 to 2009–10 in all the six HPS and LPS. The agrarian crisis which started from the early 1990s (along with initiation of economic reforms) has arguably reduced the profitability of paddy and other crops (see Kalamkar and Narayanamoorthy, 2003). Therefore, an attempt is also made to find out whether any difference exists in the profitability of paddy before and after 1990–1 among the selected states. As considered earlier, here too the VOP and cost C2 are considered for computing profitability in paddy cultivation.

Table 4.7 shows the ratio of VOP to cost C2 for different time periods for HPS and LPS. If the ratio is more than or equal to one it means that the farmers were reaping profit from paddy cultivation and vice versa. Paddy farmers were not reaping profit or were possibly incurring losses if the ratio is less than one. As noted earlier in the profitability analysis, except in Punjab, the ratio of VOP to cost C2 is found to be less than one (<1.00) in more number of years in all the other five states including HPS such as Andhra Pradesh and Tamil Nadu. Of the total 31 years (from 1971–2 to 2009–10)[7] for which

[7] Although we have covered the period from 1971–2 to 2009–10 (a total of 39 years) for profitability analysis, data on cost and income pertaining to paddy crop were not available from CACP's publications consistently for all the years for any of the six selected states. Only for those years for which data were available were considered for the analysis and, therefore, the total number of years (data time points) considered for the analysis varies considerably from one state to another.

Table 4.7 Number of Years When Profit Was Reaped or Loss Was Incurred by Paddy Farmers from 1971–2 to 2009–10

State's Category	States	Green Revolution Period (1971–2 to 1990–1)		Agrarian Crisis Period (1990–1 to 2009–10)		Entire Period of Analysis (1971–2 to 2009–10)	
		Ratio of VOP to C2		Ratio of VOP to C2		Ratio of VOP to C2	
		>1.00	<1.00	>1.00	<1.00	>1.00	<1.00
HAHP	Andhra Pradesh	5/17	12/17	11/17	6/17	16/34	18/34
		(29.41)	(70.59)	(64.71)	(35.29)	(47.06)	(52.94)
	Punjab	10/11	1/11	20/20	0/20	30/31	1/31
		(90.91)	(9.09)	(100.00)	(0.00)	(96.77)	(3.23)
	Tamil Nadu	7/11	4/11	4/12	8/12	11/23	12/23
		(63.64)	(36.36)	(33.33)	(66.67)	(47.83)	(52.17)
HALP	Odisha	10/15	5/15	4/18	14/18	14/33	19/33
		(66.67)	(33.33)	(22.22)	(77.78)	(42.42)	(57.58)
	Uttar Pradesh	6/13	7/13	9/17	8/17	15/30	15/30
		(46.15)	(53.85)	(52.94)	(47.06)	(50.00)	(50.00)
	West Bengal	8/15	7/15	1/17	16/17	9/32	23/32
		(53.33)	(46.67)	(5.88)	(94.12)	(28.13)	(71.88)

Sources: Computed using data from CACP (various years).
Note: VOP: value of output; HAHP: high area with high productivity; HALP: high area with low productivity. Figures in brackets are percentage to total number of years.

we have got data from Punjab, farmers were able to reap profit for 30 years (96.77 per cent), which is not observed in any of the remaining five states considered for the analysis. Farmers from West Bengal, which is considered as one of the LPS for the analysis, seem to have made losses more number of times than any other states. For instance, out of 32 years considered for the analysis, the ratio of VOP to cost C2 turned out to be less than one (<1.00) in 23 years for West Bengal, which is about 72 per cent of the total number of years. In states such as Andhra Pradesh, Tamil Nadu, Odisha, and Uttar Pradesh, farmers have reaped profit in only around 50 per cent of the time periods considered for the analysis. This means that except for Punjab farmers, all other farmers belonging to both HPS and LPS appeared to have incurred losses more number of times by cultivating paddy crop.

Did the profitability vary between the GRP (1971–2 and 1990–1) and ACP (1990–1 to 2009–10)? We expected farmers to have reaped profit in fewer number of years during the ACP arguably due to increased COC. But this is turned out be correct only partially. Among the HPS, Punjab and Andhra Pradesh farmers reaped profit in more number of years during ACP as compared to GRP, but farmers belonging to Tamil Nadu incurred losses in more number of years (8 out of 12 years) during ACP as compared to GRP (4 out of 11 years). However, as we expected, farmers belonging to the LPS, particularly from Odisha and West Bengal, incurred losses in more number of years during the ACP as compared to the GRP. Although the pattern of profitability is almost the same between the GRP and ACP for Uttar Pradesh, the ratio of VOP to cost C2 was less than one (<1.00) in more number of years among the remaining two LPS, namely Odisha (14 out of 18 years) and West Bengal (16 out of 17 years) during the ACP. While there is no clear pattern emerging on the profitability of paddy crop between HPS and LPS, the losses incurred by paddy farmers belonging to HALP states appear to be more frequent, especially during the ACP.

***

This study shows that although the absolute support price provided for paddy is relatively lower than wheat over the years, the rate of increase in paddy price is found to have increased at a faster rate as compared to wheat price between 1965–6 and 2011–12. The inter-crop price parity (ratio) between paddy and wheat has reduced over the years from 67 per cent in 1965–6 to just 3 per cent in 2011–12. On the procurement front, although the procurement of paddy compared to its total production was very low (about 8 per cent) in relation to its counterpart of wheat procurement (about 21 per cent) during the 1970s, it has remarkably increased to 34 per cent during 2010–11. The procurement of paddy today accounts for over one-third of its production, whereas the same is only about one-fourth of the production of wheat. Among the states, the procurement of paddy was as high as 80 per cent of the production in Punjab, whereas it was only about 7 per cent (lowest among the states) in West Bengal during 2010–11. Although the procurement scenario has changed substantially in almost all the states since 1991–2, we have found wide fluctuations in procurement of paddy in most states, especially after the introduction of economic reforms.

The study finds that the returns over the cost C2 in real terms in paddy cultivation has not consistently increased in any of the HPS (Andhra Pradesh, Punjab, and Tamil Nadu) and LPS (Odisha, Uttar Pradesh, and West Bengal) considered for analysis between 1971–2 and 2009–10. Except for Punjab, where paddy farmers have been consistently making profit since 1980–1, farmers from all other states, both low and high productivity groups, have incurred losses in relation to cost C2. The analysis carried out to ascertain the number of years that paddy farmers were able to reap profit in the entire period of analysis (1971–2 to 2009–10) shows that except in the case of Punjab the ratio of GVO to cost C2 is found to be less than one (<1.00) in more number of years in all the five other states including HPS such as Andhra Pradesh and Tamil Nadu. Punjab farmers were able to reap profit for 30 years (96.77 per cent) out of 31 years, which is not seen in any of the remaining five states considered for the analysis. Farmers from West Bengal, considered as one of the HALP states for the analysis, have incurred losses more number of times (23 years out of 32 years) than any other state. While the analysis on profitability between the GRP and ACP reveals no clear pattern in profitability of paddy crop between HPS and LPS, the farmers from LPS have incurred losses more number of times during the ACP (1990–1 to 2009–10) than that of the GRP (1971–2 to 1990–1). Given the poor returns from paddy cultivation in most states considered for the analysis, one cannot say that the recommendation of the CACP to increase the price of paddy for the 2012 kharif season involved any 'dirty economics and dirtier politics'.

The findings of our study suggest that there is a need to strengthen the procurement infrastructure to have consistent profit from paddy cultivation, which is clearly evident from the experience of Punjab farmers. Despite having higher productivity, farmers from states such as Andhra Pradesh and Tamil Nadu could not reap any appreciable profit from paddy cultivation in a consistent manner partly because of poor procurement infrastructure. Therefore, state agencies must make the effort to improve procurement arrangements along with the announcement of MSP. Apart from this, efforts should also be made to increase the productivity of paddy, which has slowed in recent years in most states. This is also one of the reasons for poor returns from paddy cultivation. There has been a sharp increase in COC, especially since 2000–1, which is upsetting the profitability of paddy. The newly introduced method of system of rice intensification (SRI) is reportedly helping to reduce the COC considerably by conserving water and other inputs (Reddy et al., 2005; World Bank, 2007; WWF, 2007). Therefore, concerted efforts should be made to bring large areas under the method of SRI to improve the returns from paddy cultivation. It is argued in some quarters that the introduction of MGNREGS has steeply increased the COC of paddy crop. While any efforts taken to reduce the COC will obviously benefit farmers, it is equally important to find out why the COC has increased at a relatively faster rate in the recent years. Farmers in West Bengal incurred losses in paddy cultivation in the most number of years than any other state we have considered for the analysis. In-depth studies with disaggregated data need to be carried out to understand why farmers in West Bengal are incurring losses in paddy cultivation and also what promotes them to cultivate paddy crop despite the losses from it.

Bibliography

Acharya, S. S. 1997. 'Agricultural Price Policy and Development: Some Facts and Emerging Issues'. *Indian Journal of Agricultural Economics*, vol. 52, no. 1 (January–March), pp. 1–47.

Alagh, Y. K. 2012. 'Problem with Raising Paddy MSP'. *The Financial Express*, 10 May.

Bhalla, S. S. 2012. 'Price of Paddy Populism'. *The Financial Express*, 10 May.

Bhalla, G. S., and G. Singh. 2012. *Economic Liberalisation and Indian Agriculture: A District-Level Study.* Sage Publications, New Delhi.

CACP (Commission for Agricultural Costs and Prices). 2012. *Report on Price Policy for Kharif Crops of 2011–2012 Season.* Ministry of Agriculture, Government of India, New Delhi.

———. Various years. *Report on Price Policy for Kharif Crops.* Ministry of Agriculture, Government of India, New Delhi.

Chand, Ramesh. 1999. 'Liberalisation of Agricultural Trade and Net Social Welfare: A Study of Selected Crops'. *Economic and Political Weekly*, vol. 4, no. 52 (25 December), pp. A153–9.

———. 2010. 'Understanding the Nature and Causes of Food Inflation'. *Economic and Political Weekly*, vol. 44, no. 9, pp. 10–13.

Deshpande, R. S. 1996. 'Demand and Supply of Agricultural Commodities: A Review'. *Indian Journal of Agricultural Economics*, vol. 51, nos 1–2 (January–June), pp. 270–87.

Dev, S. M., and A. Ranade. 1998. 'Rising Food Prices and Rural Poverty: Going Beyond Correlations'. *Economic and Political Weekly*, vol. 33, no. 39, pp. 2529–36.

GOAP (Government of Andhra Pradesh). 2011. *Report of State Level Committee to Study the Problems of Farmers in Crop Holiday Affected Mandals of East Godavari District of Andhra Pradesh* (Chairman: Mohan Kanda).

GoI. 2012. *Agricultural Statistics at a Glance: 2011–12.* Ministry of Agriculture, Government of India, New Delhi.

Gulati, A. 2012a. 'Getting Paddy Prices Right'. *The Financial Express*, 16 May.

———. 2012b. 'Hike MSPs or Free Up Agriculture'. *The Financial Express*, 15 June.

The Hindu Business Line. 2012a. 'Misdirected Farm Subsidies'. 18 June.

———. 2012b. 'Surging Cultivation Costs behind Hike in Support Price'. 20 June.

Kalamkar, S. S., and A. Narayanamoorthy. 2003. 'Impact of Liberalisation on Domestic Agricultural Prices and Farm Income'. *Indian Journal of Agricultural Economics*, vol. 58, no. 3 (July–September), pp. 353–64.

Krishnaji, N. 1990. 'Agricultural Price Policy: A Survey with Reference to Indian Foodgrain Economy'. *Economic and Political Weekly*, vol. 25, no. 26, pp. A54–63.

Narayanamoorthy, A. 2006a. 'Relief Package for Farmers: Can It Stop Suicides?'. *Economic and Political Weekly*, vol. 41, no. 31 (5 August), pp. 3353–5.

———. 2006b. 'State of India's Farmers'. *Economic and Political Weekly*, vol. 41, no. 6 (11 February), pp. 471–3.

———. 2007. 'Deceleration in Agricultural Growth: Technology Fatigue or Policy Fatigue'. *Economic and Political Weekly*, vol. 42, no. 25 (23 June), pp. 2375–9.

———. 2012. 'Is the MSP Hike Justified?'. *The Financial Express*, 3 July, New Delhi, p. 9.

NSSO (National Sample Survey Office). 2005. *Situation Assessment Survey of Farmers: Some Aspects of Farming*, Report No. 496, 59th Round. Ministry of Statistics and Programme Implementation, Government of India, New Delhi.

Rao, C. H. H. 1994. *Agricultural Growth, Rural Poverty and Environmental Degradation in India*. Oxford University Press, New Delhi.

Rao, N. Chandrasekhara, and S. Mahendra Dev. 2010. 'Agricultural Price Policy, Farm Profitability and Food Security'. *Economic and Political Weekly*, vol. 45, nos 26 and 27 (June), pp. 174–82.

Rao, V. M. 1994. 'Farmers in Market Economy: Would Farmers Gain through Liberalisation?'. *Indian Journal of Agricultural Economics*, vol. 49, no. 3 (July–September), pp. 393–402.

———. 2001. 'The Making of Agricultural Price Policy: A Review of CACP Reports'. *Journal of Indian School of Political Weekly*, vol. 13, no. 1, pp. 1–28.

Reddy, V. R., P. P. Reddy, M. S. Reddy, and D. S. R. Raju. 2005. 'Water Use Efficiency: A Study of System Rice Intensification (SRI) Adoption in Andhra Pradesh'. *Indian Journal of Agricultural Economics*, vol. 60, no. 3 (July–September), pp. 458–72.

Schiff, M., and C. E. Montenegro. 1997. 'Aggregate Agricultural Supply Response in Developing Countries: A Survey of Selected Issues'. *Economic Development and Cultural Change*, vol. 45, no. 2, pp. 393–410.

Schultz, T. W. 1964. *Transforming Traditional Agriculture*. Yale University Press, New Haven, U. S. A.

Sen, Abhijit, and M. S. Bhatia. 2004. *Cost of Cultivation and Farm Income in India.* Academic Foundation, New Delhi.

Singh, Manmohan. 1995. 'Inaugural Address at the 54th Annual Conference of the Indian Society of Agricultural Economics'. *Indian Journal of Agricultural Economics*, vol. 50, no. 1, pp. 1–6.

World Bank. 2008. *Get More from Less with System of Rice Intensification (SRI).* The World Bank, Washington, U. S. A.

WWF (World Wide Fund for Nature). 2007. *More Rice with Less Water: System of Rice Intensification.* WWF-ICRISAT, Hyderabad, India.

5

Agricultural Market Access and Farm Income Nexus

Farmers throughout the developing world face a myriad of issues when they confront markets. The most crucial among all the issues is the access to markets. Access to market is of critical importance to farmers primarily because its existence defines their market participation and its absence undermines their ability to buy inputs and sell output. Highlighting the pervasiveness of lack of access to markets in developing countries, the International Fund for Agricultural Development (IFAD, 2001) recognized that the majority of farmers in developing countries are currently passive participants in markets, often obliged to sell at low prices and buy at high prices, with little choice of where they conduct transactions, with whom, and at what prices. So vital is market access to farmers that it is perceived to be a prerequisite for enhancing agricultural output and increasing rural income (IFAD, 2003). However, agricultural output and rural income cannot be substantially increased by exclusive emphasis on subsistence food crop production, as more market-oriented production systems are needed. These require the intensification of agricultural production systems, increased commercialization, and specialization of production. Commercialization, in turn, can be built upon the establishment of efficient and well-functioning basic infrastructural[1] facilities—ones that keep transaction costs low, minimize risk, and extend information to all players, and that do not either exclude or work contrary to the interests of those living in areas of inadequate infrastructure. Mere presence of these rural infrastructures will not serve the intended purpose unless it is made easily accessible to farmers.[2] The probability of a change in farming practices is proportional to the extent of accessibility or inaccessibility to such infrastructure as, for instance, a good road network accelerates efficient delivery of farm inputs, while a 1 km increase in distance to fertilizer services decreases the spending on fertilizer by INR 24.70 (Wanmali, 1992).

Although the interest of researchers and policymakers in agricultural infrastructure and its impact on agricultural development is growing, the paramount importance of rural infrastructure in phenomenally accelerating the process of agricultural development has long been at the centre of the development debate since at least the second half of the eighteenth century.[3] This has further received very concrete and robust recognition from the World Bank (WB, 1994). Identifying that improved agricultural productivity is inconceivable without the development of such basic infrastructure, investment

[1] Although the Oxford Dictionary defines 'infrastructure' as the basic physical and organizational structures needed for the operation of a society or enterprise or the services and facilities necessary for an economy to function, owing to its multiple meanings in different fields, it is really hard to define all dimensions of infrastructure in single perspective (GoI, 2004a). In this paper, we have confined ourselves to only physical infrastructure as accepted by the Committee on Infrastructure (GoI, 2004a).

[2] Infrastructure facilities such as irrigation systems, roads, bridges, and water systems fail to generate net benefits to its beneficiaries owing to insufficient maintenance which is becoming very pervasive in recent times. Maintenance of these infrastructures is as important as it is important to design, construct, and make them accessible (Ostrom et al., 1993).

[3] Before Adam Smith, the French physiocratic school had brought the attention to the importance of investment in public works such as bridges, aqueducts, and roads in the reduction of cost of transportation of commodities (in particular agriculture commodities) and the creation of national markets.

in rural infrastructure including market facilities has featured as an important development priority in most developing countries.[4] Yet, the World Bank (WB, 2008) reported that about 439 million people in most developing countries still continue to live in areas with poor market access, requiring five or more hours to reach a market town, signifying that distance to markets and lack of roads to get to them continue to be some of the most pressing development challenges. With the issue of investment in rural infrastructure being discussed frequently in various policy forums, a plethora of development economists have left no stone unturned in providing an empirical basis to the perceived link between agricultural infrastructure and agricultural productivity. While some researchers (see Antle, 1983; Andersen and Shimokawa 2006; Acharya, 2003; Bhatia, 1999; Ulimwengu, et al., 2009, Ahmad and Donovan, 1992) have documented that productivity increase in agriculture depends solely on good and reliable infrastructure, well-functioning domestic markets, appropriate institutions, and access to appropriate technology, a few others have underlined the positive externality of increased agricultural infrastructure facilities (Venkatachalam, 2003).[5] Following the crucial observations made by Spencer (1994) and IFAD (1995)[6] on rural roads and agricultural productivity nexus, quite an impressive number of studies have been carried out with robust results stating that better

[4] Identifying that inadequate agricultural infrastructure and market access is hindering farmers, the Government of India created the Rural Infrastructure Development Fund (RIDF) in 1995–6 to assist states in rural infrastructure. Irrigation projects, rural roads, and bridges have been the main expenditure categories from RIDF.

[5] Many scholars have underlined that increased agricultural infrastructure facilities play a strong positive role not only in promoting agricultural growth of a concerned region but also other regions of the economy since enormous amount of indirect benefits are generated by the infrastructure and enjoyed by outside regions.

[6] IFAD (2003) highlighted the fact that roads form the most basic element of agricultural infrastructure and that construction of rural roads almost inevitably leads to increase in agricultural production and productivity in villages. With better access to roads, fertilizer costs were 14 per cent lower, wages were 12 per cent higher, and crop output was 32 per cent higher in developing countries.

roads[7] drastically reduce the cost of inputs such as fertilizers,[8] seeds, and extension services as well as increase the scope of profitable trade, encouraging on-farm investments to raise agricultural production (see Ahmad and Hossain, 1990; Dercon et al., 2009; Van de Walle, 2002; Gollin and Rogerson, 2010; Khandker, Bakht, and Koolwal, 2009; Khandker, 1989; Singh, 1983; Majumdar, 2002; Binswanger, Khandker, and Rosenzweig, 1993; and Khachatryan, et al., 2005). A second strain of literature on the relation of agricultural infrastructure and agricultural growth looks at the impact of irrigation technology on agriculture growth, which has also been duly recognized by development economists. The empirical results on this nexus are found to be ambiguous with few studies pointing out that investments in irrigation infrastructure result in higher agriculture output (see AFDB, 2011; Dhawan, 1988; Vaidyanathan, 1999; Thorat and Sirohi, 2002; Manalili and Gonzales, 2009; Fan and Hazell, 1999; Zhang and Fan, 2000; Fan, Hazell, and Haque, 2000; Fan, Hazell, and Thorat, 2000; Fan, Zhang, and Zhang, 2002; and Narayanamoorthy and Hanjra, 2006), while others stating that investments on irrigation and electricity only have a modest impact on growth in agriculture productivity (Fan, Hazell, and Haque, 2000a; Evenson and Quizon, 1991). Examining the impact of electricity on agriculture productivity, Barnes and Binswanger (1986), Ahmad and Hossain (1990), and Binswanger, Khandekar, and Rosenzwieg (1993) found that the availability of electricity tended to increase farmers' investments in irrigation pumps leading to enhanced agricultural productivity. That tractor farms gave higher yields and had enhanced gross output per hectare than non-tractor farms has been very well recognized by Singh and Singh (1972), NCAER (1973), Aggarwal (1983), Rao (1978), and Binswanger (1978).

[7] Dorosh et al. (2010) presented more complicated evidence that input use depends on not only distance to roads but also the density of road networks. For instance, in East Africa, reducing travel time significantly increases adoption of high-yield technology, whereas roads have an insignificant impact in West Africa, where road network density is relatively high.

[8] The price of fertilizers is more in areas with poor roads owing to high transportation costs incurred in the purchase of this input. Studies show that farmers tend to apply more fertilizer because of lower cost brought about by lower transportation cost (Manatili and Gonzales, 2009).

It is clear from the preceding discussion that majority of the studies validate the proposition that investments in hard infrastructure (roads and irrigations systems) coupled with simultaneous investments in soft infrastructure (transport, seeds, fertilizers) facilitate intensive agricultural production. From employing simple statistics to complex econometric analysis, most of these studies were hitherto able to paint a healthy macro picture of the infrastructure and agriculture nexus; but in the process they failed to analyse as to what lies beyond enhanced agriculture production. In the context of India it has been perceived by some researchers (Narayanamoorthy, 2013; Narayanamoorthy and Alli, 2012) that fluctuations in the VAO with respect to cost C2 tend to explain the variations in agricultural production and productivity as well. In that situation, does it not become imperative to analyse what would be the impact of agriculture infrastructures on VAO? Barring a few studies (Bhatia, 1999; Chand and Chauhan, 2002; Narayanamoorthy and Hanjra, 2006), not many have conducted research in this direction. Moreover, very few studies (except Chand and Chauhan, 2002) are available on the impact of density of agricultural markets on VAO. Another important issue that has not received due attention by researchers is what would be the impact of the distance of farm from market on VAO. Given the finding that the farther away a market from the farm the more depressed is profitability of farmers (Adejobi, Amazo, and Ayoola, 2006), can distance from market be considered an inherent property of depressing VAO? Furthermore, with the World Bank (2008) reporting that wide variations exist in market facilities and infrastructure across Indian states, the impact of the essential infrastructural elements on VAO will also tend to vary across states. To address these issues, this study makes an attempt to analyse the impact of the basic agricultural market and non-market elements on VAO district-wise with the following objectives:

- to study the variations in VAO in relation to market-related variables across 235 selected districts;
- to examine the plausible association between VAO and various agricultural market and non-market variables; and
- to find out which of the market and non-market variables is able to influence VAO significantly.

Data and Method

The study is entirely based on secondary data pertaining to the period 2003–6. For the purpose of the analysis, a total of 235 districts[9] have been selected from 13 states of India, which are presented in Table 5.1. These districts represent both the agriculturally well-developed and less developed ones. The data for this study has been culled and compiled from varied published sources. District-wise input-related data on irrigated area (IRR), VAO, fertilizer use per hectare (FERT), and coverage of cropped area per tractor (TRACT) have been collected from Bhalla and Singh (2010; 2012). Market-related data such as average market distance (ADM), number of wholesale markets (NWM), and market density, which is defined as net sown area per agricultural market (NSAPAM), have been compiled/estimated from

Table 5.1 Number of Districts Selected from 13 Different States

States	Number of Districts
Andhra Pradesh	15
Bihar	7
Gujarat	16
Haryana	7
Karnataka	18
Madhya Pradesh	37
Maharashtra	24
Odisha	10
Punjab	11
Rajasthan	26
Tamil Nadu	8
Uttar Pradesh	44
West Bengal	12
Total	235

Source: GoI, 2001.

[9] Comparable data for the variables that we have planned to use in the analysis were available only for 235 districts and, therefore, the remaining districts had to be discarded from the analysis without assigning any special reasons.

the *Directory of Wholesale Agricultural Produce Assembling Markets in India* published by the MoA, Government of India (GoI, 2004b). Data pertaining to availability of pucca road (ROAD) and villages electrified (ELE) have been culled from the *Census of India* (GoI, 2001).

Agricultural output is largely influenced by a large number of market and non-market variables. However, due to non-availability of data, the study could identify and employ only eight variables for the analysis, which are presented in Table 5.2. Of these, IRR, FERT, ELE, and TRACT directly influence agricultural output while ROAD, ADM, NWM, and NSAPAM greatly facilitate increasing the VOP in agriculture. It is expected that variables such as IRR, FERT, ELE, TRACT, ROAD, ADM, NWM, and NSAPAM will greatly influence VAO across space and time. Therefore, we have considered variable VAO as the dependent variable in the analysis, which is expressed in terms of INR per hectare. It is very well documented that there exists a positive correlation between irrigation infrastructure and agricultural output. In order to represent irrigation infrastructure in the analysis, the percentage of irrigated area to GCA (IRR) has been used. Fertilizer as an agricultural input positively affects the yield of crop which is represented by fertilizer per hectare of gross cropped area (FERT) in the analysis. Another important infrastructural indicator that would positively and directly contribute to agricultural development is the total number of villages electrified (ELE). Rural electrification is bound to have a direct impact on the use of motor pump sets for irrigation purpose, which will increase agricultural production and productivity. The road variable (ROAD), which is represented by the percentage of villages having road facility, is indeed an indicator of the development of transport infrastructure and undisputedly is the most important element of agricultural infrastructure. However, there is still no consensus[10] on exactly how

10 Hirschman (1958) and Owen (1965) tried to temper the high expectations with the qualification that transport holds no special inherent properties capable of initiating growth. Rather, they argued it should be considered a necessary but not sufficient component of infrastructural investment, which is as unpredictable as other components in terms of its ability to generate development.

Table 5.2 Description of Variables Used in the Study for Analysis

Variable	Description of Variables	Unit	Average	Standard Deviation	Max.	Min.
ADM	Average distance of market in 2004	km	17.78	16.30	89.67	0.00
NWM	Number of wholesale market in 2004	N	14.09	11.41	66.00	1.00
ELE	Percentage of villages electrified in 2001	%	88.00	16.50	100.00	28.38
FERT	Fertilizer per hectare of cropped area in 2003–6	kg	103.82	66.17	359.37	1.58
IRR	Percentage of irrigated area to cropped area in 2003–6	%	43.81	25.73	115.52	0.84
NSAPAM	Net sown area per agriculture market in 2003–6	ha	66,709.16	86,739.20	793,034.00	4,677.81
ROAD	Percentage of villages having road facility in 2001	%	62.32	22.88	100.00	18.93
TRACT	Gross cropped area per tractor in 2003–6	ha	266.58	677.74	6,841.38	13.92
VAO	Value of agricultural output per hectare of cropped area in 2003–6 (at 1990–3 prices)	INR	7,693.07	3,734.76	22,445.37	998.40

Sources: Computed using data from Bhalla and Singh (2012); GoI (2004b); and GoI (2001).

roads become critical to agricultural development and if they actually warrant the faith vested in them; yet, majority of the studies point out that better roads can drastically reduce the cost of inputs and can increase the scope of profitable trade.

Tractor infrastructure (TRACT) is indicated by coverage of gross cropped area by a tractor, which represents the level of technology and power available for agriculture production. The variable ADM[11] captures the distance that separates farmers from basic infrastructure, categorized by the geographical distance (km) and not by time or money spent in obtaining these services. All that is produced needs to be marketed, for which the market systems have to be competitive wherein the sellers and buyers need to be well-informed about supply, demand, and prices. The presence of large, well-organized wholesale markets facilitates the attainment of this ideal situation by providing information on market trends, prices, and quantities marketed. Hence, variable NWM has been included into our analysis. NSAPAM is a proxy for market density which is one of the most important rural infrastructure that determines agricultural output. The significance of market density in influencing VAO lies in the fact that if NSAPAM increases exponentially, then fewer markets cannot absorb the excess agricultural produce. A situation of market congestion and market glut becomes inevitable, dampening VAO and erasing all or most of the gains to farmers. Realizing that this essence of market density is a decisive factor of VAO, it was decided that NSAPAM would be included in the analysis along with the other variables.

To study the nexus between agricultural market, infrastructure development, and output, both descriptive and regression analyses have been carried out. Districts widely differ in the distribution of agricultural infrastructure, more specifically in the presence and accessibility to markets. It is this disparity that is expected to make some districts better off than others in terms of agricultural growth.

11 Average distance to market (ADM) is indeed a very vital market-related variable and in the context of India it is this variable that largely determines farmers' earnings. This particular fact has been very well proven in a study by Birthal, Joshi, and Gulati (2005), which shed light on the grave scenario that in India greater distance of the farm from the market eats up as much as 15 per cent of farmers' gross income.

In order to study the distinct characteristics of all the 235 districts with respect to VAO, we have categorized all the districts into different groups on the basis of ADM and market density (NSAPAM). In order to identify which of the market and non-market variables are greatly influencing agricultural output, regression analysis is carried out treating VAO as the dependent variable and IRR, FERT, ELE, TRACT, ROAD, ADM, and NSAPAM as independent variables. The regression model which is used for studying the influence of market and other variables on VAO is as follows:

$$\begin{aligned} VAO = a + b_1 \text{ ADM} + b_2 \text{ ELE} + b_3 \text{ FERT} + b_4 \text{ IRR} \\ + b_5 \text{ NSAPAM} + b_6 \text{ ROAD} + b_7 \text{ TRACT} + u \end{aligned} \quad (1)$$

Results and Discussion

Before studying the influence of market and non-market variables on VAO, let us briefly discuss what the infrastructural variables at the district level try to convey. To begin with, it is observed from Table 5.2 that on an average about 14 wholesale markets are available in each of the selected districts. Although the number of regulated (secondary) agricultural markets has seen a tremendous jump from just 286 in 1950 to a phenomenal 7,157 by 2010 (GoI, 2011), majority of the farmers in the country still dispose of their produce in the village, rural/primary markets, or secondary agricultural market. What could be the reason? Is it due to the inaccessibility to markets? It is understood that the ADM from farm of 235 districts is about 18 km, which is indeed a matter of concern as it was suggested by the NCF (2006) that markets should be made available within 5 km radius (approximately 80 sq km). The percentage of villages covered by supply of electricity on an average is around 88 per cent.[12] An average of about 104 kg of fertilizer has been used for a hectare of cropped area in the selected districts for cultivating various crops. About 62 per cent

[12] This particular fact indeed gives an appreciable impression that the majority of the villages in India are electrified. However, if one looks at a study by World Bank and Private Infrastructure Advisory Facility (WB, 2010) it would indeed be shocking to know that about 77 per cent of poor households in rural areas do not have electric connections.

of villages equipped with roads indicate that villages are no longer isolated from their sale points and are well connected. Market density (NSAPAM) is found to be 66,709 ha on average. This particular information on market density is very vital for our analysis as it is on the basis of this average that we will be analysing the behaviour of VAO of the selected districts. If the selected districts have an average of NSAPAM above or below the average of 235 districts, what does it imply and, more importantly, how significant is it with respect to VAO? All these questions can be answered only by analysing the data of selected districts, which are discussed in the following sections.

Agricultural Markets and Value of Output

A major objective of the study is to find out whether the distance from market has any relationship with the VAO. There is a general conception that when farms are in proximity to markets, it enables farmers to transport the agricultural produce swiftly and at a lower transportation cost. This in turn helps them to realize better prices from the market. In order to study this, we have categorized the districts into two: 1. districts with ADM above the ADM of 235 districts; and 2. districts with ADM below the ADM of 235 districts. It comes out from this analysis that VAO is relatively higher among the second group than for the first group (Table 5.3). To be more elaborate, the ADM in 170 districts is found to be below the ADM of 235 districts, which is about 18 km, suggesting that more than 72 per cent of the districts in India reaped the benefits of a higher VAO due to easy access to markets, with lesser time involved in

Table 5.3 Classification of Districts Based on ADM and Their VAO

Classification	Number of Districts	VAO (INR/ha at 1990–3 prices)
Districts with above average distance to market of 235 districts	65	6,245.25
Districts with below average distance to market of 235 districts	170	8,247.80
All districts	235	7,693.07

Sources: Computed using data from Bhalla and Singh (2010; 2012) and GoI (2004b).

getting to the market outlets leading to lesser cost of various farm inputs and transportation costs. Besides, the VAO of these districts, which is about INR 8,247/ha, is indeed above the average VAO of 235 districts of INR 7,693/ha, indicating that these districts are marching well ahead in terms of agricultural output. On the other hand, about 28 per cent of the districts whose ADM was above the ADM of 235 districts had to bear the burden of higher transportation and other related costs owing to the longer time involved in getting to the markets, resulting in the escalation in the prices of farm inputs and hence depressing VAO.

Similar to studying the relationship between ADM and VAO, we have also made an attempt to find whether the density of agricultural market has any association with the agricultural output. Generally, increased density in markets acts as a catalyst for agricultural growth as more number of markets in a given area can bring about intense competition in the market. However, if only one market serves for the whole lot of farmers in a given region, and on account of NSAPAM, when the market arrivals increase, a situation of market congestion and market glut cannot be ruled out. This would add substantially to farmers' waiting time and product deterioration (in case of perishable goods), thereby depressing VAO. Moving ahead with this conceptual clarity, when we turn towards Table 5.4, it is observed that the density of markets in 153 districts is below the average of 235 districts, which is about 66,709 ha. The VAO is found to be relatively higher in these 153 districts (above 65 per cent) owing to less market congestions and other reasons, while a greater market congestion in about 35 per cent of the districts have resulted in a depressing VAO.

Table 5.4 Classification of Districts on the Basis of NSAPAM and Their VAO

Classification	Number of Districts	VAO (INR/ha at 1990–3 prices)
Districts with above average NSAPAM of 235 districts	82	6,370.22
Districts with below average NSAPAM of 235 districts	153	8,402.04
All districts	235	7,693.07

Sources: Computed using data from Bhalla and Singh (2010; 2012) and GoI (2004).

In order to understand the relationship between market variables and the VAO in a more disaggregated manner, we have further classified the districts in ascending order based on VAO. The distribution of districts by different levels of VAO is depicted in Table 5.5. The disaggregated distribution of districts clearly indicates that both ADM and NSAPAM tend to decline when the range of VAO moves up. However, the distribution of districts in the VAO ranges of 151–200 and 201–235 is very significant and noteworthy since it is in these ranges that the VAO is found to be higher than the average of 235 districts. It is indeed an encouraging signal as it suggests a continuous move to a higher distribution indicating that these districts are seriously working towards enhancing agricultural output, which is indeed the most decisive factor of farm profitability. The same is not true with the ADM wherein the distribution of districts suggests that in an increasingly large number of districts the ADM is above the average of 235 districts, which is 17.78 km. This observation highlights the grim fact that non-access to markets continues to be a major hindrance to farmers. It is encouraging to observe that the number of districts having market density below the average of 235 districts has seen a gradual improvement during the study period.

These descriptive analyses at best point out that the VAO is relatively higher in case of the districts whose ADM and NSAPAM are below the average of 235 districts than those with above the average of all districts. However, this analysis does not convey which of the variables is able to enhance the agricultural output significantly among

Table 5.5 Classification of Districts Based on VAO and Its Relation with Market Variables

Classification of Districts	VAO (INR/ha at 1990–3 prices)	ADM (km)	NSAPAM (ha)
1–50	3,510.60	23.62	110,194.33
51–100	5,234.00	23.24	64,788.69
101–50	7,422.06	16.27	57,526.01
151–200	9,865.73	10.18	57,207.01
201–35	14,464.33	14.69	34,024.34
All districts	7,693.07	17.78	66,709.16

Sources: Computed using data from Bhalla and Singh (2010 and 2012) and GoI (2004b).

the variables considered for the analysis. Will the market-related variables such as ADM and NSAPAM, which were used as the yardsticks to categorize the districts, significantly influence agricultural output? An attempt is made to provide an answer to this question utilizing correlation and regression analysis in the following sections.

Market, Infrastructure, and Agricultural Output Nexus

As was pointed out earlier, each of the agricultural market and non-market variables that has been taken up for study would in one way or another influence agricultural output to a greater extent. There is also the likelihood that some infrastructure variables may influence the agricultural output significantly, eclipsing the presence of other variables. Before getting deeper into identifying such variables, it becomes imperative to first analyse the possible association between VAO and all the agriculture infrastructure variables. The correlation values computed between VAO and other selected variables reported in Table 5.6 vividly point out that VAO is negatively associated with ADM. A host of studies have categorically proved that lesser the distance to market, greater would be the agricultural productivity. This appears to be correct in our analysis too, as the relationship turned

Table 5.6 Correlation Values: Value of Agricultural Output (VAO) with Other Selected Variables

Variable	Description of Variables	Correlation Coefficients
ADM	Average distance of market	–0.248[a]
ELE	Percentage of villages electrified	0.147[b]
FERT	Fertilizer per hectare gross cropped area	0.710[a]
IRR	Percentage of irrigated area to gross cropped area	0.483[a]
NSAPAM	Net sown area per agriculture market	–0.289[a]
ROAD	Percentage of villages having road facility	0.382[a]
TRACT	Gross cropped area per tractor	0.002[ns]

Sources: Computed using Bhalla and Singh (2010 and 2012); GoI (2004b); and GoI (2001).

Notes: a and b are significant at 1 per cent and 5 per cent levels respectively; ns: not significant.

out to be very robust. A statistically significant but negative association is observed between the market density variable NSAPAM and VAO, which is also expected and plausible. The other variables such as ROAD, ELE, TRACT, IRR, and FERT are also positively correlated with VAO.

Having understood the association of each of the variables with VAO, we now turn towards the results of the regression presented in Table 5.7. The results of most variables that were included in the regression analysis turned out to be along the expected line. The R^2, which is estimated to be 0.538, implies that about 54 per cent of the variations in VAO can be explained by the variables included in the regression analysis. As expected, market variables have significantly influenced VAO. The coefficient of market density, which is

Table 5.7 Determinants of VAO by Market and Non-market Variables: Regression Results

Variable	Description of Variables	Estimates of Regression Coefficients	't' Values
ADM	Average distance of market	-15.41^{d}	−1.37
ELE	Percentage of villages electrified	23.25^{b}	1.91
FERT	Fertilizer per hectare gross cropped area	31.99^{a}	8.67
IRR	Percentage of irrigated area to gross cropped area	23.21^{a}	2.63
NSAPAM	Net sown area per agriculture market	-0.004^{b}	−1.86
ROAD	Percentage of villages having road facility	4.25^{ns}	0.44
TRACT	Gross cropped area per tractor	0.621^{a}	2.47
Constant		$1,413.57^{ns}$	1.18
	R^2	0.547	
	Adjusted R^2	0.533	
	F-Value	39.17	
	D-W	1.691	

Sources: Computed using Bhalla and Singh (2010 and 2012); GoI (2004b); and GoI (2001).

Notes: a, b, c, and d are significant at 1 per cent, 5 per cent, 10 per cent, and 20 per cent levels respectively; ns: not significant.

represented by NSAPAM, is negatively and significantly associated to VAO in determining agricultural output. This means that when the cropped area covered by agricultural market increases, it will have a deleterious impact on the VOP. As the cropped area per agricultural market increases, an increase in the marketable surplus is definitely expected. Fewer markets in any given region fail to absorb this excess local supply, compelling farmers to face the wrath of market glut and market congestion. An increase in the cropped area is the need of the hour but adequate agricultural markets need to also be set up to accommodate the excess produce. In the presence of only a few markets, farmers would prefer to sell their surplus agricultural produce in their local villages rather than losing their whole produce. The coefficient of ADM also turned out to be negative and significant, which we expected.

Besides market variables, non-market variables have also considerably influenced VAO, which is obviously expected. The regression coefficient of FERT suggests that 1 per cent increase in FERT would lead to an increase of nearly INR 32 in the VOP, while in case of IRR (irrigation coverage) the output would increase by INR 23. Recalling the previous discussions, road infrastructure can be expected to positively affect agriculture. The ROAD coefficient is found to be positively associated to VAO, but to our surprise it is statistically insignificant, questioning the validity of a voluminous literature that validates that road infrastructure is primarily important for efficient functioning of market. The positive coefficient indicates that the road infrastructure is no doubt highly related to VAO, but fails to explain the variations in VAO despite a phenomenal surge in the overall village accessibility to roads from 20 per cent in 1950–1 to 54 per cent in 2000–1. It seems that there are some other infrastructure variables which have almost eclipsed the impact of the ROAD variable on VAO. The estimated coefficient of electricity variable (ELE) is positively associated and is statistically significant in determining agricultural output. Electricity infrastructure undoubtedly enters the production directly as intermediate input. More specifically, it is a part and parcel of irrigation activity, wherein improvement in access to electricity brings about substantial improvements in irrigation facilities.

The importance of this infrastructure becomes even more pronounced when agricultural activities become increasingly irrigation-based.

The coefficient of irrigation infrastructure, IRR, is found to be positive and statistically significant in determining agricultural output. This result is in tune with the large body of literature which does concede the fact that irrigation influences agricultural output significantly. Irrigation infrastructure becomes necessary when crops cannot satisfy all their water needs through natural precipitation. In India, with inconsistent rainfall characterizing climate change, irrigation becomes indispensable. With a view to bringing about manifold increase in agricultural production and productivity, enormous efforts were taken by the Government of India immediately after Independence to promote major and minor irrigation projects and to bring the majority of small and marginal farmers under the ambit of irrigated agriculture. On the whole, the regression analysis suggests that along with yield-enhancing factors, market-related variables are also important in increasing the VOP in agriculture.

***

Agricultural infrastructure is considered to be one of the most important factors in influencing agricultural output. In India, it is mostly the inaccessibility to some of the basic agricultural infrastructures that results in dwindling of farm profits and even provokes the farmers to rethink their decision of continuing farming. A plethora of studies have amply corroborated the perceived nexus between each of the agricultural infrastructure elements with that of the agricultural output. Not many studies have attempted to analyse whether the market-related agricultural infrastructure, such as distance to market and market density, have any impact on agricultural output. In pursuit of an answer to this question, utilizing data from 235 selected districts from different states, this chapter has attempted to study the impact of market-related agricultural infrastructures along with input-related agricultural infrastructure on VAO.

The results of the descriptive analysis point to the fact that the VAO is relatively high for those districts whose ADM is below the average of 235 districts than those whose ADM is higher than the average. The VAO is also found to be relatively high for those districts where the cropped area per agricultural market (market density) is below the average of all the districts. The descriptive analysis, on the whole, signifies that market-related infrastructural variables do play a very important role in enhancing agricultural output. The regression results clearly bring out the very crucial finding that the market-related variables ADM and NSAPAM play a vital role in determining agricultural output along with non-market yield-enhancing variables such as irrigation, fertilizer, tractor use, and rural electricity supply. The association between market density and VAO is a robust one, which sheds light on the fact that if the cropped area per agricultural market increases then the problem of market congestion and market glut arises which becomes pivotal in depressing VAO. This is because with the increase in the cropped area, the additional agricultural produce demands additional agricultural markets. In the absence of any increase in the number of agricultural markets, farmers may often be provoked to dispose of their agricultural produce in the local villages at throwaway prices depressing their earnings.

The coefficient of fertilizer, FERT, bears a positive sign and is statistically significant. Better access to markets and less congested markets boost farmers' incentives to produce more with enhanced modern inputs such as fertilizers. The coefficient of electricity variable, ELE, is positively associated with and statistically significant to VAO. The irrigation infrastructure represented by IRR is found to be positive and significantly associated with VAO. This result goes in tune with the large body of literature which concedes the fact that irrigation influences agricultural output significantly. The findings of the study clearly suggest that besides other infrastructure variables, market variables also play a major role in enhancing VAO. However, further studies need to be undertaken to bring about a robust association between NSAPAM and VAO by employing a more disaggregated data set covering larger administrative units with more number of data time points.

Bibliography

Acharya, S. S. 2003. *Agricultural Marketing in India, Millennium Study of Indian Farmers*. Ministry of Agriculture, Government of India, New Delhi.

Adejobi, A., P. Amazo, and G. Ayoola. 2006. 'Enhancing the Access of Rural Households to Output Markets for Increased Farm Incomes'.

Paper presented at International Association of Agricultural Economists Conference, Australia, 12–18 August.

AFDB (African Development Bank). 2011. *Infrastructure and Agriculture Productivity in Africa. Market Brief.* November.

Aggarwal, B. 1983. *Mechanization in Indian Agriculture—An Analytical Study Based on Punjab.* Delhi School of Economics.

Ahmad, R., and C. Donovan. 1992. *Issues of Infrastructural Development: A Synthesis of the Literature.* International Food Policy Research Institute, Washington, D. C.

Ahmad, R., and M. Hossain. 1990. *Developmental Impact of Rural Infrastructure in Bangladesh,* Research Report 83. International Food Policy Research Institute, Washington, D. C.

Andersen, P., and S. Shimokawa. 2006. 'Rural Infrastructure and Agricultural Development'. Paper presented at the Annual Bank Conference on Development Economics, Tokyo, Japan, 29–30 May.

Antle, J. 1983. 'Infrastructure and Aggregate Agricultural Productivity: International Evidence'. *Economic Development and Cultural Change,* vol. 31, no. 3, pp. 609–19.

Barnes, D. F., and H. P. Binswanger. 1986. 'Impact of Rural Electrification and Infrastructure on Agricultural Changes, 1960–1980'. *Economic and Political Weekly,* vol. 21, no. 1, pp. 26–34.

Bhalla, G. S., and G. Singh. 2010. 'Growth of Indian Agriculture'. Final Report on Planning Commission Project. Centre for Study of Regional Development, Jawaharlal Nehru University, New Delhi.

———. 2012. *Economic Liberalisation and Indian Agriculture: A District-Level Study.* Sage Publications India Private Limited, New Delhi.

Bhatia, M. S. 1999. 'Rural Infrastructure and Growth in Agriculture'. *Economic and Political Weekly,* 27 March–2 April.

Binswanger, H. P. 1978. *The Economics of Tractors in South Asia.* Agricultural Development Council, New York, and ICRISAT, Hyderabad.

Binswanger, H. P., S. R. Khandker, and M. R. Rosenzweig. 1993. 'How Infrastructure and Financial Institutions Affect Agricultural Output and Investment in India'. *Journal of Development Economics,* vol. 41, pp. 337–66.

Birthal, P. S., P. K. Joshi, and Ashok Gulati. 2005. *Vertical Coordination in High-Value Food Commodities: Implications for Smallholders.* Markets, Trade and Institutions Division Discussion Paper No. 85. International Food Policy Research Institute, Washington, D. C.

Chand, R., and S. Chauhan. 2002. 'Socio-economic Factors in Agricultural Diversification in India'. *Agricultural Situation in India,* vol. 58, no. 11, pp. 523–9.

Dercon, S., D. Gilligan, J. Hoddinott, and T. Woldehanna. 2009. 'The Impact of Roads and Agricultural Extension on Consumption Growth and Poverty in Fifteen Ethiopian Villages'. *American Journal of Agricultural Economics*, vol. 91, no. 4, pp. 1007–21.

Dhawan, B. D. 1988. *Irrigation in India's Agricultural Development: Productivity, Stability, Equity*. Sage Publications India, New Delhi.

Dorosh, P., H. Wang, L. You, and E. Schmidt. 2010. 'Crop Production and Road Connectivity in Sub-Saharan Africa'. World Bank Policy Research WP 5385. Washington, D. C.

Evenson, R. E., and J. Quizon. 1991. 'Technology, Infrastructure, Output Supply, and Factor Demand in Philippine Agriculture'. In R. E. Evenson and C. E. Pray, eds, *Research and Productivity in Asian Agriculture*. Cornell University Press.

Fan, S., and P. Hazell. 1999. 'Are Returns to Public Investment Lower In Less-Favored Rural Areas? An Empirical Analysis of India'. Discussion Paper 43. Environment and Production Technology Division, International Food Policy Research Institute, Washington, D. C.

Fan, S., P. Hazell, and T. Haque. 2000. 'Targeting Public Investments by Agro-Ecological Zone to Achieve Growth and Poverty Alleviation Goals in Rural India'. *Food Policy*, vol. 25, no. 4, pp. 411–28.

Fan, S., P. Hazell, and S. Thorat. 2000. 'Government Spending, Growth, and Poverty in Rural India'. *American Journal of Agricultural Economics*, vol. 82, no. 4, pp. 1038–51.

Fan, S., L. Zhang, and X. Zhang. 2002. *Growth, Inequality and Poverty in Rural China: The Role of Public Investments*. International Food Policy Research Institute Research Report 125. Washington, D. C.

Gollin, D., and R. Rogerson. 2010. 'Agriculture, Roads, and Economic Development in Uganda'. National Bureau of Economic Research WP 15863. Cambridge.

GoI. 2001. *Census of India*. Ministry of Home Affairs, Government of India, New Delhi.

———. 2004a. *Committee on Infrastructure*. Prime Minister, Chairman, Planning Commission, Government of India, New Delhi.

———. 2004b. *Directory of Wholesale Agricultural Produce Assembling Markets in India*. Department of Agriculture and Cooperation, Ministry of Agriculture, Government of India.

———. 2011. *Report of the Working Group on Agricultural Marketing Infrastructure, Secondary Agriculture and Policy Requirement for Internal and External Trade*. Planning Commission, Government of India.

Hirschman, A. O. 1958. *Strategy of Economic Development*. Yale University Press, U. S. A.

IFAD (International Fund for Agricultural Development). 1995. *The State of World Rural Poverty: A Profile of Asia.* Rome.

———. 2001. *Rural Poverty Report 2001: The Challenge of Ending Rural Poverty.* Oxford University Press, New York.

———. 2003. *Promoting Market Access for the Rural Poor in Order to Achieve the Millennium Development Goal.* Rome.

Khachatryan, A., M. V. Oppen, R. Doluschitz, and N. Khachatryand. 2005. 'Response of Plant Productivity to Improved Agricultural Markets in India: Application of an Advanced Econometric Cross-Section Time Series Analysis'. Paper presented at the Tropentag Conference on International Agricultural Research for Development, Stuttgart-Hohenheim, Germany, 11–13 October.

Khandker, S. 1989. 'Improving Rural Wages in India'. WP 276. World Bank, Washington, D. C.

Khandker, S., Z. Bakht, and G. Koolwal. 2009. 'The Poverty Impact of Rural Roads: The Evidence from Bangladesh'. *Economic Development and Cultural Change*, vol. 57, pp. 685–722.

Majumdar, R. 2002. *Infrastructure and Economic Development: A Regional Analysis.* Centre for the Study of the Regional Development, Jawaharlal Nehru University, New Delhi.

Manalili, R., and L. Gonzales. 2009. *Impact of Infrastructure on Profitability and Global Competitiveness of Rice Production in the Philippines.*

Narayanamoorthy, A. 2013. 'Profitability in Crops Cultivation in India: Some Evidence from Cost of Cultivation Survey Data'. *Indian Journal of Agricultural Economics*, vol. 68, no.1, pp. 104–21.

Narayanamoorthy, A., and P. Alli. 2012. 'India's New Food Security Worries—from Crop Holiday to Declining Foodgrains Area'. *Indian Journal of Agricultural Economics*, vol. 67, no. 3, July–September.

Narayanamoorthy, A., and M. A. Hanjra. 2006. 'Rural Infrastructure and Agriculture Output Linkages: A Study of 256 Indian Districts'. *Indian Journal of Agricultural Economics*, vol. 61, no. 3, pp. 444–59.

NCF (National Commission on Farmers). 2006. *Serving Farmers and Saving Farming.* Ministry of Agriculture, Government of India, New Delhi.

NCAER (National Council of Applied Economic Research). 1973. *Report of the Impact of Mechanization in Agriculture on Employment.* New Delhi.

Ostrom, E., L. Schroeder, and S. Wyne. 1993. 'Analysing the Performance of Alternative Institutional Arrangements for Sustaining Rural Infrastructure in Developing Countries'. *Journal of Public Administration Research and Theory*, vol. 13, no. 1, pp. 11–45.

Owen, W. 1965. 'Case Studies of the Effects of Roads on Development'. Highway Research Record No. 115, pp. 10–18.

Rao, T. R. 1978. 'Agricultural Mechanization in Retrospect and Prospect'. Proceedings of Symposium on Farm Mechanisation—Problems and Prospects. Indian Society of Agriculture Economics and Punjab Agricultural University, Ludhiana, pp. 45–56.

Singh, R., and B. B. Singh. 1972. *Farm Mechanization in Western Uttar Pradesh: Problems of Farm Mechanisation.* Seminar Series IX, Indian Society of Agricultural Economics, Mumbai.

Singh, V. K. 1983. *Infrastructure and Development in India: A Study of Regional Variations.* Centre for the Study of the Regional Development, Jawaharlal Nehru University, New Delhi.

Spencer, D. S. C. 1994. 'Infrastructure and Technology Constraints to Agricultural Development in the Humid and Sub-humid Tropics of Africa'. Environment and Production Technology Division, International Food Policy Research Institute, Washington, D. C.

Thorat, S., and S. Sirohi. 2002. *Rural Infrastructure State of Indian Farmer: A Millennium Study.* Ministry of Agriculture, Government of India, New Delhi.

Ulimwengu, J., J. Funes, D. Headey, and L. You. 2009. *Paving the Way for Development: The Impact of Road Infrastructure on Agricultural Production and Household Wealth in the Democratic Republic of Congo.* International Food Policy Research Institute, Washington, D. C.

Vaidyanathan, A. 1999. *Water Resources Management: Institutions and Irrigation Development in India.* Oxford University Press, New Delhi.

Van de Walle, D. 2002. 'Choosing Rural Roads Investments to Help Reduce Poverty'. *World Development*, vol. 30, no. 4, pp. 575–89.

Venkatachalam, L. 2003. *Infrastructure and Agriculture Development in Karnataka State.* Institute for Social and Economic Change, Bangalore.

Wanmali, S. 1992. *The Settlement System and Development of the Regulated Economy in Southern India.* Research Report. International Food Policy Research Institute, Washington, D. C.

WB (World Bank). 1994. *World Development Report: Infrastructure for Development.* Oxford University Press, New York.

———. 2008. *World Development Report 2008: Agriculture for Development.* Washington, D. C.

———. 2010. *India Country Framework Report for Private Participation in Infrastructure.* World Bank and Public Private Infrastructure Advisory Facility, Washington, D. C.

Zhang, X., and S. Fan. 2000. 'Public Investment and Regional Inequality in Rural China'. Discussion Paper No. 71. Environment and Production Technology Division, International Food Policy Research Institute, Washington, D. C.

PART III

PROFITABILITY AND FARM INCOME

6

Has MGNREGS Affected Farm Profitability?

This chapter presents a detailed analysis of whether MGNREGS introduced in 2006 has affected the profitability of crops cultivated in different parts of India. It is argued vehemently in different forums that 'MGNREGA has "pushed" up the average wage of casual workers, distorted the rural labour markets by diverting them to non-farm rural jobs, thus creating an artificial labour shortage and raising the cost of production of agricultural commodities' (Gulati, Jain, and Satija, 2013, p. 9). As a result of increased cost of production, the profitability from cultivating different crops has reportedly reduced. A plethora of reports published in various vernacular dailies, especially in south India, has also indicated the issue of declining profitability due to the introduction of the national rural employment scheme. Is this argument valid?

An assured employment scheme, namely MGNREGS, was introduced in 2006 by the Government of India with the major objective of reducing rural poverty. Over INR 2 lakh crore has been spent on this programme, which has generated an amount of 1,348 crore person days of employment throughout India since its inception (MoRD, 2012; Gulati, Jain, and Satija, 2013). MGNREGS aims to reduce the migration of the rural poor and poverty among the vulnerable sections by providing assured employment opportunities. Studies carried out on the impact of this scheme also showed that it helps in getting the assured wage rate and employment in most of the states where it is implemented effectively (see Shah, 2009; Mukherjee and Sinha, 2011; Dutta et al., 2012; MoRD, 2012; Mann and Ramesh, 2013).

This employment scheme was introduced specifically to improve the standard of living of the vulnerable sections of the rural population. But it is increasingly argued that this scheme has been seriously affecting the growth of the agricultural sector that has already been passing through a major crisis since the early 1990s because of increased COC and poor remuneration from crop cultivation (see Harish et al., 2011; Narayanamoorthy and Alli, 2013; Gulati, Jain, and Satija, 2013). As this scheme is operated throughout the year including the busy seasons of agriculture, it has created unusual labour scarcity in the rural areas which has resulted in a steep increase in the wage rate of agricultural labourers (Shah, 2009; Dutta et al., 2012; Berg et al., 2012; Gulati, Jain, and Satija, 2013). The introduction of MGNREGS has also reportedly resulted in the deterioration of the quality of labour considerably, meaning that the effective working hours of labour have reduced, which is ultimately leading to an increase in the labour requirement for the given operation (Verma and Shah, 2012). Both the increased wage rate and requirement of labour have reportedly increased the COC of different crops substantially since the introduction of MGNREGS (Chandrasekar and Ghosh, 2011). As the output prices are not fixed in consonance with the rise in COC in India, the losses from crop cultivation reportedly increased for farmers. Importantly, citing increased wage rate due to MGNREGS in agriculture, farmers belonging to the fertile region of Andhra Pradesh even declared paddy crop holiday in a large area during the kharif season of 2011 (see GoAP, 2011; Narayanamoorthy and Alli, 2012).

The COC and farm wage rate are determined by irrigation coverage and a host of other factors that vary widely from one region to another in India. Given the wide variation in determining factors, is it correct to say that MGNREGS is increasing farm wage rate which has resulted in increased COC uniformly across different crops and states in India? Even if one accepts the argument that MGNREGS increases the farm wage rate, will the impact of it on wage rate and COC be the same across high and low irrigated states? Quite a few studies have analysed the implementation, equity, and governance aspects of MGNREGS after the implementation this scheme (Aiyar and Samji, 2006; Bhatia and Dreze, 2006; Chakraborty, 2007; Gopal, 2009, Khera and Nayak, 2009; Adhikari and Bhatia, 2010; Jha et al., 2009; Jha, Bhattacharya, and Gaiha, 2011; Imbert and Papp, 2011; Liu and Barrett, 2013). Several studies have shown that MGNREGS has been relatively successful since it directly provides more employment opportunities and wages to the poor in the rural areas (see Dutta et al., 2012; MoRD, 2012). Although the employment guarantee scheme has multiplier impacts on the village economy that help in ameliorating the standards of living, obviously it is expected to cause a hike in agricultural wages (Berg et al., 2012; Hirway, Saluja, and Yadav, 2008).

A study by Gulati, Gujral, and Nandakumar (2012) reported that by distorting the rural labour markets by creating an artificial labour shortage, the employment scheme has reportedly raised the cost of production of agricultural commodities. As a result, farmers have been facing an adverse effect on the farm profitability in major crops (Narayanamoorthy, 2013; Reddy and Reddy, 2007). Many vernacular dailies have also stressed the adverse effect of MGNREGS on agricultural labour supply and wages, and COC. Although a large number of studies have analysed the impact of the employment scheme on farm wage rate in particular, not many detailed studies are available as to what happened to the profitability of crops covering major states and major crops of India. Given the absence of studies based on detailed macro-level data, one cannot come to a conclusion that MGNREGS has reduced the profitability of crops uniformly across states. Moreover, the surplus labour available is less in the irrigated regions as compared to un-irrigated regions and, therefore, the impact of MGNREGS on cost of human labour will not be the same between the two regions. Since the irrigation coverage to cropped area, cropping pattern, intensity of crop cultivation, availability of labour, and rural infrastructure facilities widely vary from one state to another and the profitability is also a function of irrigation, infrastructure, and other inputs (Vishandass and Lukka, 2013), the impact of MGNREGS on profitability of crops may not be the same across the states. Keeping this in view, an attempt is made in this chapter to determine the impact of MGNREGS on the COC as well as profitability of different major crops utilizing CCS data. The specific objectives of the study are:

1. To determine the change in the cost of human labour in different crops before and after the introduction of the rural employment guarantee scheme.
2. To compare the cost of major operations with human labour cost in different crops before and after the introduction of rural employment guarantee scheme.
3. To analyse the overall pattern of COC in different crops before and after the introduction of rural employment guarantee scheme.
4. To estimate the profitability in different crops in relation to cost C2 before and after the introduction of rural employment guarantee scheme.

Data and Methodology

The entire study has been carried out utilizing crop-wise CCS data covering the period from 2000–1 to 2010–11. The main objective of the study is to find the profitability of different crops before and after the introduction of MGNREGS. The CACP has been publishing valuable time series data on operation-wise costs, productivity, income, and such others for various important crops over the years. This CCS data is regarded as very valuable information, which is generally used for fixing MSPs for different crops for both kharif and rabi seasons in India. For studying the profitability of crop cultivation, all the costs and income-related data have been compiled from various CACP publications and also from its website. The labour and other inputs required for the cultivation of different crops are not the same, which is also expected to be varied in different states depending upon the intensity of crop cultivation. The intensity of input use in HPS will be totally different from relatively LPS in any crop. Profit levels are also expected to be different for different crops because of their nature and market conditions. One of the objectives of our study is to find whether the profitability of crop varies with the states having high and low productivity. Keeping this in view, a total of five different crops (paddy, gram, groundnut, sugarcane, and cotton) consisting of cereals, pulses, oilseeds, and high-value commercial crops have been considered for the study. Based on the productivity data of TE 2010–11, for each crop, two states belonging to the category of HAHP and HALP have been considered for studying the profitability of crops. The details of crops and the states selected for the analysis are presented in Table 6.1.

As regards the method of profit calculation, CACP has been using nine different cost concepts (A1, A2, A2+FL, B1, B2, C1, C2, C2*, and C3) for measuring the economics of various crop cultivations. For this study, cost C2 has been considered for computing the profitability of various crops as it covers the entire variable and fixed costs needed for crop cultivation. Our objective is to study whether the profitability in different crops cultivated in different states has increased after the introduction of MGNREGS. For this, all the costs and income-related data have been converted into constant prices using CPIAL deflator at 1986–7 price. Profit level of the crop is computed by deducting the cost C2 from the VOP. Although the study covers data pertaining to different crops from 2000–1 to 2010–11, the study period has been divided into two sub-periods as pre-MGNREGS (2000–1 to 2005–6) and post- MGNREGS (2005–6 to 2010–11) to capture the impact of the national rural employment scheme on COC and profitability.

Analysis and Discussion

This study covers five different crops for its analysis. These five selected crops are not the same in terms of its duration, coverage of irrigation, productivity, VOP, and so on. The states that are selected for the analysis of each crop are also not the same. Therefore, it is prudent to analyse the profitability of each crop separately rather than by taking all the crops together. Let us first analyse the profitability of paddy crop before and after the introduction of MGNREGS.

Profitability in Paddy

Paddy is one among the important and labour-intensive crops cultivated in most parts of India. It has been reported especially in south

Table 6.1 Details of Crops and States Selected for the Study on MGNREGS

Crops	States Selected for Study	Category of State Selected	Area (mha)		Yield (kg/ha)	
			TE 2005–6	TE 2010–11	TE 2005–6	TE 2010–11
1. Paddy	Andhra Pradesh	HAHP	3.35 (9.12)	4.19 (11.08)	3,020	3,114
	Odisha	HALP	4.48 (10.26)	4.35 (9.87)	1,491	1,577
2. Gram	Madhya Pradesh	HAHP	2.70 (36.94)	3.01 (33.84)	927	972
	Rajasthan	HALP	1.08 (15.58)	1.31 (19.37)	607	760
	Karnataka	HALP	0.57 (16.76)	0.70 (20.37)	539	529
	Madhya Pradesh	HALP	0.68 (11.13)	0.75 (10.87)	1,039	1,085
3. Groundnut	Gujarat	HAHP	1.99 (28.93)	1.85 (30.89)	1,638	1,408
	Andhra Pradesh	HALP	1.74 (27.89)	1.56 (27.56)	760	851
4. Sugarcane	Maharashtra	HAHP	0.42 (11.90)	0.83 (19.88)	66,229	82,900
	Uttar Pradesh	HALP	2.05 (51.43)	2.06 (43.65)	58,159	56,102
5. Cotton	Gujarat	HAHP	1.82 (22.00)	2.48 (23.40)	481	576
	Maharashtra	HALP	2.83 (33.18)	3.53 (35.05)	184	303

Sources: Computed utilizing data from GoI (2012) and www.dacnet.nic.in.

Notes: HAHP: high area with high productivity; HALP: high area with low productivity; figures in brackets are percentage to India's total area; R&M: rapeseed and mustard.

India that the introduction of national rural employment scheme has created artificial demand for labour which has resulted in increased labour cost required for crop cultivation. As human labour cost generally accounts for close to one-third of cultivation cost of paddy, this increased labour cost has reportedly increased the gross COC that ultimately affected the profitability of paddy crop. Is it correct to say that the human labour cost required for paddy cultivation has increased after the introduction of the rural employment scheme? What is the increase in labour cost vis-à-vis the costs of other operations? Can we say that the profitability is affected only due to the increase in labour cost that occurred because of the rural employment scheme? What was the state of labour cost in paddy cultivation before the introduction of the employment scheme? We need to find the answers to these questions to make any judgment as to whether or not the rural employment scheme has had any impact on the profitability of paddy crop.

Profitability of any crop is always related to its productivity, which is highlighted by many studies (see Bhalla and Singh, 2012). Therefore, as mentioned in the methodology section, we have selected two states, each having the characteristics of HAHP and HALP for the analysis. While Andhra Pradesh has been considered as an HAHP state, Odisha has been selected as an HALP state in paddy crop for the detailed analysis. Table 6.2 presents the trends in operation-wise cost, productivity, VOP, and profit for paddy crops for the two selected states for both pre- and post-MGNREGS periods. For the purpose of analysis, the operation-wise cost has been classified into five categories, namely cost on human labour, cost on bullock labour, machine labour cost, costs on yield-increasing inputs, and other costs. This classification is done in order to find out the pattern of human labour cost in comparison to other operations of paddy cultivation.

It is clear from the table that there has been a substantial variation in the operation-wise COC between the two periods considered for the analysis. This is particularly true in the case of cost of human labour, which is a serious issue widely discussed after the introduction of the national rural employment programme. The cost of human labour has increased at the rate of 6.13 per cent per annum in the HAHP state during the post-MGNREGS period, but the same grew at a negative rate of −1.84 per cent during the pre-MGNREGS

Table 6.2 Cost and Profitability of Paddy Cultivation from 2000–1 to 2010–11 (values in INR at 1986–7 prices)

Costs/Profit	Particulars	Andhra Pradesh (HAHP)			Odisha (HALP)		
		2000–1 to 2005–6	2006–7 to 2010–11	2000–1 to 2010–11	2000–1 to 2005–6	2006–7 to 2010–11	2000–1 to 2010–11
Human Labour	Cost (INR)	2,709	3,157	2,913	2,034	2,141	2,083
	CGR (%)	–1.84	6.13	1.33	1.05	4.19	2.18
	Share (%)	31.25	34.14	32.30	38.59	39.37	39.07
Bullock Labour	Cost (INR)	281	158	223	636	562	598
	CGR (%)	–0.39	–10.09	–4.73	1.55	–1.03	–0.40
	Share (%)	3.25	1.71	2.47	12.06	10.43	11.22
Machine Labour	Cost (INR)	550	851	705	121	153	136
	CGR (%)	4.24	7.50	6.46	12.42	0.44	6.70
	Share (%)	6.34	9.21	7.81	2.30	2.83	2.55
Yield-Enhancing Inputs	Cost (INR)	2,005	1,765	1,850	850	766	806
	CGR (%)	2.22	–2.17	–2.85	0.32	–2.96	–1.55
	Share (%)	23.13	19.09	20.52	16.12	14.22	15.12

Other Cost	Cost (INR)	3,220	3,501	3,381	1,630	1,786	1,708
(Fixed Costs)	CGR (%)	1.00	1.13	0.62	1.06	–0.24	–0.04
	Share (%)	37.16	37.85	37.49	30.93	33.15	32.04
Cost C2	Cost (INR)	8,667	9,248	9,018	5,271	5,389	5,331
	CGR (%)	–0.58	2.62	0.57	1.21	1.12	0.76
	Share (%)	100.00	100.00	100.00	100.00	100.00	100.00
Value of Output	VOP (INR)	8,810	10,030	9,507	4,088	4,851	4,501
	CGR (%)	0.48	1.58	0.95	0.19	2.60	1.13
Yield (qtl/ha)		50.49	53.29	52.04	29.42	30.64	30.01
Profit (VOP-C2)		143	782	489	–1182	–538	–829
Number of Years Profit Realized		4/6	4/5	8/11	0/6	0/5	0/11

Sources: Computed using data from CACP (various years).

Notes: CGR: compound growth rate per cent/per annum; HAHP: high area with high productivity; and HALP: high area with low productivity.

period. What is interesting here is that this has happened despite the significant increase in the cost of machine labour, which grew at a rate of 7.50 per cent per annum during the post-MGNREGS period. It is generally expected that the cost of human labour will decline when farmers spend more on machine labour. However, this has not happened in the case of the HAHP state in paddy cultivation. This implies that the wage rate paid for human labour used for paddy cultivation has increased substantially, possibly due to the introduction of the national rural employment programme. The growth rate in human labour cost is also found to be much higher as compared to costs on all other major operations during the post-MGNREGS period. As a result of the fast increase in cost of human labour and machine labour, the gross COC (cost C2) of paddy has also increased at a rate of 2.62 per cent per annum during the post-MGNREGS period, which was not the case during the pre-MGNREGS period.

The pattern of cultivation of crops is not the same across the states in India. Some states have been following intensive agriculture by adopting modern technological inputs, while other states are following different forms of cultivation practices. Therefore, one may not be able to firmly conclude that what is happening in one state is occurring similarly in all other states. Specifically, the labour use pattern and the wage rate vary widely across states. In view of this, we have selected another state, namely Odisha, under the category of HALP to find out whether or not the pattern of operation-wise COC is same in comparison to the HAHP state. As expected, the pattern of operation-wise cost including the cost on human labour in the HALP state is different from the HAHP state during both pre- and post-MGNREGS periods. However, the cost of human labour, which is one of our main focuses in the chapter, has increased at a faster pace during the post-MGNREGS period as compared to its previous time period considered for the analysis. For instance, the cost of human labour increased at a rate of 4.19 per cent per annum during the post-MGNREGS period, but the same has increased at a rate of only 1.05 per cent per annum during the pre-MGNREGS period. In contrast to the human labour cost, the growth rate in machine labour cost has decelerated sharply after the introduction of the rural employment scheme, which is something unexpected. The gross COC (cost C2) too has decelerated in the HALP state during the post-MGNREGS period because of the slow pace of growth in the costs of all other operations except human labour cost. Overall, what is clear from the analysis of operation-wise cost is that although the cost pattern is not the same between the two states, the cost of human labour has increased at a relatively faster pace in both the states after the introduction of rural employment scheme.

As mentioned earlier, one of the major objectives of the study is to find whether the profitability in crop cultivation has been affected due to the introduction of the rural employment scheme. It has been argued in recent years that the rural employment scheme introduced throughout the country has created artificial demand for labour, which has resulted in increased cost of human labour. Though a few studies have corroborated that the agricultural wage rate increased due to the rural employment scheme, not many studies have analysed the aspect of profitability. Therefore, after studying operation-wise COC, we have turned our focus towards the profititability of paddy crop. It is known that the profitability of any crop is determined not only by the COC but also by factors such as productivity of the crop, market price, and so on. With this understanding, let us study the profitability of paddy. The results presented in Table 6.2 show that the average value of paddy output increased from INR 8,810/ha in 2000–6 to INR 10,030/ha in 2006–11 in HAHP states, showing a much faster pace of growth during the post-MGNREGS period. As a result of the faster growth in VOP, the profitability from paddy increased from INR 143/ha to INR 782/ha between the two time periods. Although the absolute profitability is very meagre, it increased manifold during the post-MGNREGS period as compared to its earlier period. Not only has the profitability increased after the introduction of the employment scheme, but the number of years in which profit has been realized by farmers has also increased during the post-MGNREGS period in HAHP states.

The profitability scenario of HALP states is totally different from HAHP states. While no significant increase is noticed in VOP between pre- and post-MGNREGS periods, the losses incurred by farmers in cultivating paddy reduced from INR 1,182/ha to INR 538/ha during this period. Surprisingly, farmers belonging to the HALP state could not reap profit even in a single year during the entire period of analysis from 2000–1 to 2010–11. Although the COC is very low in the HALP state as compared to the HAHP state, farmers are unable to reap any profit from paddy cultivation, possibly because of low productivity. This suggests that it is difficult to increase profitability without increasing productivity.

Profitability in Gram

After studying the profitability of paddy crop, we will now turn our focus on pulse crops, which accounted for about 13 per cent (24.46 mha) of cropped area as of 2011–12 in India. Although various pulse crops have traditionally been cultivated in India, one major pulse crop namely gram (Bengal gram) has been considered for the purpose of this analysis; it accounted for about 34 per cent of India's total pulses area in 2011–12.

As done earlier for paddy, two states, namely Madhya Pradesh (HAHP state) and Rajasthan (HALP state), have been considered for the study. It emerges clearly from Table 6.3 that the cost incurred and profit realized from gram is not the same between the two states. In the case of the HAHP state, the cost on human labour has increased substantially after the introduction of the employment scheme. The real human labour cost grew at a rate of 4.36 per cent/annum during the post-MGNREGS period, but the same grew at a negative rate of −1.58 per cent/annum during the pre-MGNREGS period, suggesting a fast increase of human labour cost after the employment scheme. However, the machine labour cost has surprisingly not increased substantially during the post-MGNREGS period (2.87 per cent) as compared to its previous period (2.81 per cent). Because of negative growth in bullock labour cost as well as in the cost of yield-increasing inputs, the gross COC on gram has declined at a rate of −3.88 per cent/annum during the post-MGNREGS period. As regards the profitability, although the average VOP has increased to INR 4,730/ha during the post-MGNREGS period from the pre-MGNREGS period value of INR 4,397/ha, the growth rate of VOP during the post-MGNREGS period was negative (−6.67 per cent/annum). Notwithstanding this, the average profit realized by farmers belonging to the HAHP state during the post-MGNREGS period increased to INR 1,034/ha, which was only about INR 800/ha during its previous period.

Table 6.3 Cost and Profitability of Gram Cultivation from 2000–1 to 2010–11 (values in INR at 1986–7 prices)

Costs/Profit	Particulars	Madhya Pradesh (HAHP)			Rajasthan (HALP)		
		2000–1 to 2005–6	2006–7 to 2010–11	2000–1 to 2010–11	2000–1 to 2005–6	2006–7 to 2010–11	2000–1 to 2010–11
Human Labour	Cost (INR)	552	587	568	815	725	774
	CGR (%)	–1.58	4.36	0.45	–3.92	4.41	–1.02
	Share (%)	15.35	15.87	15.59	26.77	23.56	25.30
Bullock Labour	Cost (INR)	201	113	161	155	88	125
	CGR (%)	1.02	–10.78	–7.48	–9.45	–27.15	–19.78
	Share (%)	5.60	3.06	4.43	5.11	2.86	4.08
Machine Labour	Cost (INR)	338	450	389	316	320	318
	CGR (%)	2.81	2.87	3.64	1.25	0.64	0.23
	Share (%)	9.38	12.18	10.67	10.39	10.40	10.39
Yield–Enhancing Inputs	Cost (INR)	882	914	897	672	748	707
	CGR (%)	2.22	–7.26	–1.49	3.20	–15.20	–3.57
	Share (%)	24.53	24.72	24.62	22.09	24.30	1137

(*Cont'd*)

Table 6.3 *(Cont'd)*

Costs/Profit	Particulars	Madhya Pradesh (HAHP)			Rajasthan (HALP)		
		2000–1 to 2005–6	2006–7 to 2010–11	2000–1 to 2010–11	2000–1 to 2005–6	2006–7 to 2010–11	2000–1 to 2010–11
Other Cost	Cost (INR)	1,624	1,632	1,628	1,086	1,197	3,060
(Fixed Costs)	CGR (%)	1.83	–6.16	–1.66	0.51	–10.22	–2.74
	Share (%)	45.14	44.16	44.69	35.68	38.88	37.14
Cost C2	Cost (INR)	3,597	3,696	3,642	3,044	3,079	3,060
	CGR (%)	1.44	–3.88	–0.85	–0.38	–7.24	–2.53
	Share (%)	100.00	100.00	100.00	100.00	100.00	100.00
Value of Output	VOP (INR)	4,397	4,730	4,548	3,631	4,102	3,845
	CGR (%)	2.14	–6.67	–1.09	–0.42	–11.71	–3.19
Yield (qtl/ha)		9.89	10.08	9.98	6.62	8.25	7.36
Profit (VOP–C2)		800	1,034	906	587	1,023	785
Number of Years Profit Realized		6/6	5/5	11/11	6/6	5/5	11/11

Sources: Computed using data from CACP (various years).

Notes: CGR: compound growth rate per cent/per annum; HAHP: high area with high productivity; and HALP: high area with low productivity; VOP: value of output.

It was expected that the pattern of operation-wise COC and profitability of gram in the HALP state would be different from that of the HAHP state. But the results presented in Table 6.3 do not depict much difference in profit and other major parameters. Similar to the HAHP state, the cost on human labour has increased at a faster rate during the post-MGNREGS period as compared to its previous period. The growth in gross COC (C2) has sharply declined during the post-MGNREGS period, which was also observed with the HAHP state. Due to the increase in yield of gram from 6.62 qtl/ha to 8.25 qtl/ha between the two periods, the profitability has increased from INR 587/ha to INR 1,023/ha between pre- and post-MGNREGS periods. Again the increase in profitability in gram cultivation between the HAHP state and the HALP state is more or less same after the introduction of the employment scheme. The number of years in which profit was realized by farmers through the cultivation of gram is also the same for both the states selected for this analysis. It appears from the analysis that although the human labour cost has increased at a faster rate after the introduction of the national employment scheme, the profitability of gram has not been affected in either the HAHP or the HALP state.

Profitability in Groundnut

Groundnut is an important traditional oilseed crop cultivated in most parts of India, but with less irrigation coverage. With 6.46 mha in 1960–1, its area peaked to a level of 8.71 mha during 1989–90, but thereafter its area has been coming down continuously, and in 2012–13 it was at a level of only 5.26 mha. Increased COC, repeated crop failures, low market price, poor remuneration from its cultivation, and other factors are often cited as the main reason for the decline in its area under cultivation. Whatever may be the reasons for the decline of cultivated area in the past, let us now study the scenario of groundnut cultivation after the implementation of MGNREGS. As done for other crops, we have selected Gujarat as the HAHP state and Andhra Pradesh as the HALP state in order to study the profitability of groundnut.

Table 6.4 presents the operation-wise cost, gross COC, VOP, and profit in relation to cost C2 for both the states selected for the

Table 6.4 Cost and Profitability of Groundnut Cultivation from 2000–1 to 2010–11 (values in INR at 1986–7 prices)

Costs/Profit	Particulars	Gujarat (HAHP)			Andhra Pradesh (HALP)		
		2000–1 to 2005–6	2006–7 to 2010–11	2000–1 to 2010–11	2000–1 to 2005–6	2006–7 to 2010–11	2000–1 to 2010–11
Human Labour	Cost (INR)	1,239	1,292	1,263	1,307	2,271	1,745
	CGR (%)	2.50	3.52	1.59	2.48	16.45	7.72
	Share (%)	24.22	22.06	23.17	26.15	32.17	29.40
Bullock Labour	Cost (INR)	545	608	574	342	338	341
	CGR (%)	13.02	−0.13	5.46	12.47	−3.94	4.17
	Share (%)	10.65	10.38	10.52	6.85	4.79	5.74
Machine Labour	Cost (INR)	337	432	380	166	248	203
	CGR (%)	10.69	0.52	5.61	5.92	18.11	7.11
	Share (%)	6.59	7.37	6.97	3.31	3.51	3.42
Yield–Enhancing Inputs	Cost (INR)	1,579	2,019	1,779	1,492	1,774	1,620
	CGR (%)	2.29	5.53	3.51	2.18	8.96	4.39
	Share (%)	30.86	34.48	32.63	29.85	25.12	27.29

Other Cost	Cost (INR)	1,417	1,505	1,457	1,691	2,429	2,027
(Fixed Costs)	CGR (%)	11.02	8.42	6.31	1.43	13.05	6.74
	Share (%)	27.68	25.71	26.72	33.83	34.41	34.15
Cost C2	Cost (INR)	5,118	5,855	5,453	4,998	7,060	5,936
	CGR (%)	6.06	4.79	4.01	2.78	12.08	6.31
	Share (%)	100.00	100.00	100.00	100.00	100.00	100.00
Value of Output	VOP (INR)	5,709	6,428	6,036	3,978	6,344	5,053
	CGR (%)	18.59	10.31	10.75	0.71	17.43	8.34
Yield (qtl/ha)		11.76	11.90	11.82	9.15	13.37	11.07
Profit (VOP-C2)		591	573	583	−1021	−717	−883
Number of Years Profit Realized		4/6	3/5	7/11	0/6	2/5	2/11

Sources: Computed using data from CACP (various years).

Notes: CGR: compound growth rate per cent/per annum; HAHP: high area with high productivity; and HALP: high area with low productivity; VOP: value of output.

analysis. As expected, the cost and income patterns of groundnut cultivation in the selected two states are distinctly different, which is clearly evident from the results presented in the table. In the case of the HAHP state, although the human labour cost in real value is the same for the pre- and post-MGNREGS periods, its growth rate is relatively higher during the post-MGNREGS period, which is also noticed in most crops we have analysed so far. Given the marginal increase in human labour cost, a big increase was expected in machine labour cost during the post-MGNREGS period, but it did not happen as per the data of the CACP. Mainly because of the increase in the cost of yield-increasing inputs, gross COC has increased by about INR 737/ha after the introduction of the MGNREGS over the period before it was introduced. This increase has made some impact on the profitability of groundnut in the HAHP state, which has declined from INR 592/ha to INR 573/ha after the introduction of MGNREGS. Besides decline in absolute profitability, the number of years when profit was realized by farmers in the HAHP state has also declined after the introduction of the employment scheme.

The economics of groundnut cultivation in the HALP state appears to be more dreadful as compared to its counterpart HAHP state. Except bullock labour cost, the costs of all other operations have increased considerably after the introduction of MGNREGS. Among all operations, the cost of human labour has increased substantially from INR 1,307/ha to INR 2,271/ha and its growth rate has registered at 16.45 per cent/annum during the MGNREGS period. Although the increased human labour cost is expected to reduce the cost of machine labour (as these two are substitutes), this has not happened in the HALP state. The cost of machine labour grew at a rate of 18.11 per cent/annum during the MGNREGS period, which is unprecedented. Because of the increased cost in most operations, the gross COC in the HALP state has also increased from INR 4,998/ha to INR 7,060/ha between the two periods of analysis. Despite realization of substantial increase in VOP, the increased COC has not helped farmers to realize any profit from groundnut cultivation in the HALP state during the MGNREGS period. It appears that if the human labour had not increased substantially after the introduction of MGNREGS, groundnut would have been profitable to farmers. One good thing that happened for groundnut growers during the MGNREGS period is that they were able to realize profits in at least two out of five years, which was not the case during the pre-MGNREGS period. On this basis, one can say that despite substantial increase in human labour cost, farmers cultivating groundnut in the HALP state were less affected during the MGNREGS period.

Profitability in Sugarcane

It is a well-known fact that farm profitability varies from one crop to another depending on the nature of the crop. Therefore, what is seen from the preceding discussion on cereals, pulses, and oilseeds may not be the same with high-value crops. Keeping this in view, we have selected two important high-value commercial crops, namely sugarcane and cotton, for studying their profitability. As the patterns of cultivation of these two crops is totally different, let us first study sugarcane crop. Sugarcane is a water-intensive crop mostly cultivated in the assured irrigated region. With assured prices and marketing facility from sugar industries, farmers cultivating sugarcane are able to get assured income and, therefore, its area has been consistently increasing over the years: from 2.42 mha in 1960–1 to 5.06 mha in 2012–13. Considering area and productivity, we have selected two states, Maharashtra as the HAHP state and Uttar Pradesh as the HALP state, for studying the profitability of sugarcane crop. It is appropriate to mention here that these two states together accounted for about 63 per cent of India's total sugarcane area in 2012–13.

The results presented in Table 6.5 show that costs of various operations including the human labour incurred for cultivating sugarcane in the HAHP state have not increased appreciably after the introduction of MGNREGS. While the human labour cost increased only by about INR 132/ha, the machine labour cost has declined by about INR 322/ha during the MGNREGS period as compared to the period before that. Due to minor changes in operation-wise COC, the gross COC in absolute terms has increased by about INR 1,148/ha between the two periods. This increase, however, has not made any negative impact on the profitability of sugarcane in the HAHP state, where it increased to INR 5,054/ha during the MGNREGS period from a loss of INR 266/ha during the pre-MGNREGS period. Not only has the average profit from sugarcane cultivation increased but

Table 6.5 Cost and Profitability of Sugarcane Cultivation from 2000–1 to 2010–11 (values in INR at 1986–7 prices)

Costs/Profit	Particulars	Maharashtra (HAHP)			Uttar Pradesh (HALP)		
		2000–1 to 2005–6	2006–7 to 2010–11	2000–1 to 2010–11	2000–1 to 2005–6	2006–7 to 2010–11	2000–1 to 2010–11
Human Labour	Cost (INR)	5,164	5,296	5,224	2,727	2,872	2,793
	CGR (%)	4.65	3.72	3.33	1.28	2.14	0.95
	Share (%)	26.18	25.37	25.80	26.97	26.74	26.86
Bullock Labour	Cost (INR)	645	799	715	143	234	184
	CGR (%)	21.02	–8.58	6.27	–2.30	18.93	10.19
	Share (%)	3.27	3.83	3.53	1.41	2.18	1.77
Machine Labour	Cost (INR)	1,928	1,606	1,782	257	239	249
	CGR (%)	3.92	5.53	2.29	3.82	–4.05	–0.52
	Share (%)	9.77	7.69	8.80	2.54	2.23	2.39
Yield-Enhancing Inputs	Cost (INR)	6,636	6,217	6,446	2,411	2,365	2,390
	CGR (%)	10.61	–0.29	1.97	3.12	2.76	2.18
	Share (%)	33.64	29.78	31.83	23.85	22.02	22.99

Other Cost (Fixed Costs)	Cost (INR)	5,249	6,958	6,026	4,574	5,029	4,781
	CGR (%)	4.62	6.53	4.95	6.19	0.62	2.77
	Share (%)	26.60	33.33	29.76	45.24	46.83	45.99
Cost C2	Cost (INR)	19,728	20,876	20,250	10,112	10,739	10,397
	CGR (%)	7.16	2.96	3.40	3.91	1.79	2.20
	Share (%)	100.00	100.00	100.00	100.00	100.00	100.00
Value of Output	VOP (INR)	19,462	25,930	22,402	14,141	17,448	15,645
	CGR (%)	8.74	8.90	7.66	7.22	0.22	3.31
Yield (qtl/ha)		821.92	897.20	856.13	497.76	512.24	504.34
Profit (VOP-C2)		–266	5,054	2,152	4,029	6,709	5,247
Number of Years Profit Realized		1/6	4/5	5/11	6/6	5/5	11/11

Sources: Computed using data from CACP (various years).

Notes: CGR: compound growth rate per cent/per annum; HAHP: high area with high productivity; and HALP: high area with low productivity; VOP: value of output.

the number of years in which profit was realized by the farmers also increased from one out of six years to four out of five years after the initiation of the rural employment scheme.

The pattern of profitability of sugarcane cultivation in the HALP state is somewhat different from that of the HAHP state. The costs of both human and bullock labour have increased marginally, while the costs on machine labour and yield-increasing inputs have declined marginally after the introduction of MGNREGS. The gross COC has also increased only by INR 627/ha between the two periods because of small changes in the operation-wise COC. Despite having much lower productivity of sugarcane as compared to the HAHP state, the profitability of sugarcane is relatively higher in the HALP state mainly because of lower COC. The profitability has increased from INR 4,029/ha in pre-MGNREGS period to INR 6,709/ha after its introduction in the HALP state, which is totally different from the HAHP state. Farmers cultivating sugarcane in the HALP state have also not incurred losses in any of the years from 2000–1 to 2010–11 considered for the analysis, which is also different from the HAHP state. On the whole, the analysis seems to suggest that the profitability of sugarcane in either state has not declined after the introduction of MGNREGS.

Profitability in Cotton

Cotton is an important commercial crop which has been traditionally cultivated in various parts of India. Its area was hovering around 7–8 mha till the year 2003–4, but it increased to 12.18 mha in 2012–13, possibly because of the Bt cotton revolution. Though it is a high-value commercial crop, it is predominantly cultivated under rainfed conditions; its irrigation coverage has increased only from 12.70 per cent in 1960–1 to 33.80 per cent in 2010–11 at the all-India level. In order to study the profitability of cotton crop, we have selected Gujarat as the HAHP state and Maharashtra as the HALP state. Although the irrigation coverage under this crop in Gujarat (28.70 per cent) and Maharashtra (2.70 per cent) is totally different, these two states together accounted for about 56 per cent of India's total cotton area in 2012–13. Therefore, the analysis of these two states is expected to be useful in understanding the profitability of cotton cultivation before and after the introduction of MGNREGS.

As has been done earlier, the profitability of cotton cultivation in the HAHP state (Gujarat) is taken first for analysis. From Table 6.6 it can be seen that the cost of human labour has increased by about INR 587/ha after the introduction of the rural employment scheme over its previous period, which is expected. The cost of machine labour, which has a direct relationship with the cost of human labour, has marginally declined by about INR 18/ha over its previous period. As a result of increased cost in various operations including the fixed costs, the gross COC has increased substantially by about INR 2,194/ha over the pre-MGNREGS period. This substantial increase in gross COC has not affected the profitability of cotton in the HAHP state because of significant increase in its productivity, which increased from 11.38 qtl/ha to 22.51 qtl/ha during the period selected for the analysis. The profitability of cotton computed in relation to cost C2 has also increased from INR 1,238/ha to INR 4,125/ha during the post-MGNREGS period. It appears from the analysis that the profitability in cotton cultivation in the HAHP state has increased after the introduction of MGNREGS. Moreover, farmers from the HAHP state have realized profit in all the years during the post-MGNREGS period.

Is the profitability of cotton in the HALP state different from that in the HAHP state? The results presented in Table 6.6 show that there is a vast difference in profitability of cotton between the two selected states. Although the average cost of human labour has increased more or less on the same pattern that is noted in the HAHP state, the level of profit realized by the farmers belonging to the HALP state is abysmally low. It appears that this low profit is not mainly due to the fast increase in human labour cost but mainly because of low productivity. Between the pre- and post-MGNREGS periods, productivity increased by about 11.31 qtl/ha in the HAHP state, whereas the same increased only by about 3.98 qtl/ha in the HALP state. As a result of low productivity, the realization of profit was only INR 551/ha in the HALP state during the post-MGNREGS period as against the profit of INR 4,125/ha realized by farmers belonging to the HAHP state. One positive aspect about the HALP state is that farmers were able to reap some amount of

Table 6.6 Cost and Profitability of Cotton Cultivation from 2000–1 to 2010–11 (values in INR at 1986–7 prices)

Costs/Profit	Particulars	Gujarat (HAHP)			Maharashtra (HALP)		
		2000–1 to 2005–6	2006–7 to 2010–11	2000–1 to 2010–11	2000–1 to 2005–6	2006–7 to 2010–11	2000–1 to 2010–11
Human Labour	Cost (INR)	1,935	2,522	2,202	1,384	1,981	1,655
	CGR (%)	16.22	6.48	9.30	–0.38	18.71	8.44
	Share (%)	31.62	30.34	30.94	23.54	28.03	25.79
Bullock Labour	Cost (INR)	363	418	388	1311	1302	1307
	CGR (%)	9.94	4.09	5.49	15.91	–5.41	5.25
	Share (%)	5.94	5.03	5.45	22.31	18.43	20.37
Machine Labour	Cost (INR)	428	410	420	198	209	203
	CGR (%)	5.23	–5.36	–0.65	–1.54	14.85	5.82
	Share (%)	7.00	4.93	5.90	3.36	2.95	3.16
Yield-Enhancing Inputs	Cost (INR)	1,719	2,246	1,959	1,420	1,602	1,503
	CGR (%)	16.57	0.12	6.73	1.11	8.91	3.76
	Share (%)	28.10	27.02	27.53	24.16	22.67	23.41

Other Cost	Cost (INR)	1,647	2,639	2,098	1,565	1,973	1,750
(Fixed Costs)	CGR (%)	22.11	10.67	14.90	3.32	13.61	7.30
	Share (%)	26.91	31.74	29.48	26.62	27.92	27.27
Cost C2	Cost (INR)	6,119	8,313	7,117	5,877	7,067	6,418
	CGR (%)	16.81	6.29	9.70	3.96	10.33	6.49
	Share (%)	100.00	100.00	100.00	100.00	100.00	100.00
Cost C3	Cost (INR)	6,731	9,106	7,810	6,465	6,957	6,689
Value of Output	VOP (INR)	7,357	12,439	9,667	5,244	7,618	6,323
	CGR (%)	25.74	13.74	18.32	3.94	16.28	9.78
Yield (qtl/ha)		11.38	22.51	16.44	8.49	12.47	10.30
Profit (VOP-C2)		1,238	4,125	2,550	–633	551	–95
Number of Years Profit Realized		4/6	5/5	9/11	1/6	4/5	5/11

Sources: Computed using data from CACP (various years).

Notes: CGR: compound growth rate per cent/per annum; HAHP: high area with high productivity; and HALP: high area with low productivity; VOP: value of output.

profit after the introduction of MGNREGS, which was not the case before the introduction of the employment scheme. In addition to this, the number of years when profit was realized by farmers has also increased dramatically after the introduction of MGNREGS: four out of five years as against one out of six years during the pre-MGNREGS period. The analysis suggests that the profit from cotton cultivation appears to have improved in both the HAHP and the HALP state after the introduction of MGNREGS.

Conclusions and Suggestions

It is argued in different quarters, including farmers' organizations, that the introduction of the national rural employment scheme in rural areas has increased the farm wage rate substantially, which has resulted in sharp reduction in farm profitability. Is there any substance to this argument? Although a large number of studies have analysed the impact of MGNREGS on wage rate and other parameters utilizing both the primary and secondary information in different states, detailed studies are not available focusing specifically on the profitability in different crop cultivation covering various states. In this chapter an attempt has been made to fill this gap utilizing CCS data available for different crops published by the CACP. It has considered data from 2000–1 to 2010–11 and has covered five different crops: paddy, gram, groundnut, sugarcane, and cotton for the analysis of profitability. As the productivity of a crop often determines the its profitability, two states for each crop (one each from the category of HAHP state and HALP state) has been considered for the analysis.

The results of the study have shown mixed results, not completely supporting the argument that the profitability of crops has declined after the introduction of MGNREGS. This is not only true with HAHP states but also with HALP states. Supporting the earlier studies that the farm wage rate has increased due to the introduction of employment scheme, the results from this study also showed that the real cost of human labour has increased considerably in all crops in both HAHP and HALP states after its introduction (2006–7 to 2010–11). However, it has not had any deleterious impact on profitability. The profitability calculated by deducting the VOP from cost

C2 has increased in almost all crops in HAHP states, whereas either the profitability has increased or the losses have reduced in HALP states in all crops. Not only has the average profit of most crops increased but the number of years when profit was realized by the farmers has also increased in most crops during the post-MGNREGS period as compared to the pre-MGNREGS period (2000–1 to 2005–6). While there is no distinct pattern emerging in profitability between foodgrain and non-foodgrain crops, the level of increase in profitability is found to be relatively better among the non-foodgrain crops after the introduction of MGNREGS. Increased productivity in most crops considered for the analysis has one way or the other helped to negate the increase in human labour cost, which also facilitated to increase profitability.

Although there is no clear evidence from this study to show that the profitability of crops has declined during the post-MGNREGS period, this may not be true for all regions/states in India. Regions where the employment scheme has been operated intensively may have increased the farm wage rate at a faster rate, which might have affected the profitability of crops. It is difficult to capture this effect through the CCS data used in this study. Detailed studies using farm-level data collected from different regions need to be carried out to verify the results of this study. The study finds that wherever the productivity of crop has increased during the post-MGNREGS period, profitability has not been affected despite considerable increase in human labour cost. Therefore, concerted efforts need to be introduced to increase the productivity of crops to increase the gross value of the crops and to negate the cost increase in human labour.

This study clearly reveals that the gross COC (C2) has increased substantially in most crops as compared to the increase that is observed in VOP in both HAHP and HALP states after the launch of the rural employment programme. Farmers would have earned appreciable profits during the post-MGNREGS period if the cost of human labour had not increased appreciably. The relatively lower increase in VOP in most crops suggests that farmers are not getting the price for their produce in consonance with COC. The NCF has suggested that the government should announce the MSPs for crops at 50 per cent more than the actual cost of production (cost C3). The MSPs announced every year for various crops should also be linked with the WPI so as to protect the farmers from possible inflationary pressure.

The cost of human labour incurred for cultivating different crops in south Indian states such as Andhra Pradesh and Karnataka has registered a high growth rate as compared to other selected states, especially after the introduction of MGNREGS. This has either reduced the profitability of the crop or created losses for farmers in relation to cost C2. One needs to find out why this has happed specifically in south Indian states. Is it due to labour scarcity that was accentuated by the proper implementation of the rural employment programme in these states? The Mohan Kanda Committee (GoAP, 2011) appointed for studying the reasons for the crop holiday in the east Godavari region in Andhra Pradesh pointed out 'non-availability of labour in peak season of agricultural operation on account of MGNREGS' as one of the reasons for the distress call made by the farmers. Our analysis based on CCS data also seems to indicate that labour scarcity was accentuated due to MGNREGS and this may have increased the cost of human labour at a faster rate. Therefore, arrangements may be made to link up MGNREGS with agricultural operations to reduce the labour scarcity and also to improve the profitability in crop cultivation.

Bibliography

Adhikari, A., and K. Bhatia. 2010. 'NREGA Wage Payments: Can We Bank On Banks?' *Economic and Political Weekly*, vol. 42, no. 1 (2 January), pp. 30–7.

Aiyar, Y., and S. Samji. 2006. 'Improving the Effectiveness of National Rural Employment Guarantee Act'. *Economic and Political Weekly*, vol. 41, no. 4 (28 January), pp. 320–6.

Berg, E., S. Bhattacharyya, R. Durg, and M. Ramachandra. 2012. 'Can Rural Public Works Affect Agriculture Wage: Evidence from India'. CSAE Working Paper WPS/2012–05. Centre for the Study of African Economies, University of Oxford, Oxford, U. K.

Bhalla, G. S., and G. Singh. 2012. *Economic Liberalisation and Indian Agriculture: A District-Level Study*. Sage Publications India Private Limited, New Delhi.

Bhatia, B., and J. Dreze. 2006. 'Employment Guarantee in Jharkhand: Ground Realities'. *Economic and Political Weekly*, vol. 41, no. 29 (22 July), pp. 3198–202.

Chakraborty, P. 2007. 'Implementation of Employment Guarantee: A Preliminary Appraisal'. *Economic and Political Weekly*, vol. 42, no. 7 (17 February), pp. 548–51.

Chandrasekar, C. P., and J. Ghosh. 2011. 'Public Works and Wages in India'. *The Hindu Business Line*, 11 January.

Dutta, P., R. Murgai, M. Ravallion, and D. Van de Walle. 2012. 'Does India's Employment Guarantee Scheme Guarantee Employment?'. Policy Research Working Paper No. 6003. The World Bank, Washington, D. C., U. S. A.

Fan, S., P. Hazell, and S. Thorat. 1999. *Linkages between Government Spending, Growth and Poverty in Rural India.* Research Report 110. International Food Policy Research Institute, Washington, D. C. U. S. A.

GoAP (Government of Andhra Pradesh). 2011. *Report of State Level Committee to Study the Problems of Farmers in Crop Holiday Affected Mandals of East Godavari District of Andhra Pradesh* (Chairman: Mohan Kanda).

GoI (Government of India). 2012. *Indian Agricultural Statistics at a Glance.* Ministry of Agriculture and Farmers Welfare, Government of India, New Delhi.

Gopal, K. S. 2009. 'NREGA Social Audit: Myths and Reality'. *Economic and Political Weekly*, vol. 44, no. 3 (17 January), pp. 70–1.

Gulati, A., J. Gujral, and T. Nandakumar. 2012. *National Food Security Bill Challenges and Options.* Discussion Paper No. 2. Commission for Agricultural Costs and Prices, Department of Agriculture and Cooperation, Ministry of Agriculture, Government of India, New Delhi.

Gulati, A., and S. Jain. 2013. *Buffer Stocking Policy in the Wake of NFSB: Concepts, Empirics, and Policy Implications.* Discussion Paper No. 6. Commission for Agricultural Costs and Prices, Department of Agriculture and Cooperation, Ministry of Agriculture, Government of India, New Delhi.

Gulati, A., S. Jain, and A. Hoda. 2013. *Farm Trade: Tapping the Hidden Potential.* Discussion Paper No. 3. Commission for Agricultural Costs and Prices, Department of Agriculture and Cooperation, Ministry of Agriculture, Government of India, New Delhi.

Gulati, A., S. Jain, and N. Satija. 2013. *Rising Farm Wages in India—the 'Pull' and 'Push' Factors.* Discussion Paper No. 5. Commission for Agricultural Costs and Prices, Department of Agriculture and Cooperation, Ministry of Agriculture, Government of India, New Delhi.

Gulati, A., S. Saini, and S. Jain. 2013. *Monsoon 2013: Estimating the Impact on Agriculture.* Discussion Paper No. 8. Commission for Agricultural

Costs and Prices, Department of Agriculture and Cooperation, Ministry of Agriculture, Government of India, New Delhi.

Harish, B. G., N. Nagaraj, M. G. Chandrakanth, S. P. P. Murthy, P. G. Chengappa, and G. Basavaraj. 2011. 'Impacts and Implications of MGNREGA on Labour Supply and Income Generation for Agriculture in Central Dry Zone of Karnataka'. *Agricultural Economics Research Review*, vol. 24, no. 5, pp. 485–94.

Hirway, I., M. R. Saluja, and B. Yadav. 2008. *Impact of Employment Guarantee Programmes on Gender Equality and Pro-poor Economic Development*. Research Project No. 34. UNDP, New York.

Imbert, C., and J. Papp. 2011. 'Equilibrium Distributional Impacts of Government Employment Programs: Evidence From India's Employment Guarantee'. Working Paper No. 2012–14. Paris School of Economics, Paris.

Jha, R., S. Bhattacharyya, and R. Gaiha. 2011. 'Social Safety Nets and Nutrient Deprivation: An Analysis of the National Rural Employment Guarantee Program and the Public Distribution System in India'. *Journal of Asian Economics*, vol. 22 (April), pp. 189–201.

Jha, R., S. Bhattacharyya, R. Gaiha, and S. Shankar. 2009. 'Capture of Anti-Poverty Programs: An Analysis of the National Rural Employment Guarantee Program in India'. *Journal of Asian Economics*, vol. 20, no. 4 (September), pp. 456–64.

Khera, R., and N. Nayak. 2009. 'Women Workers and Perceptions of the NREGA'. *Economic and Political Weekly*, vol. 44, no. 43 (24 October), pp. 49–57.

Liu, Y., and C. B. Barrett. 2013. 'Heterogeneous Pro-poor Targeting in the National Rural Employment Guarantee Scheme'. *Economic and Political Weekly*, vol. 48, no. 10, pp. 46–53.

Mann, N., and J. Ramesh. 2013. 'Rising Farm Wages Will Lift all Boats'. *The Hindu*, 14 May.

MoRD (Ministry of Rural Development). 2012. *MGNREGA Sameeksha: An Anthology of Research Studies on the Mahatma Gandhi National Rural Employment Guarantee Act, 2005, 2006–2012*, edited and compiled by Mihir Shah, Neelakshi Mann, and Varad Pande. Orient BlackSwan, New Delhi.

Mukherjee, D., and U. B. Sinha. 2011. 'Understanding NREGA: A Simple Theory and Some Facts'. Working Paper No. 196. Centre for Development Economics, Delhi School of Economics, Delhi.

Narayanamoorthy, A. 2013. 'Profitability in Crops Cultivation in India: Some Evidence from Cost of Cultivation Survey Data'. *Indian Journal of Agricultural Economics*, vol. 68, no. 1 (January–March), pp. 104–21.

Narayanamoorthy, A., and P. Alli. 2012. 'India's New Food Security Worries: From Crop Holiday to Declining Foodgrains Area'. *Indian Journal of Agricultural Economics*, vol. 67, no. 3 (July–September), pp. 487–98.

———. 2013. 'Rural Job Scheme Sows Misery'. *The Hindu Business Line*, 9 February.

Narayanamoorthy, A., and M. Bhattarai. 2004. 'Can Irrigation Increase Agricultural Wages: An Analysis across Indian Districts'. *Indian Journal of Labour Economics*, vol. 47, no. 2 (April–June), pp. 251–68.

———. 2013. 'Rural Employment Scheme and Agricultural Wage Rate Nexus: An Analysis across States'. *Agricultural Economics Research Review*, vol. 26, pp. 149–63.

Narayanamoorthy, A., and R. S. Deshpande. 2003. 'Irrigation Development and Agricultural Wages: An Analysis across States'. *Economic and Political Weekly*, vol. 38, no. 35 (30 August), pp. 3716–22.

Ravallion, M. 1991. 'Reaching the Rural Poor through Public Employment: Argument, Evidence and Lessons from South Asia'. *World Bank Research Observer*, vol. 6, pp. 153–75.

Reddy, V. R., and P. P. Reddy. 2007. 'Increasing Costs in Agriculture: Agrarian Crisis and Rural Labour in India'. *Indian Journal of Labour Economics*, vol. 50, no. 2, pp. 273–92.

Shah, M. 2009. 'Multiplier Accelerator Synergy in NREGA'. *The Hindu*, 30 April.

Sinha, R. K., and R. K. Marandi. 2011. *Impact of NREGA on Wage Rates, Food Security and Rural Urban Migration in Bihar.* Report Submitted to the Ministry of Agriculture. Agro-economic Research Centre for Bihar and Jharkhand, Bhagalpur.

Verma, S., and T. Shah. 2012. *Labour Market Dynamics in Post-MGNREGA Rural India.* Water Policy Research Highlight, no. 8. IWMI-Tata Water Policy Programme, Anand, Gujarat. Available at http://www.iwmi.cgiar.org/iwmi-tata/PDFs/2012_Highlight-08.pdf (last accessed on 4 May 2020).

Vishandass, A., and B. Lukka. 2013. *Pricing, Costs, Returns and Productivity in Indian Crop Sector during 2000s.* Discussion Paper No. 7. Commission for Agricultural Costs and Prices, Department of Agriculture and Cooperation, Ministry of Agriculture, Government of India, New Delhi.

7

Is Sugarcane Cultivation Profitable to Farmers?

In recent years, India has been witnessing unprecedented unrest among sugarcane farmers from the major growing areas in the country. There have been instances of agricultural labourers going on strike demanding increased wages and farmers agitating in an organized manner for higher output prices (see Oommen, 1971; Swamy and Gulati, 1986). However, when news of sugarcane crop growers of Tamil Nadu committing suicide hit national news headlines in 2012, the entire farming community went into a state of shock. And when a sugarcane farmer in Maharashtra was shot dead in a police firing during the same year, the whole country was clueless about what was happening in the fields of the country's most viable crop (Narayanamoorthy and Alli, 2013). Adding to this already distressing scenario, the sugarcane farmers of Andhra Pradesh unanimously contemplated going for a crop holiday. Although the issue of profitability in crop cultivation has been intensively discussed in the context of agrarian crisis in recent years (Deshpande, 2002; GoI, 2007; Narayanamoorthy, 2007; Reddy and Mishra, 2009; Deshpande and Arora, 2010; Rao and Dev, 2010), these unique and unprecedented incidents have never before been heard of in the history of Indian farming. Why are sugarcane farmers in these states, which, incidentally, are the major sugarcane growing regions of the country, experiencing such unparalleled turmoil? What is wrong with the sugarcane crop, which is universally claimed to substantially augment farmers' incomes? Under what circumstances were sugarcane farmers prompted to commit suicide or agitate? Is it due to the perpetual erosion of their income from sugarcane crop cultivation? Could paucity of water and absence of assured irrigation in these water-stressed regions be the reason behind such turmoil? In recent years, these factors have been silently creating turbulences in the Indian farming sector, but the likelihood that any of these were pivotal in the ongoing depressing scenario can only be determined by a thorough investigation, which is what has been attempted in this chapter. But before that, it becomes pertinent to know what the genesis of this abominable scenario was. Let us take a look at how events unfolded before the issue assumed serious proportions.

Sugarcane farmers from the major sugarcane producing states have been relentlessly lamenting that after spending about 40 per cent of their cultivation cost on harvesting, they seldom get adequate returns from the mills. They have been making repeated requests to increase the procurement price for the crop. During the sugarcane season of 2012–13 in the state of Maharashtra, which is one of the largest sugarcane growing regions of the country, sugarcane farmers demanded about INR 4,500 per tonne from sugar factories. The latter reportedly resisted the farmers' demands and were ready to buy sugarcane for only between INR 2,100 and INR 2,300 per tonne. In response to such a distressed situation, the central government came forward and declared a hike in the FRP for the 2013–14 season to the tune of about INR 40 per quintal over the previous year's price of sugarcane. However, various farmers' organizations expressed their discontentment over such a hike as they stated that the final payment, which comes to around INR 2,100 per tonne, is arrived at by deducting the cost of transportation and harvesting, and is barely enough to cover their COC. In the backdrop of this situation, we have to ask: does it mean that rising COC is afflicting these farmers? Is the COC of sugarcane rising over a period of years? What is the trend in COC across the major producing states in India? Is sugarcane cultivation not remunerative to the cultivators across different states?

Quite a few studies have analysed the economic aspects of sugarcane cultivation in India using both primary and secondary data.

While Dhawan (1968) found that greater irrigation coverage has rendered sugarcane crop remunerative in Uttar Pradesh, Ramasamy and Kumar (2011) have identified that increased demand for human labour and high wage rate[1] have escalated the COC of sugarcane crop in its major growing areas, resulting in negative returns. Utilizing farm-level data from Maharashtra, Narayanamoorthy (2004) found that sugarcane cultivated under drip method of irrigation (DMI) was highly profitable as compared to the same crop cultivated under flood method of irrigation. While studying agricultural growth in the context of technology fatigue, a study based on COC data specific to Maharashtra showed drastic reduction in profitability of sugarcane between 1975–6 and 2001–2 (Narayanamoorthy, 2007). Despite the fact that the pattern of sugarcane cultivation varies from one state to another, Vishandass and Lukka (2013), by taking the average data of various states from the CCS for the period from 2000–1 to 2010–11, asserted that 'gross returns per hectare as percentage of paid out cost plus family labour, that is, (A2+FL) was the highest in case of sugarcane' (p. 9). Although sugarcane cultivation has been the subject of intensive discussions for various reasons, including its profitability in the recent years, there are not many studies available utilizing COC data of various states covering longer periods with a specific focus on the crops returns.[2] CCS data published by the CACP contains rich information on the cost and output of various crops on a temporal

[1] Guaranteed employment under MGNREGS has in recent years come under the scanner. It is primarily accused of causing acute shortage of labour for agriculture especially during the peak and crucial time of harvesting. More particularly, it is claimed that it is hurting the cultivation of labour-intensive crops such as sugarcane. Ashok Gulati, chairman of the CACP, pointed out that between 2008 and 2011, labour cost increased by about 74 per cent at the all-India level. In order to lure labourers to the fields, farmers are forced to pay double the wage rates that prevailed during previous seasons.

[2] Quite a few studies are available for foodgrain crops, especially for paddy and wheat, utilizing CCS data covering different states and long periods of time. Rao and Dev (2010) published an excellent analysis on the returns over COC in paddy and wheat utilizing temporal data from CCS. Ironically, although sugarcane is an important commercial crop, it has not attracted the attention of researchers in India.

basis, which can point to trends in income and expenditures of crop cultivation over a period (see Rao, 2001; Sen and Bhatia, 2004).[3] Keeping this in view, an attempt has been made in this chapter to find the trends in profitability of sugarcane crop cultivated in six states utilizing CCS data published by the CACP from 1973–4 to 2010–11.

This chapter is organized in five sections. Following the introductory section, the data sources and methodology followed for this study are presented in section two. As the present chapter focuses mainly on sugarcane, section three spells out the overall trends in sugarcane cultivation covering both national- and state-level data. Utilizing the data on CCS, the profitability of sugarcane crop in HPS, medium productivity states, and LPS is analysed in section four. The last section presents the findings and policy pointers.

Data and Methodology

Secondary data covering the period from 1950–1 to 2010–11 have been used for carrying out this study. Although the main objective of the chapter is to find the profitability of sugarcane crop cultivation, it also studies the overall state of sugarcane crop cultivation in India. The data utilized for this study has been compiled from various government sources. For studying the state of sugarcane cultivation in India, related data has been culled and compiled mainly from publications such as *Agricultural Statistics at a Glance* and the *Area and Production of Principal Crops*, both published by the MoA, GoI, and *Handbook of Statistics on Indian Economy*, published by the RBI. For studying the profitability of sugarcane crop, all the cost- and income-related

[3] CCS data is generated through the COC scheme controlled by the Directorate of Economics and Statistics, Ministry of Agriculture. It contains detailed information on costs and its components and the income for different crops. This data is collected annually from 9,000 farmers from different regions in India, and is used for deciding MSPs for different crops. Unfortunately, not many scholars have analysed this rich source of information in the context of the agrarian crisis. The importance of CCS data has also been highlighted by Acharya, 1992; Rao, 2001; Sen and Bhatia, 2004; and Rao and Dev, 2010.

data on sugarcane cultivation has been compiled from the CACP's publication *Report on Price Policy for Sugarcane* of different years and also from its website. The major objective of our study is to find whether the profitability of sugarcane varies in states that have high and low productivity of the crop. Therefore, based on the productivity data of TE 2010–11,[4] a total of six states belonging to the categories of HALP (Uttar Pradesh), medium area with high productivity (MAHP; Maharashtra, Tamil Nadu, and Karnataka) and low area with medium productivity (LAMP; Haryana and Andhra Pradesh) have been considered for studying the aspect of profitability. CACP has been using nine different cost concepts (A1, A2, A2+FL, B1, B2, C1, C2, C2*, and C3) for measuring the economics of various crop cultivations. For this study, cost C2 has been considered for computing the profitability of sugarcane as it covers all the variable and fixed costs needed for crop cultivation. In order to study whether the profitability of sugarcane cultivated in different states has increased or not, all the cost- and income-related data of the crop has been converted into constant prices using CPIAL deflator at 1986–7 prices. Profit level of the crop is computed by deducting cost C2 from VOP.

Status of Sugarcane Cultivation

This chapter primarily focuses on the profitability of sugarcane crop and, therefore, it is important to understand the overall condition of

[4] The average area and productivity of sugarcane pertaining to the six selected states for the period TE 2010–11 are presented here (data from MoA [various years]):

State	Category of State	Area (in thousand hectares)	Yield (kg/ha)
Uttar Pradesh	HALP	2,062	56,102
Maharashtra	HAHP	830	82,900
Tamil Nadu	HAHP	306	105,347
Karnataka	HAHP	347	89,035
Haryana	LAMP	83	66,726
Andhra Pradesh	LAMP	182	76,836

sugarcane cultivation in the country in terms of its area, production, and productivity over the years. The area under sugarcane at the national level increased from 1.71 mha in 1950–1 to 4.88 mha in 2010–11, but its increase has not been very appreciable in recent years (see MoA, 2012). The average area under sugarcane was 2.67 mha during the GRP (1965–6 to 1979–80), which increased to 3.31 mha post the GRP (1980–1 to 1994–5) and further to 4.32 mha during the ACP (1995–6 to 2010–11) (see Table 7.1). The pace of growth in area under sugarcane has increased considerably especially during the post GRP. For instance, the area under sugarcane which registered a negative growth rate of 0.56 per cent per annum during the GRP revived substantially at the rate of 2.50 per cent per annum post GRP, but again slowed down to 1.08 per cent per annum during the ACP. As a result of this deceleration in area, there has also been a significant deceleration in the rate of increase in production and productivity of sugarcane, especially post GRP.

Table 7.1 Trends in Area, Yield, and Production of Sugarcane in India, 1950–1 to 2010–11

Period	Area (mha)	Production (mt)	Yield (kg/ha)	Irrigation Coverage (%)	Sugarcane Area to GCA (%)
Pre-GRP (1950–1 to 1964–5)	2.02	77.11	37,298	67.84	1.37
GRP (1965–6 to 1990–1)	2.88	156.56	53,400	79.00	1.69
ACP (1995–6 to 2010–11)	4.20	283.48	67,449	90.97	2.22
Compound Growth Rate (per cent/annum)					
Pre-GRP	2.83	5.19	2.27	0.40	1.57
GRP	1.01	2.59	1.56	0.77	0.69
ACP	1.21	1.50	0.30	0.25	0.44

Sources: Computed using data from MoA (2012), www.dacnet.nic.in, and RBI (2012).
Notes: ACP: agrarian crisis period; GCA: gross cropped area; GRP: Green Revolution period.

The state-wise scenario of sugarcane cultivation in terms of area and yield is somewhat different from the national-level picture. The area under sugarcane increased in absolute terms in almost all the states, except in Haryana and Punjab. While in Haryana the area under sugarcane dipped from 0.15 mha during 1990–1 to 0.09 mha during 2011–12, in Punjab the area under sugarcane fell from 0.10 mha to 0.08 mha during the same period (see Table 7.2). However, some substantial changes have taken place in the share of sugarcane area occupied by different states since the late 1990s. Except Maharashtra, the other traditional sugarcane-growing states of Uttar Pradesh, Punjab, and Haryana have considerably lost their share of sugarcane area. For instance, the share of sugarcane area occupied by Uttar Pradesh declined from 50.27 per cent during 1990–1 to 42.94 per cent during 2011–12, while in case of Punjab it declined from 2.71 per cent to 1.59 per cent. The share of sugarcane area occupied by Haryana too has declined from 4.07 per cent to 1.78 per cent during the same period. However, Gujarat and Bihar, which are not traditionally sugarcane-growing states, accounted for 2.98 and 3.80 per cent respectively of India's total sugarcane area during 1990–1, which eventually increased to 3.97 and 4.17 per cent respectively during 2011–12.

The increase in area under sugarcane in terms of percentage is observed to have accelerated in the major growing states of Maharashtra and Uttar Pradesh between 1990–1 and 2000–1 as compared to the period of 2000–1 to 2011–12. It is indeed puzzling to note that the percentage increase in the area under sugarcane in Bihar also accelerated considerably during the aforementioned period. In all the remaining states a decelerating trend is observed, which is emerging to be a matter of serious concern. A rather perplexing picture emerges from the productivity trend of the major sugarcane growing states of the country. Although Maharashtra witnessed a rapid increase in the area under sugarcane, the increase in yield is found to have sharply declined during the period of 2000–1 to 2011–12 as compared to the period of 1990–1 to 2000–1 (see Table 7.2). The same trend is observed with Uttar Pradesh as well. However, in Haryana and Punjab the increase in yield is found to be rather appreciable. Interestingly, Punjab and Haryana seem to portray a paradoxical situation of declining area under sugarcane cultivation and accelerating sugarcane yield. What could be the factors behind

Table 7.2 Trends in Area and Yield of Sugarcane by Major Growing States in India, 1990–1 to 2011–12

States	Area (in mha)			Percentage Change		Yield (kg/ha)			Percentage Change	
	1990–1	2000–1	2011–12	1990–1 to 2000–1	2000–1 to 2011–12	1990–1	2000–1	2011–12	1990–1 to 2000–1	2000–1 to 2011–12
Andhra Pradesh	0.18 (4.49)	0.22 (5.04)	0.20 (4.05)	19.38	–6.16	69,562	81,371	81,794	16.98	0.52
Bihar	0.15 (4.03)	0.09 (2.17)	0.22 (4.33)	–37.12	133.47	52,490	42,648	51,714	–18.75	21.26
Gujarat	0.12 (3.21)	0.18 (4.12)	0.20 (4.01)	50.21	13.67	89,600	71,439	63,119	–20.27	–11.65
Haryana	0.15 (4.02)	0.14 (3.31)	0.10 (1.89)	–3.38	–33.57	52,703	57,133	73,253	8.41	28.21
Karnataka	0.27 (7.39)	0.42 (9.66)	0.43 (8.54)	53.18	3.09	76,989	102,909	90,251	33.67	–12.30
Maharashtra	0.44 (12.05)	0.60 (13.79)	1.02 (20.29)	34.01	71.76	86,523	83,349	84,866	–3.67	1.82
Punjab	0.10 (2.74)	0.12 (2.80)	0.08 (1.59)	19.80	–33.88	59,406	64,215	70,663	8.10	10.04
Tamil Nadu	0.23 (6.32)	0.32 (7.31)	0.35 (6.88)	35.38	9.85	100,817	105,258	111,378	4.41	5.81
Uttar Pradesh	1.86 (50.34)	1.94 (44.92)	2.16 (42.92)	4.46	11.54	55,811	54,719	59,583	–1.96	8.89
India	3.69 (100.00)	4.32 (100.00)	5.04 (100.00)	17.08	16.73	65,395	68,578	71,668	4.87	4.51

Sources: Computed using data from MoA (2012), www.dacnet.nic.in, and RBI (2012).

such a paradoxical scenario? Has Borlaug's hypothesis been set in motion in these states, which says that as farmers over time come to know the soils in a place better, they confine agricultural production to the most fertile lands that respond better to additional inputs? With the ever increasing domestic demand for sugar, any significant reduction in area of sugarcane cultivation will have serious implications on sugarcane availability in the forthcoming years. Therefore, it is essential to find out why the increase in area under sugarcane slowed particularly during the ACP. It is also equally important to investigate why sugarcane area and productivity are declining in major sugarcane growing states of the country.

Trends in Profitability in Sugarcane

The farmers from the traditional sugarcane-growing states of Maharashtra and Uttar Pradesh have been vehemently demanding a higher price for the sugarcane crop in recent years. Sugarcane farmers of Tamil Nadu, Andhra Pradesh, and Haryana also followed suit. For quite some time now, sugarcane farmers from different parts of the country have also been urging their respective state governments to raise sugarcane price as suggested by the NCF headed by M. S. Swaminathan, which recommended a price of 50 per cent more than the COC (cost C2). Because of such repeated demands of sugarcane farmers, the government hiked the FRP from INR 170 per quintal in 2012–13 to INR 210 per quintal in 2013–14. However, it was reported that sugarcane farmers were not satisfied with such a hike and their agitation saw no respite. Why have the country's sugarcane farmers come forward with such demands all of a sudden? Why could such a hike in FRP not contain the agitation of the sugarcane farmers? The sugarcane farmers of these states argued that the steep escalation in the COC demands a higher price for the sugarcane crop. Is this claim genuine? Has the sugarcane crop been profitable to the farmers as has been widely believed? Or are profits squeezed in a manner similar to their foodgrain counterparts? All these can be examined only by studying whether or not farmers have reaped profits over the years, which forms the central focus of this chapter. In order to answer these questions, cost- and income-related data on sugarcane crop have been used from the CCS published by the

CACP covering the period from 1973–4 to 2010–11. This is presented in the following sections.

Returns from Sugarcane in HALP States

The statistics on cost C2, VOP, and profit (all at 1986–7 prices) for sugarcane cultivation belonging to the HALP state of Uttar Pradesh from 1973–4 to 2010–11 is presented in Table 7.3. Uttar Pradesh, which accounted for 43.64 per cent of the total area under sugarcane in 2010–11, is by far the largest sugarcane-growing state of the country (see MoA, 2012). Uttar Pradesh forms the focus of our study of analysing the profitability of sugarcane; the state is characterized as the largest sugarcane acreage with low crop yield. The state had irrigation coverage of 93 per cent in 2009–10, which indicates the state's discrimination in favour of sugarcane in allocating this scarce vital input among crops. Irrigation is a vital input that can bring about a substantial difference in crop returns, a fact also proved by many credible studies. For a crop such as sugarcane which is an extremely thirsty

Table 7.3 Profitability in Sugarcane Cultivation in HALP State Uttar Pradesh, 1973–4 to 2010–11 (INR/ha at 1986–7 prices)

Year	Cost C2	VOP	Profit (VOP-C2)
1973–4	7,255	9,854	2,598
1977–8	5,861	7,134	1,272
1982–3	5,301	8,679	3,378
1987–8	6,797	10,544	3,747
1991–2	6,766	9,895	3,129
1995–6	8,843	11,565	2,722
1999–2000	8,982	11,936	2,954
2004–5	10,608	15,770	5,162
2009–10	10,971	24,983	14,011
2010–11	11,844	17,859	6,016

Sources: Computed using data from CACP (various years).

Notes: VOP: value of output; due to non-availability of data for some specified years, data from the nearest point has been used for the analysis.

crop, greater irrigation coverage enhances the prospects of a noticeable increase in the net income per hectare. Studies by Rao (1965) and Dhawan (1968) have clearly demonstrated that the largely irrigated sugarcane crop is remunerative in Uttar Pradesh. In this chapter, by employing a newer data set from CACP, let us analyse whether sugarcane continues to be remunerative for the farmers of Uttar Pradesh. The results reveal that the sugarcane farmers of Uttar Pradesh have reaped profits (VOP minus cost C2) from sugarcane cultivation in most time points (periods) considered for analysis. Although cost C2 has sharply increased from INR 7,255/ha in 1973–4 to INR 11,844/ha in 2010–11, the VOP from sugarcane crop has moved at a relatively faster pace from INR 9,853/ha to INR 17,859/ha during this period, outstripping the increase in cost C2. This has enabled the farmers to reap decent profits from sugarcane (see Table 7.3). The profits from sugarcane cultivation is found to have risen from INR 2,598/ha in 1973–4 to INR 6,016/ha in 2010–11. This finding then begs the question, why then are the sugarcane farmers of the state agitating about not getting adequate profits from the crop? When the data was put to keen observation, it was indeed worrisome to note that the profits realized by the sugarcane farmers of Uttar Pradesh were not consistent throughout the period of analysis. In each of the time periods although the VAO is found to have outstripped the cost C2 considerably, profits from sugarcane still fluctuated every alternate year.

The fluctuation in profit was in the nature of a rise in one year and a fall in the following year. For instance, profits from sugarcane during 1991–2 was INR 3,129/ha but fell to INR 2,722/ha in 1995–6 and again rose to INR 2,954/ha during 1999–2000. This depressing inconsistency in profits marks the onset of the ACP (1995–6 to 2010–11). Fluctuation in profit of such a scale does have a serious ramification on farmers' income, because an erosion of cultivators' profit margin every alternate year almost wipes out whatever profit margins they enjoyed in the previous time period. It can be noted that the fluctuation in profits is more pronounced in the post-1990s period than in the pre-1990s period. Fluctuating cost C2 could be one reason for such a trend. It is observed that from 1991–2 onwards the cost C2 has risen consistently without showing any signs of respite in any of the time periods. The cost C2 which was INR 6,766/ha in 1991–2 rose unimaginably to INR 11,844/ha in 2010–11, an increase of INR 5,111/ha.

It is astonishing to note that the profits from sugarcane crop, which were hovering in the range of INR 2,954–5,160/ha between 1999–2000 and 2004–5, jumped all of a sudden to a record high of INR 14,011/ha in 2009–10. Have the profits from sugarcane really improved during 2009–10 or is it an inflated bubble? The following year, that is, during 2010–11, the profits declined sharply to INR 6,016/ha, sparking off speculation about the validity of CACP data.[5]

Returns from Sugarcane in MAHP States

As mentioned earlier, states such as Maharashtra, Karnataka, and Tamil Nadu are considered as MAHP in this study. These states together accounted for 35.04 per cent of total area of sugarcane, of which Maharashtra alone accounted for about 20 per cent of the total area in 2010–11 (see MoA, 2012). The yield from sugarcane is found to be higher in each of these three states in spite of allocating a relatively lesser area for the crop's cultivation. Hence, studying the profitability of sugarcane in MAHP states forms our next task. Despite being caught in the midst of severe regional hydro-politics, sugarcane in each of these three states had an irrigation coverage of 100 per cent in 2009–10. Although sugarcane is not the principal crop in any of these three states, yet a cent per cent irrigation coverage for the crop indicates that the crop is given preferential treatment in the allocation of the scarce water resource in relation to other competing crops. From the point of view of acreage, although these states have allocated

[5] The data for the year 2009–10 appears to have been fudged. Despite no significant change in productivity of sugarcane, the profitability jumped in most states we have taken for the analysis. Unfortunately, we have no option but to use CCS data for analysing the issue we have addressed in this chapter. For quite some time now, farmers' organizations working in different parts of the country have been arguing that the CCS data of CACP is not reliable and largely underestimated. The problems about the COC data have also been underlined in the reports of the Farmers' Commission headed by M. S. Swaminathan. Several farmers' organizations in Andhra Pradesh have also reported this problem to the Mohan Kanda Committee, which was appointed to look into the issue of unprecedented crop holiday. For more details on this issue, see GoAP (2011).

a lesser area for the sugarcane crop and are far behind Uttar Pradesh, yet the per hectare yield is found to be robust (MoA, 2012). If greater irrigation coverage has been a determining factor for the higher yields in these three states, then the obvious question is if higher yields resulted in augmenting the income of these sugarcane farmers.

An impressive picture emerges from Table 7.4 which illustrates that the sugarcane farmers of Maharashtra enjoyed positive returns over cost C2 in all the time points taken up for the study. However, an in-depth look into the profitability trend undercuts the genuineness of this impressive picture. The profit over cost C2 is found to have fluctuated devastatingly throughout the period of analysis and more particularly between 1995–6 and 1999–2000 when the profits are observed to have hovered between INR 2,650/ha and INR 1,600/ha. The prime cause behind this sharp fluctuation is the plummeting of VOP from sugarcane cultivation from INR 17,507/ha to INR 16,906/ha with a steep rise in cost C2 from INR 14,856/ha to INR 15,306/ha. The period 2009–10 shows an astonishing trend. The profit from sugarcane was INR 8,071/ha during 2004–5 which zoomed to INR 16,596/ha during 2009–10 and then declined drastically to INR 8,678/ha during 2010–11.

Further, our in-depth analysis deciphered that Maharashtra is the only state in our study that has recorded negative returns during the ACP. Why are only the farmers of Maharashtra found to be incurring continuous negative returns from 2000–1 to 2003–4?[6] The CACP

[6] While a rapid increase in the area under sugarcane is observed in Maharashtra between 1990–1 and 2000–1 as compared to the period of 2000–1 to 2011–12, its yield and profit are found to be dwindling dramatically from 2000–1 to 2003–4 as per CACP data. For further clarification, the following table presents detailed information on yield, cost C2, profit (at current prices), and ratio of profit.

Period	Yield (Quintal/ha)	Cost C2 (INR/ha in current prices)	Profit (VOP–Cost C2) (INR/ha in current prices)	Ratio of Profit (VOP/Cost C2)
2000–1	775	48,304	–5,568	0.88
2001–2	761	52,660	–3,078	0.94
2002–3	946	70,744	–8,550	0.87
2003–4	715	60,155	–11,148	0.81

Table 7.4 Profitability in Sugarcane Cultivation in MAHP States, 1973–4 to 2010–11 (in INR/ha at 1986–7 prices)

Year	Cost C2			VOP			Profit (VOP–C2)		
	MAH	KAR	TN	MAH	KAR	TN	MAH	KAR	TN
1973–4	13,171	DNA	DNA	22,752	DNA	DNA	9,580	DNA	DNA
1977–8	12,142	DNA	DNA	16,866	DNA	DNA	4,725	DNA	DNA
1982–3	14,940	7,698	12,347	15,081	17,402	17,925	141	9,704	5,578
1987–8	13,296	11,014	12,004	17,757	18,673	19,410	4,461	7,659	7,406
1991–2	12,588	DNA	DNA	15,688	DNA	DNA	3,100	DNA	DNA
1995–6	14,856	14,206	13,748	17,507	27,935	26,125	2,650	13,729	12,378
1999–2000	15,306	14,224	21,654	16,906	22,138	29,192	1,600	7,914	7,538
2004–5	21,095	17,461	18,270	29,166	27,318	22,836	8,071	9,857	4,566
2009–10	24,816	17,969	18,974	41,412	40,104	31,860	16,596	22,135	12,886
2010–11	22,872	15,297	20,046	31,549	30,559	33,856	8,678	15,261	13,810

Sources: Computed using data from CACP (various years).

Notes: MAH: Maharashtra; KAR: Karnataka; TN: Tamil Nadu; VOP: value of output; DNA: data not available; due to non-availability of data for some specified years, data from the nearest point has been used for the analysis.

data explicitly reveals that although the COC of sugarcane has been rising for all the states during the period of analysis, it is found to have risen at an alarming rate in case of Maharashtra. It is observed that during the period of continuous negative returns from sugarcane cultivation, the cost C2 rose by about 25 per cent while the VOP merely rose by about 14 per cent. Another plausible reason for the negative returns from sugarcane in Maharashtra is the dwindling yield from the crop that was observed during the aforementioned period. As no room for a steady flow of income was left, unanimous resentment among sugarcane cultivators across the state was indeed the obvious outcome.

Shifting our focus from Maharashtra, let us now explore the costs and profitability trends emerging from the sugarcane fields of Karnataka and Tamil Nadu. Table 7.4 shows that unlike Maharashtra's farmers, sugarcane farmers of Karnataka and Tamil Nadu were able to reap relatively higher profits in all the seven time points for which data was available. What is disappointing to note is that profits did not increase steadily over the years (see Acharya, 1992). The profits from sugarcane fluctuated severely for the farmers of Karnataka when the returns over cost C2 fluctuated between INR 13,729/ha in 1995–6 to INR 7,914 in 1999–2000. Similar to Maharashtra, the period 2009–10 stands out with a spectacular yet surprising rise in profit by INR 12,278/ha over its preceding time period.

The profits equally fluctuated for sugarcane farmers of Tamil Nadu, where profits declined sharply from INR 12,378/ha in 1995–6 to INR 7,538/ha in 1999–2000. Although the VOP from sugarcane increased at a faster pace than cost C2, yet a persistent increase in cost deprived the sugarcane farmers of these three states of a steady flow of profits from sugarcane. A very crucial issue which comes out from this analysis of MAHP states is that the sugarcane farmers of Maharashtra, Karnataka, and Tamil Nadu suffered sharp decline in profits from the crop between 1995–6 and 1999–2000 in spite of 100 per cent coverage of irrigation. This sends out a clear signal that water is a supplementary farm input and not the only one that can contribute to enhancement of farm profit. It also suggests that if escalating price of farm inputs is not contained, then even complete irrigation coverage will fail to provide desired profitability to farmers in the future.

Returns from Sugarcane in LAMP States

So far in this study we have analysed the profitability trends of states that have a higher and medium productivity of sugarcane. While the results of the profitability analysis till now seem to be not very encouraging, we will now proceed further with our analysis to the states of Haryana and Andhra Pradesh which have been selected as having a relatively lower area with medium productivity of sugarcane crop. These two states together accounted for 5.73 per cent of total area under sugarcane in 2010–11 and possessed an irrigation coverage of 92 to 99 per cent (see MoA, 2012). Similar to the HPS and medium productivity states, a continuous rise in cost C2 resulting in fluctuating profits has scarred the face of the sugarcane economy of Haryana and Andhra Pradesh. Table 7.5 reveals that the sugarcane crop was profitable to the farmers of Haryana in all eight time points, whereas the farmers from Andhra Pradesh have reaped profit in eight out of nine time points. However, as was observed

Table 7.5 Profitability in Sugarcane Cultivation in LAMP States, 1973–4 to 2010–11 (INR/ha at 1986–7 prices)

Year	Cost C2		VOP		Profit (VOP–C2)	
	HAR	AP	HAR	AP	HAR	AP
1973–4	DNA	DNA	DNA	DNA	DNA	DNA
1977–8	DNA	12,825	DNA	12,661	DNA	−164
1982–3	5,251	12,278	8,449	13,623	3,198	1,344
1987–8	5,805	12,849	11,315	14,636	5,510	1,787
1991–2	9,030	13,899	15,050	16,362	6,020	2,463
1995–6	12,002	16,367	17,728	20,371	5,726	4,004
1999–2000	15,373	15,501	20,770	17,135	5,397	1,634
2004–5	13,990	15,490	21,382	18,531	7,391	3,041
2009–10	17,076	20,109	34,007	28,461	16,931	8,353
2010–11	15,376	22,574	22,030	29,545	6,654	6,971

Sources: Computed using data from CACP (various years).

Notes: HAR: Haryana; AP: Andhra Pradesh; VOP: value of output; DNA: data not available; due to non-availability of data for some specified years, data from the nearest point has been used for the analysis.

in case of the other states that were taken up for study, the profits reaped by the sugarcane farmers of these states also did not move in a definite path. Profits proved to have widely fluctuated for sugarcane farmers of Haryana between 1991–2 and 1999–2000, where it varied from INR 6,020/ha to INR 5,397/ha. It is observed that during this period the cost C2 sharply escalated from INR 9,030/ha to INR 15,373/ha.

Fluctuating profits did not spare the sugarcane farmers of Andhra Pradesh either where one notices a marked variation in profits of INR 4,004/ha in 1995–6 and INR 1,634/ha in 1999–2000. Although there occurred a marginal slump in cost C2 from INR 16,367/ha in 1995–6 to INR 15,501 in 1999–2000, a drastic decline in the VOP from INR 20,371/ha to INR 17,135/ha during the same period proved to be pivotal for such damaging profits. A sharp escalation in cost C2 and its detrimental effect on profits during 1995–6 and 1999–2000 form the basic characteristics of all the six sugarcane-growing states taken up for study. Surprisingly, the profit realized by sugarcane farmers did not increase consistently even during the 2000s in any of the six states selected for the analysis (see Figure 7.1). It becomes very evident that the period 1995–6 marks the onset of the ACP when the grave issue of discontentment

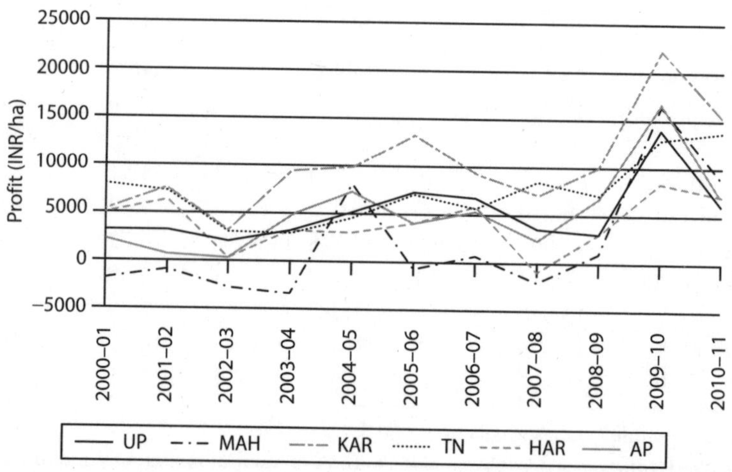

Figure 7.1 Profitability in Sugarcane Cultivation in Different States during the 2000s

Source: CACP (various years).

among sugarcane farmers across the country began to rear its head. Were the sugarcane farmers across the country with their desperate loud and clear wake-up call trying to hint at this pitiable scenario of inconsistent profits?

Number of Years Profit Was Reaped from 1973–4 to 2010–11

Besides analysing the trends in profitability of sugarcane cultivation, we have looked at how many times (years) sugarcane cultivators were able to reap profit during the entire period of analysis from 1973–4 to 2010–11 in all the six states considered for the analysis. Some studies have pointed out that the profitability of foodgrain and non-foodgrain crops has been witnessing a depressing trend, especially from the early 1990s (see Narayanamoorthy, 2006a; 2006b; 2007; and 2013). Therefore, an attempt has also been made to find whether any wide difference exists in the profitability of sugarcane before and after 1990–1 among the selected states. As considered earlier, here too the VOP and cost C2 are considered for computing profitability in sugarcane cultivation. Table 7.6 shows the ratio of VOP to cost C2 for different time periods for HPS, LPS, and medium productivity states. If the ratio is more than 1.30, it means that the farmers are reaping appreciable profit from sugarcane cultivation and if the ratio lies within the range of <1.30 to >1.00 then farmers are realizing moderate profit. If the ratio is less than one, then it means that sugarcane farmers are not reaping profit or possibly that profit is squeezed considerably to the extent incurring losses.

As noted earlier in the profitability analysis, except in Maharashtra, the ratio of VOP to cost C2 is found to be more than one (>1.00) in more number of years in all the other five states including the medium productivity states and LPS. Of the total 32 years (from 1973–4 to 2010–11)[7] for which we have got data for

[7] For this study, we have covered the period from 1973–4 to 2010–11. However, the data on cost and income of sugarcane were not available from CACP's publications consistently for all the years for any of the six selected states. Only those years for which data were available were considered for the analysis and, therefore, the total number of years (data time points) considered for the analysis varies considerably from one state to another.

Table 7.6 Number of Years Profit Was Reaped or Loss Was Incurred by Sugarcane Farmers from 1973–4 to 2010–11

State's Category	States	Green Revolution Period (GRP) (1973–4 to 1990–1)			Agrarian Crisis Period (ACP) (1991–2 to 2010–11)			Entire Period of Analysis (1973–4 to 2010–11)		
		Ratio VOP to C2			Ratio VOP to C2			Ratio VOP to C2		
		>1.30	<1.30	<1.00	>1.30	<1.30	<1.00	>1.30	<1.30	<1.00
HALP	Uttar Pradesh	14/16	2/16	0/16	19/20	1/20	0/20	33/36	3/36	0/36
		(87.50)	(12.50)	(0.00)	(95.00)	(5.00)	(0.00)	(91.66)	(8.33)	(0.00)
MAHP	Maharashtra	8/14	6/14	0/14	4/18	8/18	6/18	12/32	14/32	6/32
		(57.14)	(42.85)	(0.00)	(22.22)	(44.44)	(33.33)	(37.50)	(43.75)	(18.75)
	Karnataka	9/9	0/9	0/9	16/16	0/16	0/16	25/25	0/25	0/25
		(100.00)	(0.00)	(0.00)	(100.00)	(0.00)	(0.00)	(100.00)	(0.00)	(0.00)
	Tamil Nadu	4/4	0/4	0/4	10/14	4/14	0/14	14/18	4/18	0/18
		(100.00)	(0.00)	(0.00)	(71.42)	(28.57)	(0.00)	(77.77)	(22.22)	(0.00)
LAMP	Haryana	6/7	1/7	0/7	13/16	3/16	0/16	19/23	4/23	0/23
		(85.71)	(14.28)	(0.00)	(81.25)	(18.75)	(0.00)	(82.60)	(17.39)	(0.00)
	Andhra Pradesh	4/11	6/11	1/11	2/16	13/16	1/16	6/27	19/27	2/27
		(36.36)	(54.54)	(9.09)	(12.50)	(81.25)	(6.25)	(22.22)	(70.37)	(7.41)

Sources: Computed using data from CACP (various years).

Notes: Figures in brackets are percentages of total number of years; HALP: high area with low productivity; MAHP: medium area with high productivity; LAMP: low area with medium productivity; VOP: value of output.

Maharashtra, farmers were able to reap profit for 26 years (81.25 per cent). That is, of the total 32 years the farmers of Maharashtra have not reaped any appreciable profits in relation to cost C2 in six years (18.75 per cent); this has occurred mainly during the ACP. Such a reduced income is not observed in any of the remaining five states considered for the analysis. Farmers from Uttar Pradesh, which is considered as one of the LPS for the analysis, are found to have generated profit in all the years taken up for study. For instance, out of 36 years considered in the analysis, the ratio of VOP to cost C2 turned out to be more than one (>1.00) in all 36 years for Uttar Pradesh, which is 100 per cent of the total number of years. In a similar fashion, farmers in other states such as Tamil Nadu, Karnataka, and Haryana have also reaped profit in 100 per cent of time periods considered for the analysis. Has the profitability varied between the GRP (1973–4 and 1990–1) and ACP (1991–2 to 2010–11)? We had hypothesized that the farmers would reap profits in fewer number of years during the ACP owing to the increased COC. However, as per our analysis, except the farmers of Maharashtra and Andhra Pradesh, farmers in no other state suffered any losses in the ACP, which is indeed contradictory to the relentless battle being waged by the sugarcane farmers with respect to rising COC and dwindling price for their agricultural produce. The fact that needs to be reiterated here is that the ratio of VOP to cost C2 is no doubt expected to give a true picture of the profitability of the crop. But this is not the case in our analysis. This is because although as per the analysis almost all the states exhibit a ratio that is greater than one, yet as mentioned previously, a closer look at the data would reveal that the profits in each year for all the states have, in fact, fluctuated dramatically. A sharp fluctuation in profits across the study period does explicitly put forth the stark reality that sugarcane farmers across the major growing states are not getting consistent remunerative prices. On the whole, taking data from the last decade, from 2000–1 to 2010–11, fluctuations apart, there was a trend of increase in profitability that shows a steep decline in 2010–11. But this seems to be largely based on the fudged data for 2009–10! If the spike in profits in 2009–10 is ignored, the trend of increase in profits remains, leaving the question of how to explain the growing concern of the crisis faced by sugarcane farmers!

Findings and Policy Pointers

The study has been undertaken in the backdrop of an obvious query by the country's disgruntled sugarcane farmers as to why they should cultivate sugarcane if they are denied a reasonable return from the crop. An analysis was undertaken to cross-check this with the data from CACP to determine whether the agitation coming from the sugarcane belts of the country was justifiable or not. The ongoing fury among the country's sugarcane farmers is somewhat reflected in our analysis of profitability. It shows that although profit has been realized by farmers across all states taken up for study at constant prices, the farmers were still struggling to get consistent profits throughout the period of analysis. While the sugarcane farmers are fuming over the non-remunerativeness of the crop, our analysis reveals that the VOP from sugarcane cultivation in almost all the states has increased at a much faster rate as compared to cost C2, implying that higher income has helped farmers in reaping profits from sugarcane cultivation. A deeper analysis of profitability across the states revealed that the situation is worrisome in the farming horizon of one of the country's leading sugar-producing state, namely Maharashtra. A scenario of negative returns for four consecutive years, that is, from 2000–1 to 2003–4, and a vicious concoction of dwindling yield, soaring cost of farm inputs, and incessant drought have compelled the farmers of Maharashtra to question in great distress why they should continue to tolerate the recurring effects of financial and crop losses. Further, when we analysed how many times sugarcane farmers were able to reap profits during the period of analysis, it was really surprising to see that except Maharashtra and Andhra Pradesh all other states have made profits in all the years taken up for study. More particularly, our analysis vividly shows that sugarcane farmers of Uttar Pradesh, Karnataka, Tamil Nadu, and Haryana have even reaped profits during the ACP. If as per the CACP data all is well with sugarcane farmers of the major growing states then why should they agitate violently and commit suicide? Why have crop holidays been declared? Does it mean that the data compiled by CACP are deceptive and ambiguous?[8]

Besides the catastrophe of rising COC, an accumulation of sugarcane arrears[9] to the tune of INR 5,495 crore for the sugar season

[8] It is worth mentioning here that during the so-called crisis period, the overall area under sugarcane was on the increase across the states, with the exception of Punjab, Haryana, and Andhra Pradesh. We see no link between changes in productivity, cost, or profitability with the changes in area. The two states, Uttar Pradesh and Maharashtra, which account for a little over 60 per cent of the total area under the crop and which show continued increase in the area, have polar opposite characteristics in terms of costs, yields, and returns from this study. The state which shows decline or stagnation in the yield and also very high increase in the costs (Maharashtra) is also the state which shows the steepest increase in area under sugarcane during the last decade. Given that cane price is determined centrally by CACP (with marginal additions at the state level), the returns depend on the cost and yield levels. With more disaggregated data, it would be interesting to focus on Maharashtra and Uttar Pradesh to determine the differences in the nature of costs and the factors that would make a difference to productivity.

[9] The arrears to be paid to the sugarcane farmers by the sugar industry in different states were huge as on 31 May 2012. The details of sugarcane arrears (in INR crore) extracted from the *Report of the Committee on the Regulation of Sugar Sector in India—The Way Forward* are given as follows:

State	Cane Price Payable 2011–12	Cane Price Paid 2011–12	Cane Price Arrears 2011–12	Cane Price Arrears 2010–11	Cane Price Arrears 2009–10 and Earlier Periods	Total Cane Price Arrears
Punjab	967.32	870.58	96.74	0	0	96.74
Haryana	1,221.06	1,074.35	146.71	0	0	146.71
Uttar Pradesh	18,066.03	14,904.5	3,161.53	7.30	134.98	3,303.81
Uttarakhand	905.46	669.34	236.12	17.97	6.30	260.39
Madhya Pradesh	132.77	132.77	0	2.05	11.34	13.39
Gujarat	1,586.41	1,550.15	36.26	0	13.41	49.67
Maharashtra	13,251.39	13,080.82	170.57	32.54	17.37	220.48
Bihar	1,054.80	956.78	98.02	1.67	31.94	131.63
Andhra Pradesh	2,366.50	2,085.02	281.48	0	33.09	314.57
Karnataka	6,257.50	5,857.05	400.45	38.77	20.29	459.51
Tamil Nadu	3,790.82	3,342.77	448.05	0	2.15	450.2
India	49,760.51	44,636.64	5,123.87	100.30	270.87	5,495.04

2011–12 is hammering the sugarcane farmers' income. Unlike wheat and paddy, sugarcane is an annual crop and farmers wait for a year to get a remunerative price. The one-time payment that they receive for their crop forms the sole source of their livelihood. If arrears continue accumulating to such an extent, sugarcane farmers will have no option but to go in for alternate crops. Anticipating that this would further affect the fresh plantings in the forthcoming season, the Rangarajan Committee on the Regulation of Sugar Sector in India (see GoI, 2012) proposed a series of recommendations, the vital one being the removal of the sale of sugar under levy quota, thereby enabling the mills to pay their dues to farmers on time. While the recent budget proposals found no mention of these recommendations, it was only on 4 April 2013 that the government announced the scrapping of the levy system. While the scrapping of the release mechanism is bound to help millers with better cash flows, whether the millers will give a commensurate share of profits to the sugarcane farmers is a million dollar question. In this context the government should have also approved the profit sharing formula recommended by the Rangarajan Committee. Unhappy with the announcement, various farmers' organizations seem to be sceptical about the millers passing on the gains to them. They continue to lament that instead of providing bailout to millers the government should have passed on the benefit directly to farmers.

Amidst such a perpetuating conundrum with no signs of respite, what can be done to put the sugarcane farmers back on the track? The first and foremost step is that more credible field-level studies on the profitability of sugarcane need to be undertaken by researchers to cross-check the data of CACP. Amidst the hue and cry over soaring input prices, studies need to be also undertaken towards identifying the basic reasons behind the sharp rise in the COC of sugarcane in recent years. Productivity of sugarcane during the last one decade or so has not increased in major growing states, which is one of the reasons for low profitability. Increased productivity of sugarcane can reduce the cost of production, which will ultimately help in increasing the profitability of sugarcane growers. While field-level research studies (see Narayanamoorthy, 2004; 2005) have proved that DMI can considerably increase the productivity of sugarcane with reduced COC, one group of researchers also feels that by adopting the Sustainable Sugarcane Initiative (SSI) approach farmers will be able to produce at least 20 per cent more sugarcane while reducing water consumption by 30 per cent and chemical inputs by 25 per cent (see WWF, 2009). Besides popularizing DMI and SSI among sugarcane farmers, the centre and the respective state agencies need to make concerted efforts on a war footing in devising cost reduction measures so as to increase productivity of sugarcane and farm income.

Bibliography

Acharya, S. 1992. 'Rate of Return in Indian Agriculture'. *Economic and Political Weekly*, vol. 27, no. 3, pp. 111–19.

CACP (Commission for Agricultural Costs and Prices). Various years. *Report on Price Policy for Sugarcane.* Ministry of Agriculture, Government of India, New Delhi.

Deshpande, R. S. 2002. 'Suicide by Farmers in Karnataka: Agrarian Distress and Possible Alleviatory Steps'. *Economic and Political Weekly*, vol. 37, no. 26, pp. 2601–10.

Deshpande, R. S., and S. Arora (eds). 2010. *Agrarian Crisis and Farmer Suicides*. Sage Publications, New Delhi.

Dhawan, B. D. 1968. 'Comparative Advantage of UP in Sugarcane'. *Economic and Political Weekly,* vol. 3, no. 44, pp. 1697–8.

GoI (Government of India). 2007. *Report of the Expert Group on Agricultural Indebtedness.* Ministry of Finance, Government of India, New Delhi, July.

———. 2012. *Report of the Committee on Regulation of Sugar Sector in India: The Way Forward* (Chairman: C. Rangarajan). New Delhi.

GoAP (Government of Andhra Pradesh). 2011. *Report of State Level Committee to Study the Problems of Farmers in Crop Holiday Affected Mandals of East Godavari District of Andhra Pradesh* (Chairman: Mohan Kanda).

MoA (Ministry of Agriculture). 2012. *Agricultural Statistics at a Glance: 2011–12.* Government of India, New Delhi.

———. Various years. *Agricultural Statistics at a Glance.* Government of India, New Delhi.

Narayanamoorthy, A. 2004. 'Impact Assessment of Drip Irrigation in India: The Case of Sugarcane'. *Development Policy Review*, vol. 22, no. 4, pp. 443–62.

———. 2005. 'Economics of Drip Irrigation in Sugarcane Cultivation: Case Study of a Farmer from Tamil Nadu'. *Indian Journal of Agricultural Economics*, vol. 60, no. 2 (April–June), pp. 235–48.

———. 2006a. 'Relief Package for Farmers: Can It Stop Suicides?'. *Economic and Political Weekly*, vol. 41, no. 31 (5 August), pp. 3353–5.

———. 2006b. 'State of India's Farmers'. *Economic and Political Weekly*, vol. 41, no. 6 (11 February), pp. 471–3.

———. 2007. 'Deceleration in Agricultural Growth: Technology Fatigue or Policy Fatigue'. *Economic and Political Weekly*, vol. 42, no. 25 (23 June), pp. 2375–9.

———. 2013. 'Profitability in Crops Cultivation in India: Some Evidence from Cost of Cultivation Survey Data'. *Indian Journal of Agricultural Economics*, vol. 68, no.1, pp. 104–21.

Narayanamoorthy, A., and P. Alli. 2013. 'Sugarcane Leaves Farmers Crushed'. *The Hindu Business Line*, 16 April, p. 9.

Oommen, T. K. 1971. 'Green Revolution and Agrarian Conflict'. *Economic and Political Weekly*, vol. 6, no. 26, pp. A-99–103.

Ramasamy, C., and D. S. Kumar. 2011. 'Regional Differences in Farm Profitability in Indian Agriculture'. In B. C. Barah and S. Sirohi, ed., *Agrarian Distress in India: Problems and Remedies.* Concept Publishing Company Pvt. Ltd, New Delhi, pp. 21–47.

Rao, C. H. H. 1965. *Agricultural Production Functions, Costs and Returns in India.* Asian Publishing House, Bombay, p. 72.

Rao, N. Chandrasekhara, and S. Mahendra Dev. 2010. 'Agricultural Price Policy, Farm Profitability and Food Security'. *Economic and Political Weekly*, vol. 45, nos 26 and 27 (June), pp. 174–82.

Rao, V. M. 2001. 'The Making of Agricultural Price Policy: A Review of CACP Reports'. *Journal of Indian School of Political Economy*, vol. 13, no. 1, pp. 1–28.

RBI (Reserve Bank of India). 2012. *Handbook on Statistics of Indian Economy, 2011–12.* Mumbai, India.

Reddy, D. N., and S. Mishra eds. 2009. *Agrarian Crisis in India.* Oxford University Press, New Delhi.

Sen, Abhijit, and M. S. Bhatia. 2004. *Cost of Cultivation and Farm Income in India.* Academic Foundation, New Delhi.

Swamy, D., and A. Gulati. 1986. 'From Prosperity to Retrogression—Indian Cultivators during the 1970s. *Economic and Political Weekly,* vol. 21, nos 25–6, pp. A57–64.

Vishandass, A., and B. Lukka. 2013. *Pricing, Costs, Returns and Productivity in Indian Crop Sector during 2000s.* Discussion Paper No. 7. Commission for Agricultural Costs and Prices, Ministry of Agriculture, Government of India, New Delhi.

WWF (World Wide Fund for Nature). 2009. *Producing More Food Grain with Less Water: Promoting Farm-Based Methods to Improve the Water productivity—Sustainable Sugarcane Initiative.* WWF-ICRISAT, Hyderabad, India.

8

Farm Profitability in Andhra Pradesh

A Temporal Analysis

A significant development has been achieved in Indian agriculture in terms of production and productivity of various crops since the introduction of the Green Revolution during the mid-1960s. The production of foodgrains increased from 72 mt in 1965–6 to 252 mt in 2015–16. Significant achievements have also been made in the productivity of oilseeds, sugarcane, cotton, fruits, vegetables, and other crops (GoI, 2018). As a result of significant increase in the production of commodities, the per capita availability has also increased despite substantial increase in population. The increased volume of crop output has also helped to increase the wage rate and employment opportunities, and reduce poverty in the rural areas (Ahluwalia, 1978; Saleth et al., 2003; Narayanamoorthy, 2001; Narayanamoorthy and Deshpande, 2003). All these achievements would not have been possible without the incisive role of Indian farmers (NCF, 2006; Swaminathan, 2008).

Even with all these achievements, no great news is coming from the farm sector especially since the mid-1990s. Farmers' suicides, indebtedness, crop failures, un-remunerative prices for crops, and poor returns over COC are the foremost features of India's agriculture today. That farmers were committing suicide was not apparent before the early 1990s, but it has become a widespread phenomenon today in many states of India. Close to 300,000 farmers have committed suicide in India between 1990–1 and 2009–10, and the proportion is alarmingly high in states such as Maharashtra, Andhra Pradesh, and Karnataka (Sainath, 2010). Indebtedness among agricultural households is not only widespread but has also been increasing in the recent years (NSSO, 2005a; Narayanamoorthy and Kalamkar, 2005; GoI, 2007).

Recently, in an unprecedented move, farmers from Andhra Pradesh have started to abandon their farms by declaring crop holiday. Why is this happening in India? Is it because of poor returns from crop cultivation? A large number of studies have analysed these issues since the mid-1990s, when the problem of farmers committing suicide started appearing as a serious issue in policy circles. Some of the studies reported inadequate supply of institutional credit, decline in productivity of crops, and imperfect market conditions as the major reasons for this phenomenon (Deshpande, 2002; Deshpande and Prabhu, 2005; Reddy and Galab, 2006). Some researchers have even blamed the Green Revolution for farmer suicides.

Profit from crop cultivation is essential not only for the survival of the farmers but also to facilitate reinvestment in agriculture for the next season. If the flow of income from crop cultivation is not adequate, farmers may not be able to repay their debts (Darling, 1925; NSSO, 2005b; Narayanamoorthy and Kalamkar, 2005; GoI, 2007; Deshpande and Arora, 2010). Despite this, not many studies carried out detailed analyses to find what is happening to the profitability of different crops in relation to COC over a period of time. Without using any temporal data on COC, some recent studies have observed that stagnation in real income and rise in input prices being more than the prices of the agricultural produce could be the reasons for farmers' suicides (Kalamkar and Narayanamoorthy, 2003; Narayanamoorthy, 2006; 2007; Deshpande and Arora, 2010; Sainath, 2010). The NCF has also recognized that inadequate return from crop cultivation is the main reason for the present agrarian crisis and farmer suicides (NCF, 2006).

Although Andhra Pradesh is one of the developed states in India, the agricultural sector has not been doing well in the state, which is evident from factors such as widespread farmer suicides and higher ratio of indebtedness (GoI, 2007; NSSO, 2005b; 2014). Could this be due to reduced farm profitability? Not many detailed studies are available on farm profitability focusing on Andhra Pradesh, where farmers have been facing different problems in the last few years. Therefore, utilizing the data from CCS on eight important crops covering the period from 1970–1 to 2015–16, an attempt has been made in this chapter to ascertain the trends in farm profitability of different crops.

Data and Methodology

This study has been carried out utilizing data pertaining to Andhra Pradesh. The CCS data published by CACP has been mainly used for all analyses presented here. It covers data from 1970–1 to 2015–16 for which latest published data is available from CACP. The pattern of crop cultivation varies from crop to crop: while some crops are cost-intensive, others incur relatively less cost for cultivation. Therefore, to determine the profitability of different types of crops, eight important crops have been carefully chosen from different groups. They are paddy, jowar, maize, arhar, moong, groundnut, sugarcane, and cotton. These eight crops together accounted for about 74 per cent of the cropped area of Andhra Pradesh during 2015–16.

As regards the calculation of farm profitability, CACP has been using nine different cost concepts (A1, A2, A2+FL, B1, B2, C1, C2, C2*, and C3) for computing COC for various crops in India. In this study, we have considered two cost concepts, namely cost A2 and cost C2, to find the profitability (returns over COC) of different crops selected for the analysis. Cost A2 covers only the actual expenses in cash and kind incurred in production by the owner plus rent paid for leased-in land. Cost C2 covers all actual expenses in cash and kind incurred in production by the owner, rent paid for leased-in land, imputed value of family labour, and also the interest on value of owned capital assets (excluding land). Both cost A2 and cost C2 are considered specifically to find the difference in profitability in crop cultivation. Profit of the crop is calculated by deducting cost A2/C2 from the value of crop output. In order to study whether the profitability of various crops cultivated in the state has increased or not, all cost- and income-related data of the crop have been converted into constant prices using CPIAL deflator at 1986–7 prices.

Analysis of Returns from Crop Cultivation

As mentioned earlier, eight crops belonging to different groups were selected for the analysis of profitability. It is known that the cost required and income generated from each crop varies significantly because of various reasons. The COC and VOP are generally found to be higher in irrigated crops than for those cultivated under rainfed conditions. Therefore, we have analysed the profitability of each crop separately instead of analysing all crops together to locate the exact trends in profitability of crops.

Returns from Paddy

One of the crops considered for the analysis is paddy. After the introduction of the Green Revolution, the share of paddy area increased in the total area under foodgrains, at a time when many foodgrain crops have lost their areas. India's total area under paddy increased from 30.81 mha in 1950–1 to 43.50 mha in 2015–16. Presently, the area under paddy accounts for about 35 per cent in total foodgrain area and close to 43 per cent in the total foodgrain production in India. Though paddy is cultivated throughout India, it is predominantly cultivated in Andhra Pradesh, which alone accounted for nearly one-tenth of India's total area under paddy during 2015–16.

Table 8.1 presents profitability in paddy cultivation from 1970–1 to 2015–16. Andhra Pradesh is one of the leading states in terms of productivity of paddy and is also efficient in terms of cost of production (Rao and Dev, 2010). Therefore, it was expected that farmers would be reaping high profits from paddy cultivation. Of the 10 time points taken for the study, farmers were able to make a margin of profit in relation to cost A2 in all time points. The profitability from paddy crop increased from INR 1,963/ha in 1970–1 to INR 2,776/ha in 2015–16. However, the profit estimated in relation to cost A2 cannot be considered as a real profit as it does not cover the fixed-cost aspect of COC, which is a major cost in modern agriculture. Therefore, after having estimated the profitability

Table 8.1 Profitability in Paddy Cultivation in Andhra Pradesh, 1970–1 to 2015–16 (values at 1986–7 prices)

Year	Cost A2 (INR/ha)	Cost C2 (INR/ha)	VOP (INR/ha)	VOP–A2 (INR/ha)	VOP–C2 (INR/ha)
1970–1	2,618	4,308	4,581	1,963	273
1975–6	2,341	3,690	3,161	820	−529
1980–1	3,480	5,640	5,481	2,001	−159
1985–6	4,084	6,682	6,545	2,461	−137
1990–1	4,424	7,307	6,563	2,139	−744
1995–6	4,319	7,684	7,518	3,199	−166
2000–1	4,705	8,582	8,216	3,511	−366
2005–6	4,623	8,288	8,455	3,832	167
2010–11	5,245	9,132	9,115	3,870	−17
2015–16	4,351	7,446	7,128	2,776	−318

Sources: Computed using data from CACP (various years).
Notes: VOP: value of output in INR; ha: hectare.

in relation to cost A2, profitability of crop was estimated relating with cost C2. Predictably, then the profitability of paddy changed completely. In this scenario, farmers were making losses in 8 out of 10 time points. Even in the remaining two time points, the profits reaped by farmers were very minimal, varying only from INR 167 to INR 273/ha.

Agrarian distress and farmer suicides were observed in a larger proportion after 2000–1 in India. Therefore, apart from looking at the overall profitability of crops selected for the analysis, we have specifically looked into whether any perceptible change has taken place in profitability of paddy cultivation after 2000–1. Though no significant change was found in the trends in profitability of paddy before and after 2000–1, profitability in relation to cost A2 has increased consistently after 2000–1, which was not the case earlier. Similarly, the losses incurred by farmers in relation to cost C2 were also found to be relatively less after 2000–1 as compared to the earlier period. This is mainly because of relatively less increase in COC (both A2 and C2) after 2000–1. For instance, cost A2 increased by 2.02 times between 1970–1 and 2000–1, but the same was very less between 2000–1 and 2015–16. A similar trend is noticed in cost C2 as well.

As a result, the magnitude of loss incurred by farmers in relation to cost C3 was found to be less, especially after 2000–1. However, the results of paddy were unexpected, as we were expecting that profit from paddy would be very large because of the following three reasons. First, paddy is cultivated predominantly under irrigated condition in Andhra where crop failure seldom occurs. Second, unlike for many other crops, the MSP for paddy is effectively implemented. Third, Andhra Pradesh is also a high productivity state in paddy crop. Overall, it is very clear that cultivating paddy crop is profitable only when it is estimated in relation to cost A2.

Returns from Jowar

Jowar, the third most important foodgrain crop of India, has been chosen in order to study its profitability. The area under jowar at the national level has witnessed a decline from about 15.57 mha in 1950–1 to about 6.08 mha in 2015–16. Jowar crop occupies about 5 per cent of the total area of foodgrains and accounts for about 2 per cent of the total foodgrain production in India (GoI, 2018). The crop is predominantly cultivated under rainfed conditions in states such as Maharashtra, Karnataka, Rajasthan, Andhra Pradesh, and Tamil Nadu. These states together accounted for about 89 per cent of India's total area under jowar during 2015–16 (GoI, 2018). Andhra Pradesh alone accounted for about 4 per cent of the total area under jowar.

Andhra Pradesh is one of the leading states in terms of productivity of jowar and therefore, it was expected that farmers would be benefitting from its cultivation. Our analysis on profitability shows that out of eight time points, jowar farmers of the state were able to make profits over cost A2 in seven (see Table 8.2). The profitability from jowar increased from INR 113/ha in 1985–6 to INR 2,119/ha in 2015–16. However, when profits were estimated in relation to cost C2, the results were very disappointing. The crop proved to be a loss-making venture in all time points.

While studying profitability of jowar before and after 2000–1, some interesting observations emerged. The profitability of jowar in relation to cost A2 improved considerably after 2000–1 as compared to the previous period. While jowar continued to incur losses

Table 8.2 Profitability in Jowar Cultivation in Andhra Pradesh, 1975–6 to 2015–16 (values at 1986–7 prices)

Year	Cost A2 (INR/ha)	Cost C2 (INR/ha)	VOP (INR/ha)	VOP-A2 (INR/ha)	VOP-C2 (INR/ha)
1975–6	631	1,057	621	−10	−436
1985–6	830	1,489	943	113	−546
1990–1	1,007	1,767	1,040	33	−727
1995–6	1,199	2,440	1,329	130	−1,111
2000–1	1,523	2,979	1,910	387	−1,069
2005–6	2,064	3,675	2,797	733	−878
2010–11	3,008	5,576	5,438	2,430	−138
2015–16	2,094	4,226	4,213	2,119	−12

Sources: Computed using data from CACP (various years).
Notes: VOP: value of output in INR; ha: hectare.

in relation to cost C2 both before and after 2000–1, the extent of loss is found to be more profound during the former than the latter period. This is because VOP from crop cultivation moved at a slower pace or in close tandem with the COC, resulting in severe losses. For instance, cost A2 increased by 2.41 times between 1975–6 and 2000–1, whereas VOP from crop cultivation did so by 3.07 times. This has changed after 2000–1. However, we cannot ignore the fact that the increase in profits after 2000–1 lacked consistency as profits fluctuated between INR 2,430/ha and INR 1,368/ha during 2010–11 and 2011–12. A complete loss over cost C2 in all time points clearly explains the unviability of cultivating jowar.

Returns from Maize

Maize, 'the crop of the future', is grown in different production environments in India. The area under maize has seen a jump from 3.16 mha in 1950–1 to 8.81 mha in 2015–16 (GoI, 2018). This crop currently occupies about 7 per cent of the total area and accounts for about 8 per cent of the total production of foodgrains. Andhra Pradesh, Karnataka, Maharashtra, and Bihar are the leading producers of maize, which together accounted for 43 per cent of total area and 56 per cent of its total production in India (GoI,

2018). Andhra Pradesh alone accounted for about 14 per cent of India's total area under maize during 2015–16. As Andhra Pradesh leads the country in terms of production and productivity of maize, it is expected that the state's farmers would be getting appreciable returns from its cultivation. It is observed that maize farmers have reaped profits in relation to cost A2 in all the six time points for which the data was available (see Table 8.3). The profits over cost A2 increased from INR 1,079/ha in 1995–6 to INR 4,595/ha in 2015–16. However, in relation to cost C2, maize farmers are found to be reaping profits in only two out of the five time points. That is, the farmers are subjected to loss in the remaining three time points. The profits were also not substantial as they varied in the range of INR 1,112/ha to INR 552/ha.

As the COC data before 2000–1 is not adequately available, it was difficult to ascertain whether the profitability of maize in the state improved after 2000–1. However, there exist some differences in the profits obtained from maize after 2000–1. In relation to cost A2, farmers were able to make consistent profits, even if they were not phenomenal, while profits over cost C2 decelerated in the latest periods. What could be the reason behind such a trend? It was identified that VOP from crop cultivation was either moving on par or moving at a slower pace vis-à-vis COC. Clearly, the crop has disappointed farmers on account of meagre earnings. Similar to jowar, the maize crop also fails to bring any appreciable returns to farmers of Andhra Pradesh.

Table 8.3 Profitability in Maize Cultivation in Andhra Pradesh, 1995–6 to 2015–16 (values at 1986–7 prices)

Year	Cost A2 (INR/ha)	Cost C2 (INR/ha)	VOP (INR/ha)	VOP–A2 (INR/ha)	VOP–C2 (INR/ha)
1995–6	2,341	4,645	3,420	1,079	−1,225
2000–1	2,173	3,734	2,639	466	−1,095
2005–6	3,013	5,644	5,391	2,378	−253
2010–11	5,508	8,197	9,309	3,801	1,112
2015–16	4,293	8,336	8,887	4,595	552

Sources: Computed using data from CACP (various years).

Notes: VOP: value of output in INR; ha: hectare.

Returns from Arhar

After studying the profitability of cereal crops, we will now focus on the pulse crops, which are mostly cultivated under rainfed conditions. Arhar (tur or red gram) is an important pulse crop in India. Its cultivated area at the national level has increased gradually from 2.18 mha in 1950–1 to 3.96 mha in 2015–16, possibly because of increased demand for the crop. Arhar accounts for about 3 per cent of the total area and about 17 per cent of the total production of pulses in the country (GoI, 2018). Maharashtra, Karnataka, and Madhya Pradesh are the three leading producers of arhar, which together accounted for about 61 per cent of the total area and about 55 per cent of the production in 2015–16. Andhra Pradesh, which also cultivates arhar, accounted for about 12 per cent of its total area in the country during 2015–16.

Because of increased demand for arhar, the prices (both open market and MSP) offered for this crop have increased significantly in recent years. Therefore, it is expected that the farmers cultivating this crop would be reaping substantial profit. Our analysis shows that unlike the three cereal crops (paddy, jowar, maize) studied earlier, the arhar crop has not disappointed the state's farmers in terms of profitability. The arhar cultivators of the state were able to reap profits in all four time points (see Table 8.4). The profits over cost A2 have increased tremendously from INR 53/ha in 2000–1 to INR 3,703/ha in 2015–16. However, with regard to cost C2, arhar farmers of the state were able to reap profits in only two of the four time

Table 8.4 Profitability in Arhar Cultivation in Andhra Pradesh, 2000–1 to 2015–16 (values at 1986–7 prices)

Year	Cost A2 (INR/ha)	Cost C2 (INR/ha)	VOP (INR/ha)	VOP–A2 (INR/ha)	VOP–C2 (INR/ha)
2000–1	2,055	3,483	2,108	53	–1,375
2005–6	1,815	4,005	4,470	2,655	465
2010–11	2,601	4,396	4,024	1,423	–372
2015–16	2,544	5,392	6,247	3,703	856

Sources: Computed using data from CACP (various years).
Notes: VOP: value of output in INR; ha: hectare.

points. In the rest of the time points, the crop turned out to be a loss-making venture.

Since COC data is not available for the period prior to 2000–1, we shall see whether the profits obtained between 2000–1 and 2012–13 were impressive or not. Although the arhar farmers of the state did not incur any loss over cost A2, they were in the grip of fluctuating profits. Profits fluctuated every alternate year, leaving very little room for farmers to benefit from the crop cultivation. In relation to cost C2, arhar farmers obtained profits in the range of INR 465/ha and INR 856/ha during 2005–6 and 2015–16, which were not even sufficient to cover the escalation in COC. Besides, the profits also decelerated during the aforementioned periods. It is because VOP from crop cultivation, even after moving ahead of COC (both cost A2 and C2), moved in close tandem with cost A2 and cost C2. On the whole, arhar has provided profit to farmers of Andhra Pradesh only in relation to cost A2, and that too amidst fluctuations.

Returns from Moong

Another important pulse crop considered for the analysis is moong (green gram). It accounted for about 2 per cent of the total foodgrain area as of 2015–16 in India. Rajasthan, Maharashtra, Andhra Pradesh, Gujarat, and Bihar are the leading producers of moong. Andhra Pradesh alone accounts for about 8 per cent of the total area under moong in the country. With its ever increasing demand, moong is expected to be profitable to farmers.

The analysis reveals that the moong crop proves to be profitable to farmers in all eight time points presented in Table 8.5. The profit over cost A2 is seen to have risen from INR 467/ha in 1980–1 to INR 2,456/ha in 2005–6, and then declined to INR 862/ha in 2015–16. However, the profit over cost A2 is found to be unsteady throughout the time period, which is a matter of serious concern as it explains the instability of the income from moong cultivation. The performance of moong in Andhra Pradesh seems to be dismal when profit is estimated in relation to cost C2; the crop has benefitted farmers only in three out of eight time points. The profits obtained by farmers not only fluctuated sharply but were also not adequate. Profits over cost C2 varied from INR 179/ha in 1995–6 to INR 908/ha in 2005–6.

Table 8.5 Profitability in Moong Cultivation in Andhra Pradesh, 1980–1 to 2015–16 (values at 1986–7 prices)

Year	Cost A2 (INR/ha)	Cost C2 (INR/ha)	VOP (INR/ha)	VOP–A2 (INR/ha)	VOP–C2 (INR/ha)
1980–1	938	1,623	1,405	467	–218
1985–6	1,022	1,890	1,880	858	–10
1990–1	927	1,654	1,514	587	–140
1995–6	1,081	2,277	2,456	1,375	179
2000–1	1,565	2,955	2,512	947	–443
2005–6	1,578	3,161	4,069	2,491	908
2010–11	982	2,267	2,746	1,764	479
2015–16	2,158	3,364	3,020	862	–343

Sources: Computed using data from CACP (various years).
Notes: VOP: value of output in INR; ha: hectare.

Profit from moong crop in relation to cost A2 remained unsteady both before and after 2000–1. In relation to cost C2, the profitability situation is somewhat different. It is seen that moong farmers of the state incurred absolute losses before 2000–1; however, the crop turned out to be profitable after 2000–1. The reason behind this is that the increase in VOP was inadequate to cover the rising COC. For instance, while cost A2 rose by 1.66 times between 1980–1 and 2000–1, VOP increased by 1.78 times. However, the picture was different between 2000–1 and 2015–16. Nevertheless, similar to profit over cost A2, profit over cost C2 also remained unsteady. Thus, it is clear that farmers have been cultivating moong in Andhra Pradesh without incurring any losses only in relation to cost A2.

Returns from Groundnut

Groundnut has traditionally been an important oilseed crop in India, which we have considered for studying profitability. At the all-India level, the area under groundnut has increased only marginally from 4.49 mha in 1950–1 to 4.60 mha in 2015–16 (GoI, 2018). Gujarat, Andhra Pradesh, Tamil Nadu, and Karnataka are the major producers of groundnut, which together accounted for about 75 per cent of the area and 65 per cent of production in 2015–16. Of these, Andhra

Pradesh alone accounted for about 19 per cent of India's total area under groundnut.

The data on cost and income presented in Table 8.6 shows that in relation to cost A2, groundnut in Andhra Pradesh turned out to be profitable in all nine time points. Although the profit over cost A2 increased from INR 488/ha in 1975–6 to INR 2,776/ha in 2015–16, it did not follow a uniform trend. In contrast, when cost C2 is used for profit estimation, the crop proved to be profitable in only two out of nine time points. Even in the two time points, the profits were not substantial but rather fluctuated sharply varying from INR 1,005/ha to INR 3/ha.

Some significant difference is observed in the profit obtained before and after 2000–1. For instance, the profit over cost A2 fluctuated widely before 2000–1, and it was not the same after 2000–1. However, some gradual improvement is observed in profit in the recent period, between 2005–6 and 2015–16. This is because VOP from groundnut cultivation both before and after 2000–1 has either moved at a slower pace over cost A2 or has moved in close tandem with COC.

In relation to cost C2, we have not observed any significant difference in the profitability of groundnut before and after 2000–1. This is because cost C2 has increased at a faster pace than VOP.

Table 8.6 Profitability in Groundnut Cultivation in Andhra Pradesh, 1975–6 to 2015–16 (values at 1986–7 prices)

Year	Cost A2 (INR/ha)	Cost C2 (INR/ha)	VOP (INR/ha)	VOP–A2 (INR/ha)	VOP–C2 (INR/ha)
1975–6	2,001	3,095	2,489	488	–606
1980–1	2,106	3,411	3,192	1,086	–219
1985–6	2,395	3,861	3,215	820	–646
1990–1	3,186	5,895	6,900	3,714	1,005
1995–6	2,821	5,111	4,932	2,111	–179
2000–1	2,736	4,760	3,865	1,129	–895
2005–6	3,316	5,613	4,033	717	–1,580
2010–11	5,146	9,330	9,333	4,187	3
2015–16	4,351	7,446	7,128	2,776	–318

Sources: Computed using data from CACP (various years).

Notes: VOP: value of output in INR; ha: hectare.

Nevertheless, the profit over cost C2 was neither consistent nor substantial. Even in Gujarat, as per a study by Narayanamoorthy (2013), profit from groundnut was not impressive. The status of the crop in Andhra Pradesh on the whole is quite unsteady.

Returns from Sugarcane

The next crop that we will analyse is sugarcane, which is one of the most important commercial crops of the country. It is also considered to be one of the most viable commercial crops. However, in recent years, a uniform level of despair is observed among sugarcane cultivators across the country. Distressed voices from Maharashtra and Tamil Nadu echo that sugarcane is not remunerative any more (see *The Hindu Business Line*, 2012). It is in this context that it becomes pertinent to analyse how justifiable is the claim by sugarcane farmers that the crop is not remunerative any more. The area under sugarcane has increased from 1.71 mha in 1950–1 to 4.93 mha in 2015–16 at the all-India level. Uttar Pradesh, Maharashtra, Tamil Nadu, Andhra Pradesh, and Karnataka are the major producers of sugarcane in the country, which together occupied about 82 per cent of the total area and about 84 per cent of the total production in the country during 2015–16. Of these, Andhra Pradesh alone accounts for about 4 per cent of the total area under sugarcane.

Table 8.7 reveals that sugarcane farmers of the state have reaped adequate profits in relation to cost A2 in all nine time points analysed. The profits over cost A2 increased tremendously from INR 4,571/ha in 1975–6 to INR 13,841/ha in 2015–16. Surprisingly, farmers have not incurred losses in any of the time points considered for the analysis. This preliminary finding then begs the question, why then were sugarcane farmers of Andhra Pradesh agitating about not generating adequate profits from the crop? When the data was put to keen observation, it was revealed that the profits obtained by farmers were not consistent throughout the period of analysis. In relation to cost C2, the crop proved to be profitable in eight out of nine time points, with loss occurring in one time point. But the profits were found to have decelerated from INR 9,369/ha in 1975–6 to INR 4,012/ha 2015–16. Here too the profits are found to be fluctuating every alternate period.

Table 8.7 Profitability in Sugarcane Cultivation in Andhra Pradesh, 1975–6 to 2015–16 (values at 1986–7 prices)

Year	Cost A2 (INR/ha)	Cost C2 (INR/ha)	VOP (INR/ha)	VOP–A2 (INR/ha)	VOP–C2 (INR/ha)
1975–6	8,169	12,905	12,740	4,571	–165
1980–1	7,656	16,397	25,766	18,110	9,369
1985–6	7,131	14,193	21,180	14,049	6,987
1990–1	8,058	13,861	16,318	8,260	2,457
1995–6	7,324	16,662	20,863	13,539	4,201
2000–1	9,226	16,776	19,083	9,857	2,307
2005–6	9,989	18,968	23,091	13,102	4,123
2010–11	12,248	22,574	29,545	17,297	6,971
2015–16	12,450	22,279	26,291	13,841	4,012

Sources: Computed using data from CACP (various years).
Notes: VOP: value of output in INR; ha: hectare.

There seems to be no significant difference in the profit reaped by sugarcane farmers before and after 2000–1. Profits were absolutely unsteady before and after 2000–1 under both cost settings. What could be the plausible reason for this? It is because in most of the time points, VOP from crop cultivation moved almost on par with COC. For instance, before 2000–1, cost A2 and cost C2 rose by 1.12 and 1.29 times respectively, while VOP rose by 1.49 times. Similarly, after 2000–1, both the costs rose by almost the same level, that is, 1.32 to 1.35 times, while VOP rose by 1.38 times. This seems to be the obvious reason for the unanimous resentment among cultivators across Andhra Pradesh. Not only Andhra Pradesh, it is reported that sugarcane farmers of Maharashtra, Tamil Nadu, and Uttar Pradesh are also struggling to get substantial profits over cost C2 (for details, see Narayanamoorthy, 2013).

Returns from Cotton

Similar to sugarcane, cotton farmers from major growing regions of the country have been mulling over other alternatives to cotton crop. Several researchers have pointed out that an escalation in COC and depressing yields due to pest attack not only rendered the cotton crop uneconomical but also contributed to a large number of farmer suicides (see Gandhi and Namboodiri, 2006; Deshpande, 2002). In contrast, in a very recent study in which about 22 crops were analysed, cotton was one among the eight crops that were found to have reaped 100 per cent or more gross profit (Vishandass and Lukka, 2013). It is in this context that the cotton crop is taken up for studying its profitability. The area under cotton cultivation has increased tremendously, particularly after the introduction of Bt varieties, from 5.88 mha in 1950–1 to 12.29 mha in 2015–16 (GoI, 2018). Maharashtra, Gujarat, Andhra Pradesh, and Haryana are the major producers of cotton, which together accounted for about 80 per cent of total area and about 77 per cent of the total production of cotton.

Andhra Pradesh, which is the third largest cotton-producing state, accounted for about 20 per cent of India's total area under cotton during 2015–16. It is also one among the few states where the incidence of suicides among cotton farmers is very high. Are the cotton growers of the state able to cover COC? It is seen from Table 8.8 that cotton is profitable to farmers in all eight time points in relation to cost A2. The profit over cost A2 has increased from INR 1,040/ha in 1975–6 to INR 1,751/ha in 2015–16. However, the profits were

Table 8.8 Profitability in Cotton Cultivation in Andhra Pradesh, 1975–6 to 2015–16 (values at 1986–7 prices)

Year	Cost A2 (INR/ha)	Cost C2 (INR/ha)	VOP (INR/ha)	VOP–A2 (INR/ha)	VOP–C2 (INR/ha)
1975–6	1,066	1,762	2,106	1,040	344
1980–1	1,810	2,762	2,894	1,084	132
1985–6	1,647	2,360	1,970	323	–390
1990–1	NA	NA	NA	NA	NA
1995–6	2,870	4,434	5,281	2,411	847
2000–1	3,031	4,667	3,983	952	–684
2005–6	4,078	5,891	5,023	945	–868
2010–11	5,613	9,323	11,114	5,501	1,791
2015–16	5,445	8,822	7,195	1,751	–1,627

Sources: Computed using data from CACP (various years).

Notes: VOP: value of output in INR; ha: hectare.

neither substantial nor consistent. In relation to cost C2, the profitability situation is somewhat different, wherein farmers have reaped profits in only four time points. In the remaining time points, the crop has suffered losses, which is varying between INR 390/ha and INR 1,627/ha. The profit so obtained was far more inadequate and even fluctuated sharply.

Profit from cotton cultivation in relation to cost A2 fluctuated very sharply both before and after 2000–1. It is because VOP from cotton cultivation in most time points has either moved at a slower pace or has moved in close tandem with cost A2. A similar trend is also observed in the case of cost C2. It is thus inferred from the analysis that cotton farmers of Andhra Pradesh are ravaged by relentless oscillations in COC and profits over the years.

Profit Reaped or Loss Incurred by Farmers (Number of Years)

Besides analysing the trends in profitability of crop cultivation in Andhra Pradesh, an attempt has also been made here to determine how many times (years) farmers cultivating the selected crops were able to reap profit (both in relation to cost A2 and cost C2) during the entire period of analysis, from 1970–1 to 2015–16. As seen earlier, here too VOP and costs A2 and C2 are considered for computing profitability in crop cultivation. Let us first study the profits reaped by farmers in relation to cost A2. Table 8.9 shows the ratio of VOP to cost A2 for different time periods for various crops. If the ratio is more than 1.30, it means that farmers are reaping good profit from crop cultivation and if the ratio is in the range of <1.30 to >1.00 then farmers are realizing moderate profit. A ratio of less than one means farmers are incurring losses by cultivating crops.

It is seen that out of the eight crops selected for analysis, seven have generated profits for farmers throughout the period of analysis. They include paddy, maize, arhar, moong, groundnut, sugarcane, and cotton. Jowar turned out to be profitable in 26 out of 32 years (81.25 per cent). An important issue that we have studied is whether the profitability varied between the pre-liberalization period (1970–1 and 1995–6) and the economic liberalization period (1995–6 to 2015–16). It is hypothesized that farmers would have reaped profit

Table 8.9 Number of Years Profit (in relation to cost A2) Reaped or Loss Incurred by Andhra Pradesh Farmers from 1970–1 to 2015–16

Crops	Pre-liberalization Period (1970–1 to 1995–6)			Economic Liberalization Period (1995–6 to 2015–16)			Entire Period of Analysis (1970–1 to 2015–16)		
	>1.30	>1 to <1.30	<1.00	>1.30	>1 to <1.30	<1.00	>1.30	>1 to <1.30	<1.00
Paddy	17/20	03/20	0/20	20/20	0/17	0/17	37/40	03/40	0/40
	(85.00)	(15.00)	(0.00)	(100.00)	(0.00)	(0.00)	(92.50)	(8.11)	(0.00)
Jowar	04/13	07/13	02/13	10/19	05/19	04/19	14/32	12/32	6/32
	(30.77)	(53.85)	(15.38)	(52.63)	(26.32)	(21.05)	(43.75)	(37.50)	(18.75)
Maize	02/02	0/02	0/02	18/19	01/19	0/19	20/21	01/21	0/21
	(100.00)	(0.00)	(0.00)	(94.74)	(5.26)	(0.00)	(95.24)	(4.76)	(0.00)
Arhar	0/0	0/0	0/0	16/17	01/17	0/17	13/17	01/17	0/17
	(0.00)	(0.00)	(0.00)	(94.12)	(5.88)	(0.00)	(94.12)	(5.88)	(0.00)
Moong	08/09	01/09	0/09	19/20	01/20	0/20	27/29	02/29	0/29
	(88.89)	(11.11)	(0.00)	(95.00)	(5.00)	(0.00)	(93.10)	(6.90)	(0.00)
Groundnut	10/12	02/12	0/12	15/20	05/20	0/20	25/32	07/32	0/32
	(83.33)	(16.67)	(0.00)	(75.00)	(25.00)	(0.00)	(78.13)	(21.87)	(0.00)
Sugarcane	14/14	0/14	0/14	18/18	0/18	0/18	32/32	0/32	0/32
	(100.00)	(0.00)	(0.00)	(100.00)	(0.00)	(0.00)	(100.00)	(0.00)	(0.00)
Cotton	09/11	02/11	0/11	14/18	04/18	0/18	23/29	06/29	0/29
	(81.81)	(18.18)	(0.00)	(77.79)	(22.22)	(0.00)	(79.31)	(20.69)	(0.00)

Sources: Computed using data from CACP (various years).
Note: Figures within the parentheses are percentages of total number of years.

in fewer number of years during the economic liberalization period owing to increased COC. However, as per the analysis, except jowar, no other crop growers have suffered any losses during ACP. This is indeed contradictory to the relentless battle being waged by some growers of such crops as paddy, sugarcane, and cotton.

The results of profitability from crop cultivation are entirely different when cost C2 is used to estimate profit. None of the selected crops were able to reap profit in 100 per cent of the time points considered for analysis (see Table 8.10). However, sugarcane reaped profits in more number of years in comparison to other crops, that is, in 30 out of 32 years (93.09 per cent). All the remaining crops, including the principle foodgrain crop paddy, were able to do so in less than 50 per cent of the time periods. In fact, nearly five out of eight crops have incurred loss of more than 50 per cent in the time period analysed. Of these, it is jowar that has suffered loss in most number of years: 29 out of 32 years (90.60 per cent). The losses from groundnut and maize are also very extensive. Importantly, almost all the crops considered for analysis have incurred losses during the economic liberalization period. However, jowar, maize, and groundnut have incurred losses in more number of years during the economic liberalization period than other crops. Among these, jowar suffered losses in over 90 per cent of the time period. Overall, in relation to cost C2, sugarcane performed excellently in Andhra Pradesh in terms of benefitting farmers in more number of years.

Conclusion and Suggestions

The analysis of different crops from Andhra Pradesh reveals that farmers have either reaped miniscule profits or suffered massive losses in cultivating most of the crops we have investigated. Under the cost A2 scenario, most crops proved to be profitable in most time points from 1970–1 to 2015–16. But the same is not true under the cost C2 scenario, where almost all the crops suffered extensive losses. Significant differences in profits were observed across selected crops. Sugarcane farmers have realized better profit than any other crop farmers in relation to both cost A2 and cost C2.

The analysis of the number of years farmers reaped profit from the entire period of analysis shows that in relation to cost A2, seven

Table 8.10 Number of Years Profit (in relation to cost C2) Reaped or Loss Incurred by Andhra Pradesh Farmers from 1970–1 to 2015–16

Crops	Pre-liberalization Period (1970–1 to 1995–6)			Economic Liberalization Period (1995–6 to 2015–16)			Entire Period of Aanalysis (1970–1 to 2015–16)		
	>1.30	>1 to <1.30	<1.00	>1.30	>1 to <1.30	<1.00	>1.30	>1 to <1.30	<1.00
Paddy	0/20	06/20	14/20	0/20	14/20	06/20	0/40	20/40	20/40
	(0.00)	(30.00)	(70.00)	(0.00)	(70.00)	(30.00)	(0.00)	(50.00)	(50.00)
Jowar	0/13	01/13	12/13	0/19	02/19	17/19	0/32	03/32	29/32
	(0.00)	(7.69)	(92.31)	(0.00)	(10.53)	(89.47)	(0.00)	(9.38)	(90.63)
Maize	0/02	0/02	02/02	0/19	07/19	12/19	0/21	07/21	14/21
	(0.00)	(0.00)	(0.00)	(0.00)	(36.84)	(63.16)	(0.00)	(33.33)	(66.67)
Arhar	0/0	0/0	0/0	01/17	07/17	09/17	01/17	07/17	09/17
	(0.00)	(0.00)	(0.00)	(5.88)	(41.16)	(52.94)	(5.88)	(41.16)	(52.94)
Moong	0/09	02/09	07/09	02/20	12/20	06/20	02/29	14/29	13/29
	(0.00)	(22.22)	(77.78)	(10.00)	(60.00)	(30.00)	(6.90)	(48.28)	(44.83)
Groundnut	0/12	01/12	11/12	0/20	04/20	16/20	0/32	05/32	27/32
	(0.00)	(8.33)	(91.67)	(0.00)	(20.00)	(80.00)	(0.00)	(15.63)	(84.37)
Sugarcane	04/14	09/14	01/14	04/18	13/18	01/18	08/32	22/32	02/32
	(28.57)	(64.28)	(7.14)	(22.22)	(72.22)	(5.56)	(25.00)	(68.75)	(6.25)
Cotton	03/11	06/11	02/11	0/18	07/18	11/18	03/29	13/29	13/29
	(27.27)	(54.54)	(18.18)	(0.00)	(38.89)	(61.11)	(10.34)	(44.83)	(44.83)

Sources: Computed using data from CACP (various years).

Note: Figures within the parentheses are percentages of total number of years.

of the eight crops have generated profits throughout the period of analysis (100 per cent). It was seen that except jowar no other crop growers have suffered any losses during the economic liberalization period from 1995–6 to 2015–16. However, when cost C2 is used to estimate profit, none of the selected crops were able to show profit in 100 per cent of the time periods. Sugarcane farmers reaped profits in more number of years in comparison to other crops. Fluctuating profits, rising COC, and dwindling price for their agricultural produce seem to be wreaking havoc on the earnings of farmers.

Continued losses or meagre earnings from crop cultivation would definitely discourage farmers from engaging in farming. A consistent profit and a steady flow of remunerative income from crops will definitely provide a boost for farmers to encourage them to go in for cultivation in the following season. The agrarian crisis, which the country has been facing for more than a decade now, cannot be solved without providing incentives to farmers in the form of higher profitability for crops. The unabated number of farmer suicides reported from various parts of the country also suggest that one-time support such as farm loan waiver will not help in solving the problem of farmers.

Farmers need sustained support in the form of increased returns from crop cultivation. In this context, prices for the crops should be fixed in consonance with COC. As suggested by the NCF (2006), the government should announce MSPs for crops at 50 per cent more than the actual cost of production (cost C3). Besides this, the MSPs announced every year should also be linked with the WPI to protect farmers from possible inflationary pressure. To protect farmers from distress sale, there is also a need to closely watch the price behaviour of sensitive commodities, especially during glut periods, by making swift intervention through the MIS as suggested by the Radhakrishna Committee on Agricultural Indebtedness (GoI, 2007).

Apart from price incentives, the government should also focus on non-price incentives to increase productivity of crops and to reduce COC. The COC appears to have increased after the introduction of MGNREGS. By restructuring this employment programme, the cost of labour, which impinges on the overall COC, can be brought down. Studies show that farmers are not able to get even 40 per cent of the money that the consumer pays for various agricultural commodities in the market. The role of middlemen can be controlled to a large extent by directly extensively involving producers in market activities. The experience of farmers' markets in Tamil Nadu and other parts of the country is very encouraging (Kallummal and Srinivasan, 2007). Therefore, as underlined in the National Agricultural Policy (2000), producers' markets on the lines of rythu bazaars should be encouraged throughout the country to improve the income levels of farmers and to break the back of middlemen (GoI, 2000). Unless the issue of profitability of crops is addressed immediately, it will be difficult to rescue farmers from the current mire they are in. It is high time that policymakers begin to work towards the prime concern of farmers, which extends from plough to plate.

Bibliography

Ahluwalia, M. S. 1978. 'Rural Poverty and Agricultural Performance in India'. *Journal of Development Studies*, vol. 14, no. 2 (April), pp. 298–323.

CACP (Commission for Agricultural Costs and Prices). Various years. *Report of the Commission for Agricultural Costs and Prices.* Ministry of Agriculture, Government of India, New Delhi.

Darling, M. L. 1925. *The Punjab Peasant in Prosperity and Debt.* Oxford University Press, Delhi.

Deshpande, R. S. 2002. 'Suicide by Farmers in Karnataka: Agrarian Distress and Possible Alleviatory Steps'. *Economic and Political Weekly*, vol. 37, no. 26, pp. 2601–10.

Deshpande, R. S., and S. Arora (eds). 2010. *Agrarian Crisis and Farmer Suicides.* Sage Publications, New Delhi.

Deshpande. R. S., and N. Prabhu. 2005. 'Farmers' Distress: Proof beyond Question'. *Economic and Political Weekly*, vol. 40, nos 44–5, pp. 4663–5.

Gandhi, V. P., and N. V. Namboodiri. 2006. *The Adoption and Economics of Bt Cotton in India: Preliminary Results from a Study.* Working Paper Series No. 2006–09–04. Indian Institute of Management, Ahmedabad, India, pp. 1–25.

GoAP (Government of Andhra Pradesh). 2011. *Report of State Level Committee to Study the Problems of Farmers in Crop Holiday Affected Mandals of East Godavari District of Andhra Pradesh* (Chairman: Mohan Kanda). Government of Andhra Pradesh, Hyderabad.

GoI (Government of India). 2000. *National Agricultural Policy: 2000.* Ministry of Agriculture, Government of India, New Delhi, July.

———. 2007. *Report of the Expert Group on Agricultural Indebtedness*. Ministry of Finance, Government of India, New Delhi, July.

———. 2018. *Agricultural Statistics at a Glance: 2017*. Directorate of Economics and Statistics, Ministry of Agriculture, Government of India, New Delhi.

The Hindu Business Line. 2012. 'Maharashtra Cane Farmers Firm on Prolonging Fight on Price Issue'. 16 November.

Kalamkar, S. S., and A. Narayanamoorthy. 2003. 'Impact of Liberalisation on Domestic Agricultural Prices and Farm Income'. *Indian Journal of Agricultural Economics*, vol. 58, no. 3 (July–September), pp. 353–64.

Kallummal, M., and K. S. Srinivasan. 2007. *The Dynamics of Farmers Market: A Case of 'Uzhavar Sandhai' of Tamil Nadu*. Make Trade Fair Campaign, CENTAD, New Delhi.

Narayanamoorthy, A. 2001. 'Irrigation and Rural Poverty Nexus: A Statewise Analysis'. *Indian Journal of Agricultural Economics*, vol. 56, no. 1 (January–March), pp. 40–56.

———. 2006. 'Relief Package for Farmers: Can It Stop Suicides?'. *Economic and Political Weekly*, vol. 41, no. 31 (5 August), pp. 3353–5.

———. 2007. 'Deceleration in Agricultural Growth: Technology Fatigue or Policy Fatigue'. *Economic and Political Weekly*, vol. 42, no. 25 (23 June), pp. 2375–9.

———. 2013. 'Profitability in Crops Cultivation in India: Some Evidence from Cost of Cultivation Survey Data'. *Indian Journal of Agricultural Economics*, vol. 68, no. 1, pp. 104–21.

Narayanamoorthy, A., and R. S. Deshpande. 2003. 'Irrigation Development and Agricultural Wages: An Analysis across States'. *Economic and Political Weekly*, vol. 38, no. 35, pp. 3716–22.

Narayanamoorthy, A., and S. S. Kalamkar. 2005. 'Indebtedness of Farmer Households across States: Recent Trends, Status and Determinants'. *Indian Journal of Agricultural Economics*, vol. 60, no. 3 (July–September), pp. 290–301.

NCF (National Commission of Farmers). 2006. *Serving Farmers and Saving Farming: Towards Faster and More Inclusive Growth of Farmers Welfare*. Government of India, New Delhi.

NSSO (National Sample Survey Office). 2005a. *Situation Assessment Survey of Farmers: Some Aspects of Farming*, Report No. 496. New Delhi.

———. 2005b. *Situation Assessment Survey of Farmers: Indebtedness of Farmer Households*, Report No. 498. New Delhi.

———. 2014. *Key Indicators of Situation Assessment of Agricultural Households*, 70th Round (January–December 2013). Government of India, New Delhi.

Rao, N. Chandrasekhara, and S. Mahendra Dev. 2010. 'Agricultural Price Policy, Farm Profitability and Food Security'. *Economic and Political Weekly*, vol. 45, nos 26 and 27 (June), pp. 174–82.

Reddy, V. R., and S. Galab. 2006. 'Agrarian Crisis: Looking beyond the Debt Trap'. *Economic and Political Weekly*, vol. 41, no. 19 (13 May), pp. 1838–41.

Sainath, P. 2010. 'Farm Suicides—a 12 Year Saga'. *The Hindu*, 25 January.

Saleth, M. R., M. Samad, D. Molden, and I. Hussain. 2003. 'Water, Poverty and Gender: A Review of Issues and Policies'. *Water Policy*, vol. 5, nos 5–6, pp. 385–98.

Swaminathan, M. S. 2008. 'Ending the Debt Trap and Attaining Food Security'. *The Hindu*, 3 March, p. 12.

Vishandass, A., and B. Lukka. 2013. *Pricing, Costs, Returns and Productivity in Indian Crop Sector during 2000s*. Discussion Paper no. 7. Commission for Agriculture Costs and Prices, Government of India, New Delhi, pp. 11–61.

PART IV

FOOD SECURITY, PROCUREMENT, AND FARM INCOME

9

Crop Holiday and India's New Food Security Worries

The agricultural sector of India, which has witnessed a spectacular achievement in the production of foodgrains and other commodities over the last 50 years, is at a crossroads today. In an unprecedented situation, over 256,000 farmers have committed suicide in the last one decade or so, citing poor remuneration from crop cultivation as the main reason. Indebtedness among agricultural households is not only widespread but has also been increasing in the recent years (NSSO, 2005b; Narayanamoorthy and Kalamkar, 2005). A nation-wide survey carried out in 2003 underlined that close to 40 per cent of farmers are willing to quit agriculture because of poor profitability from crop cultivation (NSSO, 2005a). The NCF (2006) has reported that young farmers are not willing to take up agriculture as a profession because it is not profitable. Surprisingly, the adoption of new technology in agriculture has also slowed down substantially in the recent years (GoI, 2008). With all these discouraging signals, can we produce the required quantity of foodgrains to have complete food security in our country?

Though Indian agriculture has produced record amounts of foodgrain, which increased from 50.82 mt in 1950–1 to over 242 mt in 2010–11, its demand has also been continuously rising due to increase in consumers' income, population growth, and other reasons. A projection made by NCIWRD indicates that the total demand for foodgrains would be about 316 mt by 2025 and 441 mt by 2050. Given the severe agrarian crisis experienced over the last one decade in agriculture, there are apprehensions now about whether production of foodgrains can be increased to meet the projected levels of demand. On the one hand, the area allotted for foodgrain crops has been declining persistently in relation to GCA; on the other hand, the growth rate in production and productivity of various foodgrain crops has decelerated during the last decade (GoI, 2011).

Adding to this problem, the paddy cultivating farmers from Andhra Pradesh, the rice bowl of India, declared a crop holiday for the kharif season of 2011–12 in an area of 400,000 acres. Such a crop holiday, which has never been heard of in the history of Indian agriculture, declared by the farmers neither belonged to rainfed areas nor the drought-prone regions but were in the districts of highly irrigated region in Andhra Pradesh. The farmers leading the crop holiday campaign also urged their peers in Punjab, Tamil Nadu, and Karnataka to go on crop holiday so as to protest against the poor remuneration from paddy cultivation. Since the contribution of irrigated agriculture to the total production of foodgrains is large, this move can potentially harm the production of foodgrains, which may lead to food security problems. Why do farmers suddenly declare crop holiday? Will crop holiday affect the production of foodgrains? What are the implications of crop holiday on foodgrain production? Do we have any other threats to foodgrain production besides crop holiday? Utilizing the available secondary data pertaining to crop holiday and other related parameters, an attempt is made in this chapter to answers these questions as well as to decode India's emerging food security concerns.

Method and Data

The entire study has been carried out utilizing secondary data pertaining to crop holiday and foodgrain production. Besides studying the possible impact of crop holiday on the production of foodgrains, an attempt has been made to figure out the other possible threats on the foodgrain production. An important reason reported by the farmers of Andhra Pradesh for declaring crop holiday is poor remuneration from paddy cultivation. Is this true? In order to find the answer to this question, we have utilized the COC data on paddy crops published by the CACP for the period 1975–6 to 2008–9. Among the factors, gross production of foodgrains is determined by land use pattern, irrigated area, area used for different foodgrain crops, share of foodgrain area to GCA, productivity of foodgrain crops, and so on. Changes in these parameters would obviously affect the production of foodgrains, which may lead to food security problems in the future. One of the objectives of this study is to decode the possible threats to foodgrain production besides crop holiday. For this purpose, utilizing all-India level data from 1950–1 to 2010–11, we have studied the trends in selected categories of land use, area under major foodgrain crops, and production and productivity of foodgrains to understand the pattern of change in these parameters. As we are interested to know the trends that are emerging across different time points based on the above-mentioned parameters, we have divided the period of analysis into six decades, namely 1950s (1950–1 to 1960–1), 1960s (1960–1 to 1970–1), 1970s (1970–1 to 1980–1), 1980s (1980–1 to 1990–1), 1990s (1990–1 to 2000–1), and 2000s (2000–1 to 2010–11).

Why Crop Holiday?

Before studying the possible impact of crop holiday on foodgrain production, let us briefly understand why farmers declare crop holiday. Although there are no systematic studies on crop holiday as such, a great deal of newspaper articles written by various scholars (*Economic Times*, 2011, Sharma, 2011; Kurmanath, 2011; Pillai, 2011) have clearly pointed out that rising COC and an unviable MSP are, more than any other reason, vital causes in prompting the self-imposed stoppage of growing paddy. The Mohan Kanda Committee appointed by the Government of Andhra Pradesh to study the problem of crop holiday has also underlined that poor remuneration from crop cultivation is one of the main reasons for announcing crop holiday by the farmers (GoAP, 2011). The real story behind this kind of 'industrial action' by farmers is much more complex than what a simple reading of the facts suggests. The fertile and irrigated East Godavari and West Godavari districts of Andhra Pradesh are neither devoid of water resources nor is there a dearth of seed and varietal availability; moreover, the region is bestowed with most fertile lands supported by well-marked irrigation systems.

It is to be remembered that Andhra Pradesh, Karnataka, Kerala, Tamil Nadu, and Punjab were, in fact, the largest beneficiaries of the loan-waiver scheme of the Government of India. So it begs the question as to why in spite of all these the farmers reportedly seem to be saying that they cannot incur continuous losses anymore and cannot also afford the recurring effects of financial and crop losses for someone else's welfare. The fertile and irrigated East Godavari and West Godavari districts of Andhra Pradesh actually had a bad time during the 2010 kharif season due to crop failure, and the government did announce a compensation of INR 18,000 per acre due to crop failure for that kharif season. Then the farmers are reported to have produced a bumper crop of about 14 mt in the 12 months ending with March 2011, one-third more than the production of the previous year. This bumper crop turned into a problem as prices crashed due to imperfect market conditions. The soaring prices of seeds, fertilizers, and wage rates added fuel to the already existing problems. All this compelled the peasants to refrain from sowing paddy in the kharif season of 2011 as by spending INR 25,000 per acre, it seemed that they were barely getting INR 18,000, thereby making them unable to meet their expenses from the sale of their crop (*The Hindu*, 2011). To be more accurate, as per the estimates of the Andhra Pradesh agricultural department, the cost of production of a quintal of paddy in Konaseema area, where crop holiday was declared on a large scale, works out to be INR 1,583. But the MSP for paddy announced by the government for 2011–12 was only INR 1,110. This has meant a loss of INR 473 a quintal or nearly INR 10,000 per acre. It is for this reason that the farmers have demanded at least INR 2,042 a quintal as MSP (following the recommendations of NCF headed by M. S. Swaminathan) as against INR 1,100 announced by the government (Chintala, 2011). A large number of farmers' organizations that represented their view points to the Mohan Kanda Committee (GoAP, 2011) have also unequivocally pointed out that the poor remuneration from paddy cultivation has forced them to take this serious act of crop holiday.[1]

Is Paddy Cultivation Non-remunerative?

Farmers in Andhra Pradesh have reported that poor remuneration is the main reason for declaring crop holiday. Is there any truth in this? Paddy is an ecologically sensitive preeminent crop which is cultivated in over 42 mha in India (2010–11). It accounts for about 37 per cent of the cropped area and about 42 per cent of production of foodgrains (2009–10). With paddy being an irrigated crop, the coverage of irrigation saw a jump from 31.7 per cent in 1950–1 to 58.7 per cent in 2008–9. The yield is also assured with an increase from 668 kg/ha in 1950–1 to 2,240 kg/ha in 2010–11. Effective in its implementation, the MSP has also been increased over the years for paddy crop. Even considering all these healthy facts and figures on paddy, our analysis on profitability of paddy carried out utilizing the data on COC published by the CACP of the Ministry of Agriculture seems to support the claim made by the Andhra Pradesh farmers. Our exercise reveals that except for 2007–8 and 2008–9, farmers were unable to get any appreciable profit over cost C2 during 1975–6 to 2008–9 in Andhra Pradesh (see Table 9.1). Interestingly, the quantum of cost C2 was found to be relatively large over the VOP during the post-1990s because of steep rise in COC. This is the true status of one of the most efficient paddy producing states of India. What is clear from this analysis is that paddy cultivation is not greatly profitable to farmers in Andhra Pradesh, which is also mentioned as the main reason for declaring crop holiday by the farmers.

Crop Holiday versus Foodgrain Production

Will the crop holiday affect foodgrain production and thereby food security? Paddy crop currently occupies one quarter of the total

[1] Several farmers' organizations have made their pleas to the Mohan Kanda Committee on the issue of crop holiday. The details of demands made by each farmers' organizations can be seen from GoAP (2011).

Table 9.1 Value of Output and Cost of Cultivation in Paddy Cultivation, Andhra Pradesh State

Year	Cost C2 (INR/ha)	VOP (INR/ha)	VOP/ cost C2	VOP/ cost C3
1975–6	2,193	1,879	0.86	0.78
1980–1	3,895	3,785	0.97	0.88
1985–6	5,291	4,913	0.93	0.84
1991–2	10,258	10,321	1.01	0.91
1995–6	17,980	17,592	0.98	0.89
2001–2	27,043	25,408	0.94	0.85
2006–7	30,492	32,024	1.05	0.95
2007–8	37,444	41,995	1.12	1.02
2008–9	46,450	53,772	1.16	1.06

Source: Computed using data from CACP (various years).
Notes: Due to non-availability of data for some specified years, data from the nearest point is used for the analysis; VOP: value of output

cropped area and contributes close to 43 per cent of total foodgrain production in India. Therefore, the crop holiday announced by the farmers would obviously reduce the production of paddy and thereby overall production of foodgrains. However, if the reduction in area under paddy or in any other foodgrain crops is compensated for by the rise in other foodgrain crops or increase in productivity of foodgrains, then it will not have any severe impact on the gross production of foodgrains. The question is, is this happening for foodgrain crops in India? Unfortunately, the trends in area, productivity, and production of foodgrains appear to show that there is going to be a slowdown in the gross production of foodgrains, including paddy, in India (see Table 9.2). Though the production of foodgrains touched a new peak of 241 mt in 2010–11, the overall picture is depressing in both productivity and production of foodgrains. The average productivity of foodgrains increased from 1,535 kg/ha during the 1990s to 1,748 kg/ha during the 2000s, but the increase in terms of percentage reduced to 13.90 per cent during 2000s as compared to the 1990s when it increased to over 30 per cent. Similarly, the increase in gross production of foodgrains also decelerated to 12.70 per cent during the 2000s as compared to its preceding decade when the increase was

Table 9.2 Decadal Trends in Production and Productivity of Foodgrains in India

Period	Production in Million Tonnes (mt)					Productivity (kg/ha)				
	Food-grains	Paddy	Wheat	Coarse Cereals	Pulses	Food-grains	Paddy	Wheat	Coarse Cereals	Pulses
1950–1 to 1960–1	66.67	27.04	8.60	20.66	10.67	616	847	739	481	481
1960–1 to 1970–1	87.13	36.44	14.26	25.27	11.16	732	1,010	971	552	484
1970–1 to 1980–1	113.17	45.57	28.56	28.09	10.96	904	1,172	1,398	652	481
1980–1 to 1990–1	149.26	61.09	45.70	30.11	12.35	1,176	1,492	1,951	765	531
1990–1 to 2000–1	189.30	80.54	64.44	31.11	13.22	1,535	1,856	2,515	976	572
2000–1 to 2010–11	213.34	89.75	74.56	35.10	13.94	1,748	2,069	2,746	1,226	596
	Percentage Change over the Previous Decade									
1960–1 to 1970–1	30.10	34.75	65.76	22.32	4.61	18.87	19.34	31.37	14.61	0.72
1970–1 to 1980–1	29.89	25.05	100.25	11.16	–1.79	23.52	16.06	44.03	18.08	–0.71
1980–1 to 1990–1	31.89	34.08	60.05	7.20	12.65	30.07	27.24	39.54	17.44	10.41
1990–1 to 2000–1	26.83	31.83	40.99	3.32	7.02	30.48	24.43	28.91	27.56	7.74
2000–1 to 2010–11	12.70	11.44	15.71	12.82	5.44	13.94	11.47	9.19	25.57	4.13

Sources: Computed using data from GoI (2011); RBI (2011); CWC (2010), and www.agricoop.nic.in

close to 27 per cent. This depressing trend observed in total foodgrain production is also seen for all the major foodgrain crops reported in Table 9.2. Notably, the average incremental increase in production and productivity of foodgrains was the lowest during the 2000s as compared to any other decade considered for the analysis. All these clearly show that the production of foodgrains has, in fact, decelerated substantially during the 2000s over the previous decade. Given this dismal trend, can we achieve the foodgrain production of 340 mt needed for India by 2020? Can anyone simply ignore instances such as the crop holiday announced by Andhra Pradesh farmers? Will this decelerating trend in foodgrain production not create food security problems? Going by the recent trends in foodgrain production, the newly emerging problems such as crop holiday will certainly make a dent in foodgrain production in the future if attempts are not made to solve it.

Is the Land Use Pattern Favourable to Food Security?

Crop holiday is an issue that has emerged only very recently in Indian agriculture. There may be many other new issues besides crop holiday that can also hamper foodgrain production. Changes in land use pattern, irrigated area, and area allotted for different foodgrain crops are important factors expected to affect the production of foodgrains. Therefore, as mentioned earlier, one must study what kind of changes are taking place in these parameters using the national level data from 1950–1 to 2010–11. Let us first study the trends in selected categories of land use in India. Net sown area (NSA), area sown more than once (ASMTO), and gross cropped area (GCA) are the major determinants of gross production of foodgrains in India over the years. Therefore, any reduction in these three parameters can potentially affect foodgrain production and food security. Decade-wise trends presented in Table 9.3 show a dismal picture in NSA, especially during the first decade of the 2000s. The average NSA of the country was about 142 mha during the 1990s, but it declined to about 140 mha during the 2000s, indicating a reduction of about two million hectares. This kind of sharp reduction in area under cultivation had not been seen during the earlier decades, which is a serious concern. The trends in GCA and ASMTO are also not very

Table 9.3 Decadal Trends in Selected Categories of Land Use in India

Period	Area in Million Hectares (mha)					
	NSA	ASMTO	GCA	NIA	GIA	TFL
1950–1 to 1960–1	127.57	16.90	144.48	22.50	25.34	25.05
1960–1 to 1970–1	137.25	21.47	158.72	27.13	32.16	22.55
1970–1 to 1980–1	140.29	28.35	168.64	34.76	43.45	23.74
1980–1 to 1990–1	140.83	36.80	177.63	42.93	55.78	25.03
1990–1 to 2000–1	142.26	45.07	187.33	53.27	71.97	24.09
2000–1 to 2010–11	140.26	50.49	190.75	59.64	82.76	26.03
Percentage Change over the Previous Decade						
1960–1 to 1970–1	7.58	27.01	9.86	20.57	26.92	–9.99
1970–1 to 1980–1	2.22	32.06	6.25	28.10	35.12	5.26
1980–1 to 1990–1	0.38	29.79	5.33	23.51	28.38	5.44
1990–1 to 2000–1	1.02	22.48	5.46	24.09	29.01	–3.76
2000–1 to 2009–10	–1.41	12.02	1.82	11.97	14.99	7.97

Sources: Computed using data from GoI (2011); RBI (2011), CWC (2010), and www.agricoop.nic.in.

Notes: NSA: net sown area; ASMTO: area sown more than once; GCA: gross cropped area; NIA: net irrigated area; GIA: gross irrigated area; TFL: total fallow lands.

encouraging. Though there has been a consistent increase in both GCA and ASMTO since 1950–1, the rate of increase of these two parameters has sharply decelerated during the 2000s as compared to the previous decade of the 1990s. For instance, the average increase of GCA was 5.46 per cent between the 1980s and 1990s, but the same increased only at the rate of 1.82 per cent between the 1990s and 2000s. This deceleration in NSA and GCA is expected to affect foodgrain production in the future.

Apart from gloomy trends in GCA and NSA, the trends in total fallow lands (TFL) and area under irrigation have also been dismal in recent years. The average area under fallow land increased close to 2 mha during the 2000s as compared to the 1990s, which is also the largest increase noticed in any of the decades we considered for the analysis. This sharp increase in area under fallow lands during the 2000s also reinforces the fact that farmers are in distress and they are not willing to cultivate crops in their available lands. One must not forget that any increase in area under fallow lands can potentially affect the production of foodgrains.

Irrigation coverage has proved to be a decisive factor in determining the production and productivity of crops. Therefore, any reduction in the coverage of irrigation, especially under foodgrain crops, can reduce the production of foodgrains. But, unfortunately, the trends across different decades show a dismal picture in the area under irrigation too. Sharp slowdown is noticed in all the three irrigation parameters—namely net irrigated area (NIA), gross irrigated area (GIA), and area irrigated more than once (AIMTO)—during the first decade of the 2000s as compared to the 1990s. One is not very clear whether the slowdown in irrigated area is taking place uniformly across different crops. However, this slowdown will certainly have a significant impact on the production of foodgrains as the irrigated area is increasingly used for cultivating non-foodgrain crops due to economic reasons.[2]

Declining Foodgrain Area

Besides studying the selected categories of land use, we have also studied the trends in area under major foodgrain crops in India so as to ascertain whether any serious threats are arising from it from the point of view of food security. Paddy, wheat, coarse cereals, and pulses are the main contributors to foodgrain production in the country and, therefore, these crops are considered for the analysis. As observed in land use pattern, the data presented in Table 9.4 shows a clear dismal trend in almost all major foodgrain crops, particularly during the 2000s. This dismal trend is also seen among the two major foodgrain crops, namely paddy and wheat, as the incremental area under these two crops has consistently reduced over the last 40 years. The average increase in area under paddy between the 1980s and

[2] Irrigated area is increasingly used for cultivating high-value non-foodgrain crops in India, possibly due to economic reasons. As per the data on crop-wise irrigated area, the foodgrain crops together accounted for close to 79 per cent of the irrigated area in 1970–1, but it reduced drastically to 67 per cent in 2008–9, the years for which we have the latest information.

Table 9.4 Decadal Trends in Area under Foodgrains

Period	Area in Million Hectares (mha)				
	Foodgrain Area	Paddy	Wheat	Coarse Cereals	Pulses
1950–1 to 1960–1	108.24	31.81	11.59	42.73	22.10
1960–1 to 1970–1	118.76	36.02	14.39	45.31	23.04
1970–1 to 1980–1	124.98	38.78	20.30	43.14	22.76
1980–1 to 1990–1	126.90	40.84	23.38	39.46	23.23
1990–1 to 2000–1	123.38	43.35	25.56	31.96	22.49
2000–1 to 2010–11	121.86	43.34	27.11	28.69	22.72
	Percentage over the Previous Decade				
1960–1 to 1970–1	9.72	13.23	24.07	6.04	4.24
1970–1 to 1980–1	5.24	7.66	41.15	–4.80	–1.21
1980–1 to 1990–1	1.54	5.32	15.15	–8.53	2.04
1990–1 to 2000–1	–2.77	6.15	9.34	–18.99	–3.16
2000–1 to 2009–10	–1.24	–0.04	6.05	–10.24	1.02

Sources: Computed using data from GoI (2011); RBI (2011); and www.agricoop.nic.in.

1990s was about 6.15 per cent, but it recorded negative growth during the 2000s over the period of the 1990s. Though the absolute area under wheat has been increasing over the years, its area growth too has slowed down substantially during the last three decades. In fact, the average increase of area under wheat between the 1990s and 2000s was only 6.05 per cent, which is much less than the increase achieved (9.34 per cent) between the 1980s and 1990s. Despite announcing higher MSPs for pulse crops in recent years, we do not see any big leap in its area between the 1990s and 2000s—area under pulses has been hovering around 22–3 mha during the last 50 years.[3] Because of reduction in area under major foodgrain crops, the gross area under foodgrains has reduced by close to two million hectares between the

[3] Among the major crops, MSPs have been substantially increased for pulse crops over the years. Despite this, we have not seen any significant increase in either the area under pulses or its production mainly because of the absence of good varieties and marketing problems. A glance at the MSPs

1990s and 2000s, from 123.38 mha to 121.86 mha. This substantial reduction in area under foodgrain crops is not an encouraging trend as far as the food security of the country is concerned.

The GCA of the country increased by close to 45 mha between the 1950s and 2000s, which is very significant. One has to determine where this cropped area has been utilized. If most of this area is used for cultivating foodgrain crops, the production of foodgrains would go up, which would ultimately ease the food security concerns. Is this happening? Data on the share of important foodgrain area to GCA reported in Table 9.5 shows a disappointing trend in all major crops except for wheat. While the share of paddy area to GCA has not changed much since the 1950s, there has been a sharp decline in the share of coarse cereals and pulse crops. The share of area under coarse cereals to GCA has declined from about 29 per cent in the 1950s to 15 per cent in the 2000s, while the same has declined from about 15 per cent to about 11 per cent in pulse crops during this period. Among the various foodgrain crops considered for the analysis, wheat is the only crop where the share of area has increased sharply from 8 per cent in the 1950s to 14.21 per cent in the 2000s. However, this

---

(INR/quintal) of selected crops for two time points, 2000–1 and 2011–12, is presented here for reference:

Crops	2000–1	2011–12	Percentage increase over 2000–1
Paddy (common)	510	1,080	111.80
Wheat	580	1,120	93.10
Maize	445	980	120.20
Tur	1,200	3,200	166.70
Moong	1,200	3,500	191.70
Urad	1,200	3,300	175.00
Gram	1,015	2,100	106.90
Lentil	1,200	2,250	87.50
Groundnut	1,220	2,700	121.30
Sunflower	1,170	2,800	139.30
Rapeseed/Mustard	1,100	1,850	68.20
Sugarcane	59.50	145.00	143.70

Table 9.5 Trends in Share of Foodgrain Area to Gross Cropped Area

Period	Percentage to Gross Cropped Area (GCA)				
	Foodgrains	Paddy	Wheat	Coarse Cereals	Pulses
1950–1 to 1960–1	74.88	22.03	8.00	29.59	15.27
1960–1 to 1970–1	74.82	22.69	9.05	28.55	14.53
1970–1 to 1980–1	74.11	22.99	12.03	25.66	13.49
1980–1 to 1990–1	71.46	22.99	13.17	22.24	13.07
1990–1 to 2000–1	65.87	23.14	13.64	17.07	12.01
2000–1 to 2010–11	63.90	22.73	14.21	15.05	11.91

Sources: Computed using data from GoI (2011); RBI (2011); and www.agricoop.nic.in.

sharp increase in the share of wheat area could not help in improving the share of total foodgrains area to GCA, which has consistently declined from about 74.88 per cent in the 1950s to about 63.90 per cent in the 2000s. The reduction in foodgrain area both in absolute terms and in relation to GCA is a serious issue concerning food security which the policymakers must take note of it.

The Way Forward

It is clear from the analysis presented in this chapter that it is low farm profitability which led to the practice of crop holiday by farmers in Andhra Pradesh. Recently, some have argued that 'the crop holiday movement is essentially an attempt by the landowning classes and market intermediaries to discipline workers, tenants and the welfare state' (Vakulbharanam et al., 2011). This appears to be an unrealistic argument as the evidence available from the field and from the macro data on paddy cultivation does not support this. The crop holiday is clearly an economic issue, similar to the agrarian crisis which resulted in large number of farmer suicides over a decade ago (Narayanamoorthy, 2006a; 2007). Besides crop holiday, our analysis also shows a sharp decelerating trend in cropped area (both NSA and GCA), area utilized for cultivating foodgrain crops, and also in the production and productivity of foodgrain crops during the first decade of the 2000s as compared to the 1990s. Therefore, ignoring issues such as the crop holiday can have a devastating impact on foodgrain production in the future. We suggest later a few price and non-price measures which may be useful in solving issues such as crop holiday and also in improving the production of foodgrains and thereby food security.

There is a common feeling among farmers in Andhra Pradesh that the prices of crops are not announced in accordance with the COC. The Confederation of Indian Farmers Association (CIFA) has urged the centre and the CACP to change the way MSP is calculated, citing that it relies on three-year-old data that is not adequate to meet the fast rise in cost of production. Moreover, the CACP also takes the average cost of production of various states for recommending MSPs for paddy and other crops, which invariably affects the states that incur higher cost of production. The CIFA and the affected farmers have demanded that MSPs should be announced in advance of the season and should be flexible so as to take into consideration subsequent and unforeseen changes in the cost of inputs such as fertilizers, diesel, labour charges, and so on. The CIFA has also urged the government to follow the guidelines of the NCF (2006), chaired by M. S. Swaminathan, which had underlined in its fifth report that the cost of production was invariably higher than the MSP in the case of 12 crops including rice and wheat. The report stated, 'It would be extremely unlikely that in long run farmers would continue to cultivate those crops where the C2 costs (cultivation costs) are not covered.' The report also highlighted that MSPs should be regarded as the bottom line for procurement both by government and private traders. If there persists a delay in fixing MSPs of at least 50 per cent more than the actual cost of production (cost C3) then there is a likelihood of declining production with crop holiday on the rise. Therefore, the prices need to be fixed in accordance with COC and the guidelines suggested by the NCF so as to avoid this kind of problem in the future.

A higher MSP alone may not help to solve the problem in the long run, as farm produce has to be competitive both in the domestic as well in the international markets. The real solution lies in reducing COC through systematic mechanization and using only the prudent mix of required level of inputs. Increased labour cost (wage rate) needed for paddy cultivation appears to be one of the prime reasons for steep rise in COC in recent years. As per the data of CCS published by CACP, the share of labour cost in total COC (cost A2) has increased from 35 per cent in 1980–1 to 62 per cent in 2008–9 in paddy cultivation in Andhra Pradesh.[4] Many argue that the introduction of MGNREGS has not only increased the wage rate in agriculture but also deteriorated the quality of labour. If this is true, one must find out ways and means to restructure the employment programme currently in operation, without affecting agriculture.

In order to save the farmers from the spate of huge losses, there is a need to link MSP with the WPI. However, the WPI should not be taken as the only basis for determining MSP. There is a need to periodically review and revise the list of indicators for determining MSP so as to give the farmers the remunerative prices of their produce. Improper or volatile market condition is also reported as one of the reasons for crop holiday. Therefore, the MIS is to be implemented so as to protect the farmers from making distress sale in the event of bumper crop when the prices tend to fall below the economic cost of production. Losses, if any, incurred by the procuring agencies are to be shared by the central government and the concerned state government on a fifty-fifty basis.

Efforts are also needed to reduce COC through increased public investment and surface irrigation development; both have not increased by a desired level during the last two decades. Effective regulations also need to be brought in to control both input and output markets where farmers are exploited unscrupulously. Farmers' markets (rythu bazaars) and farmers' involved regulated markets (FIRMs) need to be promoted to increase the remuneration of farmers. The protest in the form of crop holiday was a wake-up call for the government—the very same government which intervenes immediately if there is any small change in the share market, but does not care about the vast market fluctuations dis-favouring the farming community. While on the one hand the government plans to increase

[4] As per the data of CACP, the share of labour cost in relation to cost C2 also increased substantially from 21 per cent in 1980–1 to 34 per cent in 2008–9 for paddy in Andhra Pradesh.

farm production to meet the obligations under the proposed bill on food security, which stands at around 65 to 70 mt, on the other hand the crop satyagraha by the paddy farmers of Andhra Pradesh has started spreading to sugarcane farmers too now. Therefore, the policymakers of the country must recognize the fact that it is impossible to achieve complete food security without providing security to its own farmers in the form of better remuneration.

Bibliography

CACP (Commission for Agricultural Costs and Prices). Various years. *Report of the Commission for Agricultural Costs and Prices.* Ministry of Agriculture, Government of India, New Delhi.

Chintala, P. 2011. 'AP Farmers Go on "Crop Holiday"—the State's Rice Bowl Is Left Empty'. *Business Standard*, 27 September.

CWC (Central Water Commission). 2010. *Water and Related Statistics.* Ministry of Water Resources, Government of India, New Delhi.

The Economic Times. 2011. 'Raise MSP above Cost of Production'. 21 September.

GoAP (Government of Andhra Pradesh). 2011. *Report of State Level Committee to Study the Problems of Farmers in Crop Holiday Affected Mandals of East Godavari District of Andhra Pradesh* (Chairman: Mohan Kanda). Hyderabad.

GoI (Government of India). 2008. *Economic Survey 2007–08.* Ministry of Finance, New Delhi.

———. 2011. *Agricultural Statistics at a Glance.* Ministry of Agriculture, New Delhi.

The Hindu. 2011. 'Paddy Growers Seek State Intervention'. 21 August.

Kurmanath, K. V. 2011a. 'Crop Holiday Effect: AP Loss Estimated at INR 530 Crore'. *The Hindu Business Line*, 19 August.

———. 2011b. 'Meaning of a "Crop Holiday" This Kharif'. *The Hindu Business Line*, 18 July.

Narayanamoorthy, A. 2006a. 'Relief Package for Farmers: Can It Stop Suicides?'. *Economic and Political Weekly*, vol. 41, no. 31 (5 August), pp. 3353–5.

———. 2006b. 'State of India's Farmers'. *Economic and Political Weekly*, vol. 41, no. 6 (11 February), pp. 471–3.

———. 2007. 'Deceleration in Agricultural Growth: Technology Fatigue or Policy Fatigue'. *Economic and Political Weekly*, vol. 42, no. 25 (23 June), pp. 2375–9.

Narayanamoorthy, A., and S. S. Kalamkar. 2005. 'Indebtedness of Farmer Households across States: Recent Trends, Status and Determinants'. *Indian Journal of Agricultural Economics*, vol. 60, no. 3 (July–September), pp. 290–301.

NCF (National Commission on Farmers). 2006. *Serving Farmers and Saving Farming, Report V Excerpts.* Ministry of Agriculture, Government of India, New Delhi.

NSSO (National Sample Survey Office). 2005a. *Situation Assessment Survey of Farmers: Some Aspects of Farming.* Report no. 496, 59th Round. Ministry of Statistics and Programme Implementation, Government of India, New Delhi.

———. 2005b. *Situation Assessment Survey of Farmers: Indebtedness of Farmer Households.* Report no. 498, 59th Round. Ministry of Statistics and Programme Implementation, Government of India, New Delhi.

Pillai, Viswanath. 2011. 'The Rice Bowl of India May See a Crop Holiday on Bumper Harvest'. Available at https://www.livemint.com/Politics/dLvgZ8qAUzUVTMSk2iHCVM/The-rice-bowl-of-India-may-see-a-crop-holiday-on-bumper-harv.html (last accessed on 28 May 2020).

RBI (Reserve Bank of India). 2011. *Handbook of Statistics on the Indian Economy: 2010–11.* Mumbai, India.

Sharma, Devinder. 2011. 'Distressed Farmers Declare a Crop Holiday'. Available at http://d-sector.blogspot.com/2011/10/distressed-farmers-declare-crop-holiday.html (last accessed on 28 May 2020).

Vakulabharanam, V., N. P. Prasad, K. Laxminarayana, and S. Kilaru. 2011. 'Understanding the Crop Holiday Movement'. *Economic and Political Weekly*, vol. 46, no. 50 (10 December), pp. 13–16.

10

Procurement of Foodgrains and Farm Income Nexus

The major objective of this chapter is to study the impact of public procurement of major foodgrains on farm income across different states over a period of time. Since income is necessary for farmers' livelihood and farm sector development, various initiatives have been taken to augment it at different periods. With the advent of Green Revolution technology, attempts have been made to increase farm income by way of increasing cropping intensity and productivity of crops (see Bhalla and Singh, 2012). Subsidies for various farm inputs have been provided to encourage the use of modern technology in crop cultivation with a view to increasing productivity as well as farm income. But as the elasticity of demand for foodgrains is less than unit, the increased production during bumper harvests often brings down the prices of agricultural commodities sharply and affects the income of farmers severely (Deshpande, 1996). Given the imperfect agricultural market conditions existing in India, assured prices are considered to be very necessary for farmers to get guaranteed income from crop cultivation (Acharya, 1997; Sen and Bhatia, 2004). Assured prices are also the known instrument of organizing and integrating production activities of farmers and have proved to be the most imperative factor for increasing the production of foodgrains and other agricultural commodities (Schultz, 1964).

In view of the importance of assured prices, the government has been providing MSPs (with the recommendations of the CACP) since the early 1970s for 23 crops that account for about 85 per cent of cropped area today. Have MSPs helped farmers in getting increased income? Quite a few studies have analysed the role of MSPs in farm income and other parameters (see Chand, Saxena, and Rana, 2015). Gaiha and Kulkarni (2005) have reported that MSPs have had significant positive impact on the procurement of wheat and rice, but these effects seem to have weakened during the late 1990s due to the removal of restrictions on domestic and international trade. Mere announcement of MSPs alone will not assure better price for farmers as the latter depends upon a number of associated factors (Narayanamoorthy, 2012; Narayanamoorthy and Alli, 2017). While studying the price variation in agricultural commodities relating to MSPs, government procurement, and agricultural markets, Chatterjee and Kapur (2016) have underlined that the producers get different prices depending upon the location in which they are situated, investment made in the physical infrastructure of mandis, and the regulatory framework including the internal governance of the market.

While evaluating the efficiency of MSP for farmers, NITI Aayog's (2016) study underlines that the major objective behind MSP is to give guaranteed prices and assured market to farmers and save them from price fluctuations. While insulating farmers from unwarranted fluctuations in prices caused by the variation in supply, the announcement of MSP also helps to tackle the lack of market integration, information asymmetry, and other elements of market imperfections plaguing agricultural markets. Similar to the study of NITI Aayog (2016), a field data–based study (Singh et al., 2015) carried out in Chittorgarh district of Rajasthan showed that farmers who sold wheat at MSP procurement centres earned higher profit (19 per cent of cost of production) than those farmers who sold it at open market price where they received less profit (14 per cent of cost of production).

Though theoretically MSPs are expected to protect farmers from sharp plunges in market prices of agricultural commodities occurring during bumper harvest, it does not always ensure reasonable profit margin, neither does it help to prevent distress selling (Chand, 2003).

Because of poor procurement arrangements, farmers are forced to sell their produce below MSP at many times, which is also underlined in different reports published by CACP. For instance, during 2010–11, farmers belonging to Karnataka, Maharashtra, Odisha, Uttar Pradesh, and West Bengal sold their paddy below the MSP rate of INR 1,000 per quintal (see CACP, 2012b; Narayanamoorthy and Suresh, 2012). Therefore, the periodical announcement of MSP alone does not help farmers unless procurement arrangements are also adequately made by state agencies, especially during harvesting season.

Timely arrangements for procurement of foodgrains are expected to help farmers to earn better income from crop cultivation in many ways. First, the improved public procurement facilities allow the farmers to dispose of their produces in time without wastages occurring due to delayed sale. Second, the excess supply arising due to bumper harvest can be sold to procurement centres immediately, which is expected to discourage distress sale. Third, by reducing the excess supply occurring at the time of bumper harvest, the timely arranged procurement facility is expected to help reduce the volatility as well as sharp dip in open market prices, thereby helping the farmers get better prices. Fourth, the public procurement facility reduces the marketing costs which are exorbitantly high in the open market environment. Fifth, the sale of produce in the public procurement centres is more transparent (pre-fixed prices, proper quality checks, better weighing machines, and so on) allowing minimal level of malpractices which is expected to help especially the marginal and small farmers who have less bargaining power in the open market environment. Sixth, with the complete absence of intermediaries who unscrupulously exploit farmers in the open market environment, farmers are expected to maximize their crop income when they sell foodgrains through public procurement centres.

Despite the fact that the impact of MSPs on crop income and other parameters of agriculture would be very little without sufficient public procurements, not many macro studies have analysed the role of public procurement of foodgrains on farm income. As mentioned earlier, improved public procurement facilities are expected to help farmers in reaping increased profit both directly and indirectly. The state in which the level of procurement of foodgrains is higher in relation to its production, profitability (the terms 'farm income' and 'profitability' have been used interchangeably in this chapter) is also expected to be higher because of the aforesaid reasons. Is this happening in India? In this chapter, an attempt has been made to examine the effect of public procurement of paddy and wheat on farm income by examining different states in India. The specific objectives of the study are as follows:

1. To study the trends in public procurement of major foodgrains such as paddy and wheat in relation to its production over the years in India.
2. To study the state-wise public procurement of major foodgrains such as paddy and wheat in relation to its production across different time periods.
3. To measure the impact of public procurement of major foodgrains such as paddy and wheat on its farm income with the help of regression analysis among major states at different time periods.

Data and Method

The study has been completely carried out by using secondary data published by different departments and ministries of the Government of India. The national-level analysis has been carried out using data from 1970–1 to 2013–14, while the state-level analysis has been carried out by taking data of six time points from 1991–2 to 2013–14 due to non-availability of data on farm income for the selected foodgrain crops. Although we want to include as many crops as possible for the analysis, owing to data constraints at the level of public procurement, we have considered only two major foodgrain crops, namely paddy and wheat, for the detailed analysis. Production, procurement, and income of paddy and wheat are the three major data categories that have been used in the analysis. While data on production has been compiled from the publication of *Agricultural Statistics at a Glance* (published by the Directorate of Economics and Statistics, Ministry of Agriculture, Government of India), public procurement–related data has been compiled from the publication of *Bulletin on Food Statistics* (published by the Ministry of Consumer Affairs, Food and Public Distribution,

Government of India). Farm income from paddy and wheat is one of the key variables used in the analysis, which is estimated using CCS data published by the CACP, an organ of the Ministry of Agriculture, Government of India. Here, farm income per hectare has been computed by deducting the cost A2 + FL from the gross VOP per hectare at constant prices.

The core objective of the study is to find whether any nexus exists between public procurement of paddy and wheat and farm income from those crops across different states. To accomplish this, both descriptive and regression analysis have been performed. In order to understand the trends in public procurement of paddy and wheat over the years at the all-India level, growth rate (log linear) has been computed covering data from 1970–1 to 2015–16. Descriptive analysis has been performed to study the changes in the level of procurement and farm income in paddy and wheat across different states at six different time points. In order to see the real change in farm income of paddy and wheat over time, all income-related data have been converted into real values using CPIAL deflator with the base year of 2004–5. To measure the impact of public procurement on farm income, simple linear regression (ordinary least squares [OLS] method) analysis has been performed separately for paddy and wheat using state-wise data covering six different time points, namely 1991–2, 1995–6, 2000–1, 2005–6, 2010–11, and 2014–15. The reduced form of two regression models used in this study are as follows:

$$FIE_{it} = \alpha_{it} + \beta_1 PPMT_{it} + \mu_{it} \quad (1)$$

$$FIE_{it} = \alpha_{it} + \beta_1 APMT_{it} + \mu_{it} \quad (2)$$

Where,

i = 1,.........n states of India

t = time points from 1 to 6 (48 observations for paddy; 30 observations for wheat)

FIE_{it} = Farm income (INR/ha) by states from paddy/wheat at six time points

$PPMT_{it}$ = Percentage of procurement of paddy/wheat to its production by states at six time points

$APMT_{it}$ = Absolute procurement (in mt) of paddy/wheat by states at six time points

α = Constant
β = Regression coefficient to be estimated
μ = Error term

We are aware of the fact that many factors determine farm income from any crop. However, we relate it only with the level of procurement of the selected crops as we want to capture the independent relationship between the two. Over the years, the absolute quantity of procurement of paddy and wheat has increased consistently. This may have impacted farm income markedly, which would be captured by regression analysis. Model (1) mentioned above tries to capture the role of percentage of procurement of the selected crops to its gross production on farm income, while model (2) attempts to measure the role of absolute procurement on farm income among the selected states. These two models have been separately estimated specifically to determine which one of the factors is more important in explaining the variation in farm income. As mentioned earlier, farm income data for the major states where paddy and wheat crops are cultivated predominantly are not consistently available over a time from CACP. Therefore, pooled regression has been estimated taking into account the data of eight states with six time points for paddy ($8 \times 6 = 48$ observations) and five states with six time points for wheat ($5 \times 6 = 30$ observations).

Trends in Procurement of Paddy and Wheat in India

Although the major objective of the study is to determine the impact of public procurement of paddy and wheat crops on their farm income, we have also studied the procurement of these two major crops to understand the trends over the years in India. The Food Corporation of India (FCI), which is a nodal agency of the Government of India, with the support of state agencies has been procuring paddy and wheat over the years by establishing a large number of centres in key areas where these crops are predominantly cultivated. During the year 2015–16, for instance, wheat procurement has been made from more than 20,000 centres and paddy has been procured from about 44,000 procurement centres in different parts of India (see www.fci.gov.in). These extensive price supportive procurement operations are believed to have helped in sustaining the income of farmers over the years since it procures paddy and wheat with the pre-announced MSPs.

Since the establishment of FCI in 1964, the procurement of paddy and wheat has increased substantially in the country (see Table 10.1). The procurement of paddy was only about 3.46 mt during 1970–1, which massively increased to about 34.14 mt during 2015–16. That is, from less than 10 per cent of total paddy production, the procurement level increased to almost one-third (32.73 per cent) of its production during this period. Similarly, the procurement of wheat also increased from 5.09 mt in 1970–1 to 28.09 mt in 2015–16. However, the procurement level of wheat in relation to its production was relatively high as compared to paddy till the end of the 1990s. For instance, the procurement of wheat accounted for about one-fifth of its production during 1970–1, whereas it reached over 20 per cent for paddy production only after 2000–1. In the recent years, the percentage of procurement of paddy in relation to its gross production has been higher than that of wheat. It seems that the procurement policy on paddy has changed considerably after 2000–1, possibly because of the stringent demands of paddy-growing farmers, especially from south India.

Besides looking at the overall procurement of paddy and wheat over time, we have analysed its growth pattern by taking time series data from 1970–1 to 2015–16. As the farmers started facing many problems in cultivating and marketing crops especially after the mid-1990s (see Narayanamoorthy, 2006; 2007; 2013; and 2017; Narayanamoorthy and Suresh, 2012; 2013), the growth analysis has been performed by dividing the entire period into two as pre-ACP and post-ACP to see whether any discernible difference exists in the procurement of paddy and wheat. Table 10.2 shows that there are discernible differences between paddy and wheat in the growth pattern of procurement. The procurement of paddy in absolute terms registered a growth of 6.50 per cent per annum during the pre-ACP (1970–1 to 1994–5), whereas it decelerated to 5.50 per cent per annum during post-ACP (1994–5 to 2015–16). But this trend is somewhat different in the case of wheat crop, where the growth rate accelerated from 3.60 per cent in pre-ACP to 5.10 per cent in post-ACP. However, when we compute growth rate taking into account

Table 10.1 Trends in Procurement of Paddy and Wheat in India, 1970–1 to 2015–16

Year	Paddy			Wheat		
	Production (in mt)	Procurement (in mt)	Procurement as Percentage of Production	Production (in mt)	Procurement (in mt)	Procurement as Percentage of Production
1970–1	42.22	3.46	8.20	23.83	5.09	21.36
1976–7	41.92	6.00	14.31	28.84	6.62	22.95
1980–1	53.63	6.20	11.56	36.31	6.59	18.15
1986–7	60.56	9.14	15.09	44.32	10.53	23.76
1990–1	74.29	12.80	17.23	55.14	11.07	20.08
1995–6	76.98	10.04	13.04	62.10	12.32	19.84
2000–1	84.98	21.18	24.92	69.68	16.70	23.97
2005–6	91.79	27.65	30.12	69.35	15.27	22.02
2010–11	95.98	34.20	35.63	86.87	22.51	25.91
2015–16	104.32	34.14	32.73	93.50	28.09	30.04

Sources: Computed using data from GoI (various years) and RBI (2015).

Notes: mt: million tonnes.

Table 10.2 Growth Rate of Production and Procurement of Paddy and Wheat in India

Year	Production		Procurement		Procurement as Percentage of Production	
	Paddy	Wheat	Paddy	Wheat	Paddy	Wheat
1970–1 to 1994–5	3.00[a]	4.40[a]	6.50[a]	3.60[a]	3.50[a]	–0.70[ns]
1994–5 to 2015–16	1.40[a]	1.80[a]	5.50[a]	5.10[a]	4.10[a]	3.20[a]
1970–1 to 2015–16	2.20[a]	3.10[a]	5.60[a]	4.20[a]	3.40[a]	1.10[a]

Sources: Computed using data from GoI (various years) and RBI (2015).
Notes: Growth rate is computed using log-linear function (lnY = a + bt); a: significant at 1 per cent level; ns: not significant.

the percentage of procurement to gross production, the growth rate turns out to be better during post-ACP as compared to pre-ACP in both paddy and wheat. All these seem to suggest that the procurement levels of both paddy and wheat have been stepped up during the last two decades compared to the earlier decades in India. Has the improved procurement of paddy and wheat helped farmers increase their farm income? This is the question that we have attempted to answer in the following sections.

Procurement of Paddy and Wheat in Major States

Although the procurement levels of paddy and wheat have increased over time at the all-India level, it may not be true for all the states across India. The procurement policy of the government varies from state to state depending on the availability of marketable surplus of foodgrains. Since this chapter focuses on the impact of procurement of paddy and wheat on farm income among the major states, it is necessary to understand the procurement of these crops before getting into the core discussion in the chapter. Here, as mentioned earlier, due to data constraints, especially on farm income for different states for paddy and wheat, we have considered eight major producing states for paddy and five states for wheat covering three time points, namely 1991–2, 2000–1, and 2014–15.

As expected, the data presented in Table 10.3 clearly depicts that the level of procurement of paddy and wheat widely varied from state to state. However, the procurement, both in terms of absolute amount as well as in relation to gross production, has increased in almost all the selected states for both paddy and wheat between 1991–2 and 2014–15. Over 50 to 65 per cent of paddy production was procured from Punjab and Haryana by the state agencies during 1991–2. Although West Bengal, Uttar Pradesh, and Andhra Pradesh accounted for about 41 per cent of India's total paddy production during 1991–2, the procurement level was very miniscule in these states, except for Andhra Pradesh where the procurement was about 23 per cent. This situation has changed since 2000–1 in most states. Though the procurement level continues to be very high in Punjab and Haryana, the other states have improved their procurements substantially during 2014–15, which is also reflected from the value of CV presented in Table 10.3. In fact, the procurement level was less than 10 per cent of paddy production in states such as Madhya Pradesh and Odisha during 1991–2, which increased to over 40 per cent in 2014–15. The procurement levels of Uttar Pradesh, Tamil Nadu, and West Bengal continued to be very low despite large production of paddy.

Similar to paddy, the procurement level of wheat has also been high in both Punjab and Haryana. During 1991–2, about 45 per cent of wheat from Punjab and about 28 per cent from Haryana was procured, which increased to about 77 per cent and 62 per cent respectively during 2014–15. States such as Rajasthan and Madhya Pradesh had very low procurement of wheat (less than 1 per cent of its production) during 1991–2, but it increased dramatically during 2014–15. Although the contribution of Uttar Pradesh was over 25 per cent to India's total wheat production during 2014–15, its procurement was only about 3 per cent, which may have affected the wheat growers of the state. On the whole, the levels of procurement of both paddy and wheat increased substantially in all the states considered for the analysis between 1991–2 and 2014–15, albeit with wide variations among the states. To what extent is this variation expected to influence farm income of the crops is an important issue which should be investigated.

Table 10.3 Procurement of Paddy and Wheat in Major Producing States at Different Periods

States	1991–2			2000–1			2014–15		
	PDN (mt)	PMT (mt)	PMT to PDN (%)	PDN (mt)	PMT (mt)	PMT to PDN (%)	PDN (mt)	PMT (mt)	PMT to PDN (%)
				Paddy					
Andhra Pradesh	9.65	2.26	23.44	12.46	7.17	57.57	7.23	3.60	49.71
Haryana	1.83	0.92	50.33	2.70	1.48	54.77	4.01	2.02	50.30
Madhya Pradesh	5.73	0.40	7.05	0.98	0.18	17.82	3.63	0.81	22.26
Odisha	5.27	0.27	5.05	4.61	0.92	19.90	8.30	3.36	40.45
Punjab	6.53	4.25	65.05	9.15	6.94	75.76	11.11	7.79	70.10
Tamil Nadu	5.78	0.99	17.13	7.37	1.72	23.35	5.73	1.05	18.35
Uttar Pradesh	10.26	0.83	8.10	11.68	1.17	10.04	12.17	1.70	13.95
West Bengal	10.43	0.08	0.77	12.43	0.35	2.82	14.68	2.03	13.84
Other States	18.81	0.25	1.30	23.60	1.26	5.32	38.64	9.70	25.10
India	74.29	10.25	13.80	84.98	20.82	24.51	105.48	32.04	30.37
CV of 8 States	43.06	110.79	105.86	58.86	114.99	80.27	47.76	80.33	59.79

				Wheat					
Haryana	6.44	1.83	28.48	9.67	4.50	46.52	10.35	6.50	62.73
Madhya Pradesh	5.83	0.00	0.00	4.87	0.00	0.00	17.10	7.09	41.48
Punjab	12.15	5.54	45.62	15.55	9.42	60.60	15.05	11.64	77.35
Rajasthan	4.30	0.01	0.19	5.55	0.54	9.72	9.82	2.16	21.98
Uttar Pradesh	18.60	0.37	1.98	25.17	1.55	6.14	22.42	0.63	2.80
Other States	7.81	0.00	0.02	8.88	0.35	3.94	11.78	0.01	0.05
India	55.13	7.75	14.06	69.68	16.36	23.47	86.53	28.02	32.39
CV of 5 States	62.44	151.87	136.45	69.26	121.37	110.30	34.75	77.81	72.84

Sources: Computed using data from GoI (various years) and RBI (2015).

Notes: PDN: production; PMT: procurement; CV: coefficient of variation.

Procurement and Farm Income Nexus

The core objective of the study is to find the nexus between the farm income and the levels of procurement of paddy and wheat among the major states where these two crops are predominantly cultivated. Our hypothesis here is that the state which has higher levels of public procurement of paddy and wheat will have higher farm income as well. In order to study this, we have carried out both descriptive and regression analyses. As part of the descriptive analysis, farm income at constant prices (CPIAL 2004–5 = 100) has been worked out by grouping all the states into two, based on the level of procurement (per cent to production), the states with the above national average in procurement (SANAP) and the states with the below national average in procurement (SBNAP), for all the six different time points. As mentioned earlier, regression analysis has been carried out treating farm income as the dependent variable and the percentage of procurement of paddy/wheat as an explanatory variable.

Let us first discuss the results of descriptive analysis presented in Table 10.4. As expected, the average farm income from paddy and wheat cultivated in SANAP was considerably higher than that from SBNAP. For paddy, the farm income difference between the two groups of states varied from 24.77 per cent to as high as 187.39 per cent across six time points. Similarly, in the case of wheat too, the difference in farm income between SANAP and SBNAP varied from 14.14 per cent to 95.63 per cent. Although the level of procurement across the states has increased over the years in both paddy and wheat, this has not increased farm income in a consistent manner. This could be because of two reasons. First, the fluctuations in COC (year on year fluctuations in COC of different crops is common in India) may have affected farm income and second, the productivity variation due to changes in rainfall and other climatic factors may have also impacted farm income. On the whole, the descriptive analysis shows that farm income from both paddy and wheat is considerably higher in those states where the percentage of procurement to its gross production is higher than the national level average procurement.

What is the exact impact of public procurement on farm income is one of the objectives of the study, for which we have employed

Table 10.4 Average Farm Income of States with Above and Below National Average in Procurement of Paddy and Wheat (value in INR at 2004–5 prices)

States' Group	1991–2	1995–6	2000–1	2005–6	2010–11	2014–15
			Paddy			
SANAP	9,840	13,453	16,078	15,137	18,219	18,803
SBNAP	5,943	10,782	7,785	5,267	12,932	7,608
Increase over SBNAP (INR)	3,897	2,671	8,293	9,870	5,287	11,195
Increase over SBNAP (%)	65.57	24.77	106.53	187.39	40.88	147.15
			Wheat			
SANAP	12,064	10,125	18,227	14,003	19,276	13,600
SBNAP	7,440	8,871	9,317	11,003	15,226	8,101
Increase over SBNAP (INR)	4,624	1,254	8,910	3,000	4050	5,499
Increase over SBNAP (%)	62.15	14.14	95.63	27.27	26.60	67.88

Sources: Computed using data from GoI (various years); RBI (2015); and CACP (various years).

Note: SANAP: states with above national average of procurement; SBNAP: states with below national average of procurement.

regression analysis. We are aware of the fact that a number of factors determine farm income of a crop besides the level of procurement by public agencies. Here, since our main aim is to measure the independent relationship between public procurement and farm income in two selected crops, we have not included other determinants in the regression analysis. Owing to non-availability of farm income–related data for all the major states where paddy and wheat crops are predominantly cultivated, pooled regression has been estimated taking into account the data of eight states with six time points for paddy (8 × 6 = 48 observations) and five states with six time points for wheat (5 × 6 = 30 observations). Though we expect that the percentage of procurement to gross production of the crop would have more influence on farm income than the absolute amount of procurement

Table 10.5 Impact of Public Procurement on Farm Income: Pooled Regression Results

Parameters	Paddy		Wheat	
	Model (1)	Model (2)	Model (1)	Model (2)
PPMT	220.99	–	100.34	–
	(6.69)[a]		(3.82)[a]	
APMT	–	1,519.17	–	675.15
		(4.05)[a]		(3.41)[a]
Constant	4,415.17	7,615.50	9,249.15	9,728.15
	(3.46)[a]	(5.914)[a]	(9.42)[a]	(10.13)[a]
R^2	0.49	0.26	0.34	0.29
Adjusted R^2	0.48	0.25	0.32	0.26
F-Value	44.75[a]	11.64[a]	14.59[a]	11.64[a]
N	48	48	30	30

Sources: Computed using data from GoI (various years); RBI (2015), and CACP (various years).

Notes: Figures in the parenthesis are t-values; a: significant at 1 per cent level; ns: not significant; PPMT: percentage of procurement; APMT: absolute procurement.

of the crop, regression analysis has also been carried out separately by taking absolute amount of procurement (APMT) specifically to determine which is the most influential variable in impacting the farm income of the selected crops.

The regression results presented in Table 10.5 show the significant influence of public procurement on farm income from paddy and wheat. In the case of paddy, the regression results suggest that a 1 per cent increase in the percentage of procurement to its gross production has increased farm income to the tune of about INR 221 per acre during the period of analysis. This also turned out to be statistically significant. Similarly, in the case of wheat, the estimated regression coefficient suggests that a 1 per cent increase in procurement has increased farm income by about INR 100 per acre, which is also statistically significant. Among the two crops selected for the analysis, the influence of public procurement on farm income appears to be substantially higher in paddy than wheat. This is possibly because of substantial increase in farm income from paddy in certain states, especially in recent years. On the question of whether

PPMT or APMT is an important factor on impacting farm income, the estimated value of R^2 suggests that PPMT is more important in explaining the variation on farm income in both paddy and wheat. For paddy, the value of R^2 turned out to be 0.49 when PPMT was used as an explanatory variable, whereas the same was only 0.26 when APMT was used as an explanatory variable in the regression model. The same kind of trend in value of R^2 was observed in wheat as well. This was expected because PPMT is a standardized variable that can capture the sudden surge or decline in the supply of crop output, whereas APMT cannot capture the supply dynamics. The regression results on the whole suggest that it is PPMT in each state which is more important than APMT in increasing the farm income in both paddy and wheat.

Conclusion and Policy Directions

Public procurement of foodgrains with pre-announced MSPs in many ways helps farmers reap increased income from farm enterprises. A structured public procurement policy of the government allows farmers to sell their foodgrains and other commodities directly in the procurement centres eliminating interferences from middlemen, who are traditionally known to take away a huge chunk of farm income. Although studies are available on the impact of MSPs and public procurement on farm income from different crops, not many studies are available relating to public procurement of major foodgrains with farm income covering different states over time. In this chapter, therefore, an attempt has been made to examine the impact of public procurement of paddy and wheat on its farm income. First, it studies the trends in public procurement of paddy and wheat in relation to its production at the all-India level covering data from 1970–1 to 2015–16. Then, with the use of regression analysis, the study attempts to measure the impact of public procurement of paddy and wheat on its farm income across six time points, namely 1991–2, 1995–6, 2000–1, 2005–6, 2010–11, and 2014–15.

The study shows that there has been a significant increase in the public procurement of paddy and wheat, both in relation to the gross production as well as in absolute quantity, from 1970–1 to 2015–16 at the all-India level. Though the procurement of paddy (33 per cent of production) and wheat (30 per cent of production) was more or less the same in 2015–16, paddy registered a much better growth rate (5.60 per cent per annum) as compared to wheat (4.20 per cent per annum) during the period of analysis from 1970–1 to 2015–16. The procurement of paddy and wheat was not the same among the major states; Punjab and Haryana continued to account for a much larger share in the procurement of these two foodgrains, while the same was very low in some major states. However, the state-wise concentration of procurement of paddy and wheat has diffused over time.

The descriptive analysis on the relationship between the level of procurement and farm income of the two selected crops, paddy and wheat, shows that the states which have the procurement percentage above the national average also have higher farm income than other states. The regression analysis carried out to measure the exact impact of public procurement on farm income suggests that every 1 per cent increase in procurement has increased farm income by about INR 221 per acre for paddy and about INR 100 per acre for wheat during the period of analysis. The regression analysis also suggests that the increased procurement in relation to its total production for each state is more important than the absolute quantity of procurement in bringing about enhanced farm income from both paddy and wheat.

This study clearly suggests that farm income can be increased significantly by raising public procurement of paddy and wheat. Farmers from Punjab and Haryana are able to reap better income mainly because of the high levels of public procurement of these crops. However, the 'Situation Assessment Survey of Agricultural Household' carried out at the all-India level during January to December 2013 underlines the pitiable condition of public procurement system in India (NSSO-SAS, 2014). The survey has mentioned that only about 17 per cent of paddy and about 19 per cent of wheat was sold to government agencies, including cooperatives. About 70 per cent of paddy and 73 per cent of wheat was sold to local private traders and mandis. Farmers are forced to sell their crops to local traders mainly because of non-availability of a procurement system. Without making assured arrangements for procurement and its infrastructure, the increased MSPs announced periodically every year will not be useful to farmers at all. Since farmers are exploited by traders and middlemen in the open market, the central and state governments must make all efforts to strengthen the public procurement system in every part of the country. The procurement of paddy and wheat is heavily concentrated in a few states presently which should be streamlined by covering all the states where adequate surplus exists. In those places/regions where establishing a procurement centre is not economically viable for the government, arrangements should be made to procure the foodgrains and other commodities through 'mobile procurement facility', where officials with trucks can visit different places periodically on a pre-scheduled day and time to procure the foodgrains during harvesting season. The government should also make an effort to bring out an act giving farmers the 'right to sell at MSP' (Narayanamoorthy and Alli, 2017). Besides establishing permanent procurement centres in each district headquarters, the government can also think of establishing procurement centres for some stipulated cropped areas in each state. The policymakers must also realize that without strengthening the public procurement and market infrastructure in every part of India, the ambitious goal of doubling of farmers' income by 2022–3 cannot be achieved.

Bibliography

Acharya, S. S. 1997. 'Agricultural Price Policy and Development: Some Facts and Emerging Issues'. *Indian Journal of Agricultural Economics*, vol. 52, no. 1 (January–March), pp. 1–47.

Banerji, A., and J. V. Meenakshi. 2004. 'Buyer Collusion and Efficiency of Government Intervention in Wheat Markets in Northern India: An Asymmetric Structural Actions Analysis'. *American Journal of Agricultural Economics*, vol. 86, no. 1, pp. 236–53.

Bhalla, G. S., and G. Singh. 2012. *Economic Liberalisation and Indian Agriculture: A District-Level Study*. Sage Publications India Private Limited, New Delhi.

CACP (Commission for Agricultural Costs and Prices). Various years. *Report of the Commission for Agricultural Costs and Prices*. Ministry of Agriculture, Government of India, New Delhi.

———. 2010. 'Understanding the Nature and Causes of Food Inflation'. Economic and Political Weekly, vol. 44, no. 9, pp. 10–13.

———. 2012a. 'Development Policies and Agricultural Markets'. Economic and Political Weekly, vol. 47, no. 52, pp. 53–63.

———. 2012b. *Report on Price Policy for Kharif Crops of 2011–2012 Season.* Ministry of Agriculture, Government of India, New Delhi.

Chand, R., R. Saxena, and S. Rana. 2015. 'Estimates and Analysis of Farm Income in India: 1983–84 to 2011–12'. *Economic and Political Weekly,* vol. 40, no. 22, pp. 139–45.

Chatterjee, S., and D. Kapur. 2016. *Understanding Price Variation in Agricultural Commodities in India: MSP, Government Procurement, and Agriculture Markets.* India Policy Forum, NCAER, New Delhi.

Deshpande, R. S. 1996. 'Demand and Supply of Agricultural Commodities: A Review'. *Indian Journal of Agricultural Economics,* vol. 51, nos 1–2 (January–June), pp. 270–87.

Gaiha, R., and V. S. Kulkarni. 2005. *Foodgrain Surpluses, Yields and Prices in India, Global Forum on Agriculture: Policy Coherence for Development.* Organized by UECD, Paris, France.

GoI (Government of India). Various years. *Bulletin on Food Statistics.* Ministry of Consumer Affairs, Food and Public Distribution, Government of India, New Delhi.

———. 2007. *Report of the Expert Group on Agricultural Indebtedness* (Chairman: R. Radhakrishna). Ministry of Finance, Government of India, New Delhi.

———. 2014. *Pricing of Agricultural Produce,* Sixteenth Report of the Committee on Agriculture (2013–14). Lok Sabha Secretariat Government of India, New Delhi.

Kallummal, M., and K. S. Srinivasan. 2007. *The Dynamics of Farmers Market: A Case of 'Uzhavar Sandhai' of Tamil Nadu.* Make Trade Fair Campaign, CENTAD, New Delhi.

Krishnamurthy, M. 2012. 'States of Wheat: The Changing Dynamics of Public Procurement in Madhya Pradesh'. *Economic and Political Weekly,* vol. 47, no. 52, pp. 72–83.

MoA&FW (Ministry of Agriculture and Farmers' Welfare). 2016. *State of India Agriculture: 2015–16.* Government of India, New Delhi.

Narayanamoorthy, A. 2006. 'State of India's Farmers'. *Economic and Political Weekly,* vol. 41, no. 6 (11 February), pp. 471–3.

———. 2007. 'Deceleration in Agricultural Growth: Technology Fatigue or Policy Fatigue'. *Economic and Political Weekly,* vol. 42, no. 25 (23 June), pp. 2375–9.

———. 2011. 'Development and Composition of Irrigation in India: Temporal Trends and Regional Patterns'. *Irrigation and Drainage*, vol. 60, no. 4, pp. 431–45.

———. 2013. 'Profitability in Crops Cultivation in India: Some Evidence from Cost of Cultivation Survey Data'. *Indian Journal of Agricultural Economics*, vol. 68, no. 1 (January–March), pp. 104–21.

———. 2017. 'Farm Income in India: Myths and Realities'. *Indian Journal of Agricultural Economics*, vol. 72, no. 1 (January–March), pp. 49–75.

Narayanamoorthy, A., and P. Alli. 2017. 'Loan Waiver Can't Fix Farmers Problems'. *The Hindu Business Line*, 11 July, p. 9.

Narayanamoorthy, A., P. Alli, and S. K. Beero. 2013. 'Agricultural Market Access, Infrastructure and Value of Output Nexus: A District-Level Study'. *Indian Journal of Agricultural Marketing*, vol. 27, no. 3 (September–December), pp. 75–93.

Narayanamoorthy, A., and R. Suresh. 2012. 'Agricultural Price Policy in India: Has It Benefitted Paddy Farmers?'. *Indian Journal of Agricultural Marketing*, vol. 26, no. 3 (September–December), pp. 87–106.

———. 2013. 'An Uncovered Truth in Fixation of MSP for Crops in India'. *Review of Development and Change*, vol. 18, no. 1 (January–June), pp. 53–62.

NITI Aayog. 2015. *Raising Agricultural Productivity and Making Farming Remunerative to Farmers.* Government of India, New Delhi.

———. 2016. *Evaluation Report of Efficacy of Minimum Support Prices (MSP) on Farmers.* Development Monitoring and Evaluation Office, New Delhi.

NSSO-SAS (National Sample Survey Office-Situation Assessment Survey). 2014. *Key Indicators of Situations of Agricultural Households in India*, 70th Round. Ministry of Statistics and Programme Implementation, Government of India, New Delhi, May.

Pathak, Vikas. 2017. 'Maximum Support, Maximum Price'. *The Hindu*, 15 July, p. 11.

Rao, N. Chandrasekhara, and S. Mahendra Dev. 2010. 'Agricultural Price Policy, Farm Profitability and Food Security'. *Economic and Political Weekly*, vol. 45, nos 26 and 27 (June), pp. 174–82.

RBI (Reserve Bank of India). 2015. *Handbook on Statistics of Indian Economy, 2014–15*. Mumbai, India.

Schultz, T. W. 1964. *Transforming Traditional Agriculture.* Yale University Press, New Haven, U. S. A.

Sen, Abhijit. 2016. 'Some Reflections on Agrarian Prospects'. *Economic and Political Weekly*, vol. 51, no. 8 (20 February), pp. 12–15.

Sen, Abhijit, and M. S. Bhatia. 2004. *State of the Indian Farmer: Cost of Cultivation and Farm Income in India*. Academic Foundation, New Delhi.

Singh, R., U. S. Mehta, G. Shukla, and N. K. Singh. 2015. *Minimum Support Price and Farmers' Income*. CUTS International, Jaipur, India.

PART V

INPUT USE, INFRASTRUCTURE, AND FARM INCOME

11

Rural Infrastructure and Agricultural Output Nexus

The nexus between infrastructure development and sustained output growth has been documented by many global empirical studies (Aschauer, 1989; Canning, 1998; Calderon and Chong, 2004) and worldwide reviews (Sawada, 2000; Asian Development Bank, Japan Bank for International Cooperation, and World Bank, 2005; Estache, Perelman, and Trujillo, 2005; Pinstrup-Andersen and Shimokawa, 2006). Cross-country analyses have also documented strong linkages between infrastructure and agricultural output growth. For example, using cross-sectional data for 47 less developed countries, including India, Antle (1983) found a strong and positive relationship between infrastructure development and aggregate agricultural productivity. Using annual data for 58 countries, Binswanger et al. (1987) report a positive and significant correlation between road development and aggregate crop output. These views have been substantiated by many Asian studies (Ruttan, 2002; Mundlak, Larson, and Butzer, 2004).

Studies from Indian settings also document evidence of positive linkages between various types of infrastructure and agricultural output growth (Antle, 1984). Rural infrastructure (both physical and institutional) such as irrigation, watershed development, rural electrification, roads, markets, credit institutions, rural literacy, agricultural research, and extension together play a key role in determining the agricultural output in India. For instance, irrigation infrastructure increases land use intensity and CI, and provides incentives to farmers to use yield increasing inputs, and thus results in higher agricultural output (Dhawan, 1988; Shah, 1993; Vaidyanathan, 1999; Narayanamoorthy and Deshpande, 2005). Rural electrification increases the energization of pump sets, which helps to increase the irrigated area using groundwater; the output of crops cultivated under groundwater irrigation is always higher than those under canal or tank irrigation, because of its better reliability and controllability (Barnes and Binswanger, 1986; Dhawan, 1988; Vaidyanathan et al., 1994; Shah, Singh, Mukherji, 2006). Rural roads increase the diffusion of agricultural technology by improving access to markets, enhance more efficient allocation of resources, reduce the transaction costs, as well as help farmers realize better input and output prices (Ahmed and Donovan, 1992; ESCAP, 2000; van de Walle, 2002). Improved road infrastructure also increases the transport facility through which rural farm households are able to get better health care, education, and credit facility. Rural–urban linkages are developed through road development, which also helps in strengthening the backward and forward linkages in the agricultural sector.

Institutional infrastructure, such as markets and credit facility, also plays a pivotal role in the growth of the agricultural sector (Binswanger, Khandker, and Rosenzweig, 1993). Better access to institutional credit reduces the cost of borrowing (Ramachandran and Swaminathan, 2002) and increases farmers' investments in production durables such as bullocks, tractors, and implements (Rosenzweig and Wolpin, 1993). Better access to markets bolsters farm productivity and profitability (Ahmed and Hossain, 1990; Ali and Pernia, 2003). However, as pointed out by Binswanger, Khandker, and Rosenzweig (1993), the rural infrastructure package as a whole matters, some elements being more important than others; and the overall impact of infrastructure on output is more pronounced in a better endowed region than in a poorly endowed one.

The above-mentioned stance is corroborated by other Indian studies which document evidence of strong complementarities between various forms of rural infrastructure and their linkages to output growth. For example, using Indian state-level time-series data for

1957–91, Datt and Ravallion (1998) show that states with better initial endowments of physical and human infrastructure (towards the early 1960s) achieved higher rates of agricultural output growth than poorly endowed states; higher initial irrigation, higher initial literacy, and lower initial infant mortality, all contributed to higher long-term growth rates. Using state-level data for 1970–93 in India, Fan, Hazell, and Thorat (1999; 2000) studied the relationship between government expenditures on agricultural research and development, irrigation, roads, education, power, soil and water conservation, rural development spending on agricultural growth, and rural poverty. The study concludes that improved rural infrastructure and technology have all contributed to agricultural growth, but their impacts have varied by settings (Fan, Hazell, and Thorat, 2000: 1050).

> Government expenditures on roads and R&D [research and development] have by far the largest impact on poverty reduction and growth in agricultural productivity; they are attractive win-win strategies. Government spending on education has the third largest impact on rural poverty and productivity growth. Irrigation investment has had only modest impacts on growth in agricultural productivity and rural poverty reduction, even after allowing for trickle-down benefits.

A study by Bhatia (1999) shows that Indian states with highest rural infrastructure index (a composite measure for rural electrification, roads, transport, health, irrigation, farm credit, fertilizer, and agricultural marketing, research, and extension) such as Punjab, Haryana, and Tamil Nadu have highest foodgrain productivity per hectare; and the states with the lowest index such as Rajasthan, Bihar, and Madhya Pradesh have lowest foodgrain productivity per hectare; the rural infrastructure index explains about 68 per cent of the variability in the yield in different states; and 10 per cent improvement in the rural infrastructure index in states with lower score would increase their foodgrain productivity by about 470 kg per hectare on average. This study thus establishes a strong relationship between the level of rural infrastructure development and the level of agricultural output.

The linkages between the Green Revolution technology package (irrigation, research and extension, improved varieties, and fertilizers) and other rural infrastructure and agricultural output/growth are well accepted, for India and elsewhere (Evenson and Gollin, 2003; Murgai, Ali, and Byerlee, 2001; Hussain and Hanjra, 2003; 2004; Saleth et al., 2003). Similar evidence distills from studies conducted at various spatial scales, such as the all-India level (Datt and Ravallion, 1998; Fan, Hazell, and Thorat, 1999; 2000); state-level (Ghosh, 2002; Bhatia, 1999); project/scheme level (Nayyer, 2002); taluka/sub-district level (Gidwani, 2002; Shah and Singh, 2004); and village level (Barnes and Binswanger, 1986; Ballabh and Padney, 1999). Likewise, studies using the typology of agro-ecological zones (AEZs) also provide further evidence on the varied contribution of infrastructure to agricultural output growth in India (Fan, Hazell, and Haque, 2000; Palmer-Jones, 2003; Saleth et al., 2003). Such studies typically divide the whole country into 14–19 or at best 45 zones. These studies are highly insightful, but the level of aggregation involved as well as non-correspondence of National Sample Survey data used for the AEZs remains problematic. India-wide studies on the infrastructure–output nexus, at lower spatial scale, are fewer. In particular, studies at the district level—the basic administrative unit—are either not there or there are few at best. Building on our earlier work (Bhattarai and Narayanamoorthy, 2003) and armed with comprehensive data sets, we aim to better understand the linkages between rural infrastructure and agricultural output levels of 256 districts in India for three time points. This framework offers several advantages.

Though empirical studies have clearly demonstrated the nexus between infrastructural development and agricultural growth, not many studies are available covering different time points, which also use a large number of districts, in recent times in the Indian context. One can understand whether the effect of infrastructure factors on agricultural output is increasing or decreasing over time only by covering different time points. The impact of infrastructure development (such as irrigation, road, rural electrification, schools/literacy, and others) on output cannot materialize instantaneously after making it available to the farmers because of the time lag involved in making adjustments to the factors of production. Therefore, while linking infrastructural development with agricultural output, one must allow for enough time lag for infrastructure variables so that their impact can be clearly measured. But, unfortunately, most of the available studies have analysed the impact of infrastructure factors on the agricultural growth/output without accounting for any time lag. This study covers these caveats and attempts to better understand the nexus between infrastructure development and agricultural output across 256 districts at three time points, 1970–1, 1980–1, and 1990–1. The overall goal of the study is to better understand the pattern of rural infrastructure development in India over the years to help identify future priorities. The main objectives of the study are: (*a*) to analyse the infrastructure and other characteristics of districts having above and below average agricultural output to help account for the differences in output; (*b*) to measure the independent relationship between infrastructure factors (irrigation, road, rural electrification, and rural literacy) and agricultural output (measured in terms of INR/hectare); and (*c*) to analyse the contribution of infrastructure and other factors to agricultural output over time.

The chapter is divided into six sections. Section two explains the data, variables, and method used in this study. The infrastructure and other characteristics of the districts are discussed in section three. The independent relationship between different infrastructure variables and agricultural output is discussed in section four while the contribution of infrastructure and other factors to agricultural output is analysed in section five. The conclusions and implications are presented in section six.

Data, Variables, and Method

The whole analysis of the study is based on secondary data. The study covers 256 districts drawn from 13 states in India.[1] These districts together accounted for nearly 93 per cent of the rural population

[1] These 256 districts have been selected at random. We could get comparable data only for these districts for all three time points and therefore, the remaining districts could not be included in the analysis. These districts have been selected from 13 states namely Andhra Pradesh (16), Bihar (12), Gujarat (18), Haryana (7), Karnataka (18), Madhya Pradesh (43), Maharashtra (24), Orissa (10), Punjab (11), Rajasthan (26), Tamil Nadu (11), Uttar Pradesh (47), and West Bengal (13).

in 1999–2000 and for more than 80 per cent of the cropped area in India. The data for this study has been compiled from various sources. Data on irrigated area has been compiled from various issues of *Indian Agricultural Statistics* published by the Ministry of Agriculture, Government of India. District-wise data on VAO of 35 crops (at 1990–3 prices),[2] FERT, and cropping intensity (CI) have been compiled from Bhalla and Singh (2001). Data on rural literacy, schooling facility, availability of pucca road, and villages electrified have been compiled/computed from various issues of *Census of India* for the years 1971, 1981, and 1991.

Agricultural output is determined by a number of infrastructure and other growth-related factors. However, due to data constraint, the study uses a total of eight variables for the analysis (see Table 11.1). Of these, five are treated as infrastructure variables (IRRI, ROAD, ELE, LITE, and SCHOOL—see Table 11.1 for the descriptions of these variables), while the remaining three are treated as growth-related variables (FERT, CI, and VAO). The rationale for using these variables is as follows.

The VAO, defined as the value of output in INR per hectare, is the dependent variable in the analysis. All the variables used in the study (both infrastructure and other growth variables) are expected to positively influence VAO for all three time points. The variable IRRI, defined as the percentage of irrigated area to cropped area, is one of the key infrastructure variables for increasing crop output and thus, IRRI is used along with other variables in the regression analysis.[3] Also, ROAD (percentage of villages having pucca road in each district) is another important infrastructure variable, expected to increase the growth of agriculture through improved transport facility

[2] As mentioned by Bhalla and Singh (2001), VOP (at 1990–3 prices) has been estimated by covering the production of 35 important crops that accounted for over 95 per cent of the gross VOP at the country level. The detailed method followed for estimating VAO including the data sources is systematically presented in Bhalla and Singh (2001).

[3] The importance of irrigation infrastructure in increasing the crop output has been corroborated by a number of studies using micro- as well as macro-level data in India at different time points. Readers are requested to see Dhawan (1988) and Vaidyanathan et al. (1994) for more details on this.

Table 11.1 Descriptive Statistics of Variables Used in the Study on Rural Infrastructure

Variable	Description	Averages (N = 256)			
		Unit	1970–1	1980–1	1990–1
VAO	Value of agricultural output (in 1990–3 prices)*	INR/ha	3,997.18 (3,392.61)	5,239.37 (2,591.58)	6,990.84 (3,482.49)
IRRI	Ratio of irrigated area to cropped area#	%	23.51 (20.92)	30.15 (23.09)	37.03 (25.14)
ROAD	Road facility**	%	28.72 (13.19)	37.92 (22.40)	45.95 (23.70)
ELE	Villages electrified**	%	23.25 (23.58)	53.28 (27.46)	80.38 (21.90)
SCHOOL	Villages having school facility**	%	60.12 (18.86)	74.79 (17.75)	80.63 (14.96)
LITE	Rural literacy**	%	21.23 (8.01)	27.42 (11.73)	41.95 (12.52)
FERT	Fertilizer use*	kg/ha	17.36 (18.08)	39.18 (44.87)	76.25 (66.40)
CI	Cropping intensity#	%	119.26 (18.45)	126.28 (19.08)	131.99 (23.07)

Sources: *Bhalla and Singh (2001); ***Census of India, Primary Census Abstract*, India (various years); #GoI (various years).
Note: Figures in brackets are standard deviations.

as well as via forward and backward linkages between agriculture and other sectors. Likewise, ELE (percentage of villages electrified) is expected to increase the energization of pump sets through which irrigated area under groundwater can be increased, which is again an important factor for increasing agricultural output. Human capital variables, SCHOOL (per cent of villages having school facility), and LITE (per cent of rural literacy) are expected to improve the knowledge of farmer households and enhance the diffusion of improved agricultural technology, both of which are essential to increase agricultural output (Narayanamoorthy, 2000). Yield-increasing inputs such as fertilizer, improved seeds, and pesticides as well as use of machines such as tractors all play a key role in increasing agricultural output. However, due to data constraints, none of the yield-increasing inputs could not be included in the analysis except FERT. The inclusion of FERT is a reasonable proxy, since the other input factors tend to move in tandem with it. Cropping intensity, defined as the ratio of GCA to net cropped area in percentage term, explains how intensively crops are cultivated in a year. Since agricultural output is determined by the intensity of crop cultivation, CI has also been included for analysis along with other defined variables.

In order to study the relationship between infrastructure development and agricultural output, both descriptive and regression analyses have been carried out. To understand the characteristics of the districts, all 256 districts have been divided into two groups, namely, districts with above average (AA districts) VAO; and districts with below average (BA districts) VAO, at each time point. This analysis is expected to show how the districts rank in terms of their agricultural output, FERT, CI, and other characteristics of interest, at each time point. In order to study the independent linkages between various infrastructure factors and agricultural output, the following eight univariate regressions are estimated, taking the VAO as dependent variable and irrigation, road, literacy rate, and rural electrification as independent variables separately, with and without time lags, for all three time points.

$$VAO = a + b1\ IRRI \tag{1}$$
$$VAO = a + b1\ IRRI_{t-10} \tag{2}$$
$$VAO = a + b1\ ROAD \tag{3}$$
$$VAO = a + b1\ ROAD_{t-10} \tag{4}$$
$$VAO = a + b1\ ELEC \tag{5}$$
$$VAO = a + b1\ ELEC_{t-10} \tag{6}$$
$$VAO = a + b1\ LITE \tag{7}$$
$$VAO = a + b1\ LITE_{t-10} \tag{8}$$

The equations (1), (3), (5), and (7) explore the independent relationship between VAO and infrastructure variable without giving any time lag, while equations (2), (4), (6), and (8) are estimated by treating infrastructure as lagged variables (by giving a 10-year time lag). As mentioned earlier, since the impact of infrastructure development cannot be seen instantaneously after providing it, infrastructure is used as a lagged variable to capture the real impact of it on the VAO.

$$\text{VAO} = a + b1\ \text{ROAD} + b2\ \text{LITE} + b3\ \text{ELEC} + b4\ \text{IRRI} + b5\ \text{FERT} + b6\ \text{CI} \quad (9)$$

$$\text{VAO} = a + b1\ \text{ROAD}_{t\text{-}10} + b2\ \text{LITE}_{t\text{-}10} + b3\ \text{ELEC}_{t\text{-}10} + b4\ \text{IRRI}_{t\text{-}10} + b5\ \text{FERT} + b6\ \text{CI} \quad (10)$$

Besides studying the independent relationship between each infrastructure variable and the agricultural output, the above-mentioned two multivariate regressions, equations (9) and (10) are also estimated to know the contribution of each variable factor to the agricultural output, wherein FERT[4] and CI are included along with other variables. Again, equation (9) is estimated without any lagged variable, while equation (10) is estimated treating all infrastructures as lagged variables but not the technology variables FERT and CI. It is expected that the impact of infrastructure variables on agricultural output will be stronger when using them as lagged variables in the regression analysis.

Infrastructural Characteristics of the Districts

How the AA and BA districts rank in terms of infrastructural parameters over time is evident from data presented in Table 11.2. It is clear that there has been an appreciable improvement in infrastructure development such as irrigation, school facility including literacy rate, road, and rural electrification across the districts between 1970–1 and 1990–1. While IRRI increased from 23.51 per cent in 1970–1 to 37.03 per cent in 1990–1, ROAD increased from 28.72 per cent to around 46 per cent during the same period. Similarly, LITE increased from 21.23 per cent to 42 per cent, and the coverage of ELE increased from 23.25 per cent to 80.38 per cent during this period. Along with the infrastructural development, output-determining factors such

[4] The contribution of fertilizer to agricultural output at different time points is clearly analysed by Vaidyanathan (1993).

Table 11.2 Characteristics of the Districts Classified Based on Value of Agricultural Output

Classification	No. of districts	VAO (INR/ha)	IRRI (%)	SCHOOL (%)	ROAD (%)	ELE (%)	LITE (%)	FERT (kg/ha)	CI (%)
1970–1:									
AA Districts	105	6,099	36.39	64.84	36.02	33.21	24.65	28.04	126.07
		(44.19)	(23.46)	(17.92)	(13.95)	(26.55)	(8.17)	(20.01)	(20.31)
BA Districts	151	2,535	14.56	56.84	23.65	16.32	18.85	9.94	114.52
		(885)	(12.86)	(18.86)	(9.87)	(18.39)	(7.01)	(11.97)	(15.41)
All Average	256	3,997	23.51	60.12	28.72	23.25	21.23	17.36	119.26
		(33.93)	(20.92)	(18.86)	(13.19)	(23.57)	(8.02)	(18.08)	(18.44)
1980–1:									
AA Districts	110	10,099	47.30	76.70	53.17	68.18	31.67	65.08	135.72
		(2,854)	(22.19)	(19.68)	(22.94)	(24.63)	(13.62)	(33.87)	(20.28)
BA Districts	146	3,472	17.23	73.23	26.52	42.05	24.22	19.67	119.16
		(1,016)	(13.27)	(13.27)	(13.39)	(23.98)	(8.87)	(42.26)	(14.58)
All Average	256	5,239	30.15	74.79	37.97	53.28	27.42	39.18	126.28
		(2,592)	(23.09)	(17.75)	(22.40)	(27.46)	(11.73)	(44.87)	(19.08)

1990–1:									
AA Districts	108	10,291	55.70	80.85	60.44	84.92	45.54	114.51	143.19
		(2,679)	(24.62)	(16.29)	(24.20)	(20.33)	(12.99)	(47.65)	(24.85)
BA Districts	148	4,583	23.40	80.47	35.36	77.07	39.22	48.33	123.83
		(1,405)	(14.55)	(13.95)	(16.75)	(22.47)	(11.52)	(64.31)	(17.74)
All Average	256	6,991	37.03	80.63	45.94	80.38	41.94	76.25	131.99
		(3,482)	(25.13)	(14.95)	(23.70)	(21.90)	(12.52)	(66.40)	(23.07)

Sources: Bhalla and Singh (2001); *Census of India*, *Primary Census Abstract*, India (various years); and GoI (various years).

Notes: AA: above average; BA: below average; figures in brackets are standard deviations.

as FERT and CI have also substantially increased between 1970–1 and 1990–1. All these amply suggest that rural infrastructure has expanded considerably between the 1970s and 1990s in India.

As regards the characteristics of the districts, a distinct difference in all the parameters between the AA and BA districts across all three time points is evident. Among the five infrastructure variables, IRRI, SCHOOL, ROAD, ELEC, and LITE, the difference between AA and BA districts is more pronounced in IRRI for all the three time points. While the difference between AA and BA districts in IRRI was 21.83 percentage points in 1970–1, the same increased to 32.30 percentage points in 1990–1. This suggests that districts having higher agricultural output invariably have higher irrigation coverage as well. Following irrigation, the difference is found to be relatively large in road infrastructure, which has empirically been proven to be a crucial factor in determining agricultural output (see Binswanger et al., 1993; Fan, Hazell, and Thorat, 1999; and van de Walle, 2002). However, in the case of school facility and literacy rate, the difference between AA and BA districts are minimum, suggesting that the human development infrastructure has not changed very much between the districts having higher and lower VAO. Apart from variation in infrastructural development, significant difference is also noticed in fertilizer use between the AA and BA districts at all three time points, suggesting that VAO is highly related to the use of fertilizer.[5] On the whole, though the infrastructure and other characteristics of the districts having above average VAO are better than those districts having output below average VAO, one may not be able to judge decisively whether infrastructure plays a greater role than other factors from this descriptive analysis. Therefore, the independent relationship between infrastructure variables and agricultural output using univariate regression analysis is investigated in the following section.

[5] As a part of the analysis we have computed the correlation matrix for all the variables so as to understand their interrelationship at different time points. We have observed significant correlation between VAO and the use of fertilizer at all the three time points. However, the correlation matrix results are omitted here for the sake of brevity.

Infrastructure and Agricultural Output Nexus

The impact of infrastructure development on agricultural output would likely vary for each of the infrastructural variables because the role played by each infrastructural element is different. It is expected that the role played by the irrigation infrastructure will be totally different from the role of roads on agricultural output. Irrigation directly helps to increase crop output by reducing moisture stress, whereas roads help to increase the VOP by providing transport and market accessibility as well as enhancing more efficient allocation of resources. Therefore, the independent relationship between each infrastructural variable and agricultural output is investigated using the eight univariate regression equations mentioned earlier. As noted elsewhere in the chapter, the impact of infrastructure development on output cannot materialize instantaneously after making it available to farmers because of the time lag involved in making adjustments to the factors of production. Generally, farmers take some time to respond to the available infrastructure because of resource and other constraints. Therefore, in order to capture the real effect of infrastructure variable on agricultural output, univariate regression is estimated both with and without time lag for infrastructural variables.

The results of regression presented in Table 11.3 clearly show that among the four infrastructure variables, the impact of IRRI on agricultural output appears to be stronger than the remaining three variables ROAD, LITE, and ELE. Interestingly, only in the case of IRRI, both the R^2 as well as the regression coefficients have consistently increased from 1970–1 to 1990–1. For instance, the regression coefficient increased from 71.57 in 1970–1 to 97.69 in 1990–1, while the R^2 of the same improved from 0.20 to 0.50. This higher level of R^2 (0.50) arrived at from 1990–1 data suggests that 50 per cent of variation in agricultural output is due to variation in the level of irrigation. The regression estimated by treating ROAD as an independent variable also turns out to be significant in impacting VAO, but its impact (coefficient) on VAO has not improved over time. This implies that the impact of ROAD on VAO is not consistently higher as in the case of irrigation, which is plausible because the inter-district variation in ROAD might have increased over the years. The regression results of the two other infrastructure

Table 11.3 Agricultural Output and Infrastructure Development Nexus: Univariate Regression Results

Year	Constant	Coefficient	R^2	Adjusted R^2	F value	D–W stat
		VAO = a + b1 IRRI … (1)				
1970–1	2,314.37 (8.06)	71.57 (7.84)[a]	0.20	0.19	61.41[a]	1.85
1980–1	2,888.09 (15.02)	77.98 (15.39)[a]	0.48	0.48	236.97[a]	1.34
1990–1	3,373.87 (12.23)	97.69 (15.84)[a]	0.50	0.50	250.95[a]	1.36
		VAO = a + b1 $IRRI_{t-10}$ … (2)				
1980–1	3,146.22 (18.51)	89.03 (16.46)[a]	0.52	0.51	271.07[a]	1.44
1990–1	3,708.60 (14.92)	108.86 (16.62)[a]	0.52	0.52	276.10[a]	1.42
		VAO = a + b1 ROAD … (3)				
1970–1	1,112.30 (2.37)	100.44 (6.76)[a]	0.15	0.15	45.70[a]	1.81
1980–1	2,321.44 (9.71)	76.84 (14.16)[a]	0.44	0.44	200.55[a]	1.44
1990–1	2,964.81 (7.75)	87.63 (11.84)[a]	0.37	0.35	140.17[a]	1.22
		VAO = a + b1 $ROAD_{t-10}$ … (4)				
1980–1	1,769.65 (5.82)	119.86 (12.27)[a]	0.37	0.37	150.55[a]	1.46
1990–1	3,286.17 (9.82)	97.56 (12.85)[a]	0.39	0.39	165.04[a]	1.31
		VAO = a + b1 ELE … (5)				
1970–1	3,141.69 (10.88)	36.79 (4.22)[a]	0.07	0.07	17.76[a]	1.67
1980–1	2,533.64 (8.47)	50.79 (10.18)[a]	0.29	0.29	103.53[a]	1.32
1990–1	3,900.44 (4.84)	38.45 (3.97)	0.06	0.06	15.78[a]	0.981

		$VAO = a + b1\ ELE_{t-10}$ … (6)				
1980–1	3,888.41 (20.08)	58.10 (9.92)[a]	0.28	0.28	98.47[a]	1.15
1990–1	3,678.82 (8.85)	62.17 (8.96)[a]	0.24	0.24	80.34[a]	1.12
		$VAO = a + b1\ LITE$ … (7)				
1970–1	1,485.77 (2.57)	118.28 (4.64)[a]	0.08	0.07	21.53[a]	1.61
1980–1	2,661.09 (7.12)	94.02 (7.50)[a]	0.18	0.18	56.20[a]	1.25
1990–1	2,874.01 (4.02)	98.15 (6.01)[a]	0.13	0.13	36.13[a]	1.04
		$VAO = a + b1\ LITE_{t-10}$ … (8)				
1980–1	1,974.32 (4.88)	153.78 (8.62)[a]	0.23	0.22	74.29[a]	1.16
1990–1	4,088.64 (7.88)	105.83 (6.08)[a]	0.13	0.12	36.99[a]	1.08

Source: Computed using data from Bhalla and Singh (2001); *Census of India*, *Primary Census Abstract*, India (various years); and GoI (various years).

Notes: a: significant at 1 per cent level; figures in brackets are 't' values.

variables ELE and LITE estimated separately show a weak relationship with VAO. The R^2 of regression estimated using ELE as independent variable explains only 6 and 7 per cent of the variation in agricultural output in 1970–1 and 1990–1 respectively. Similarly, the value of R^2 is also relatively low for regression treating LITE as an independent variable, which suggests that literacy independently (without other determining factors) will only have a limited role in impacting agricultural output.

The regression results estimated by treating infrastructure as a lagged variable appear to be better than the results arrived at without allowing for time lag in all cases (see Table 11.3). In the case of IRRI, the magnitude of regression coefficient (along with R^2) increased from 97.69 (when irrigation is not used as lagged variable) to 108.86 when IRRI is used as lagged variable in 1990–1. Similarly, the coefficient of ROAD also increased from 87.63 to 97.56 while estimating regression with a 10-year time lag in 1990–1 [see the results of equations (3) and (4) in Table 11.3]. Similar results are also arrived at while estimating regression by treating ELE and LITE as lagged variables. This was expected because the impact of any infrastructural development on agricultural output would reflect only after a certain time lag. On the whole, the univariate regression results suggest that irrigation and road infrastructure independently play a greater role in impacting the VOP than the other infrastructure variables taken for the analysis—all variables matter, *but* differently.

Contribution of Infrastructure and Other Factors to Output

Having studied the independent linkages between agricultural output and rural infrastructure development, an attempt is made to study the contribution of infrastructure and other factors to agricultural output using multivariate regression analysis. Here, since agricultural output is also determined by yield-determining factors such as fertilizer and CI, these two factors are included along with four infrastructure variables in the regression model so as to capture the impact of each variable on agricultural output. Specifically, the following four questions are probed using the multivariate regression analysis: (*a*) What is the role of infrastructural factors vis-à-vis other factors in determining agricultural output? (*b*) Does the role of infrastructural factors increase in impacting the VOP over time? (*c*) Which is the most important infrastructure variable in determining VOP? (*d*) How does the impact on agricultural output change when lagged infrastructure variables are used in the regression analysis?

The results of the multivariate regression model estimated using both infrastructure and other yield-determining factors are presented in Table 11.4. The coefficients of regression suggest that except the rural electrification variable,[6] all other infrastructure variables do significantly influence VOP at all three time points taken for the analysis. Though the coefficient of fertilizer is also highly significant in determining the output, especially in 1980–1 and 1990–1, its magnitude is relatively lower than the infrastructure variables in all three time points. The regression results pertaining to the year 1990–1 suggest that a 1 per cent increase in IRRI would increase VOP by nearly INR 62, but in the case of LITE and ROAD the output would increase only by INR 43 and INR 37 respectively. In contrast, the regression coefficient of FERT suggests that one unit increase in FERT use would increase agricultural output only by about INR 9 during the year 1990–1. This trend is almost the same in all the three time points. The significant regression coefficient of infrastructure variables seems to suggest that infrastructure development remains important for increasing agricultural output.

Whether the role of infrastructure variables increases in determining the output over time is another question studied using

[6] The coefficient of the variable ELE turned out to be negative, but not significantly (except for 1970–1) in our analysis. Some of the earlier studies have also found a negative relationship between ELE and VAO (see Evenson, 1986). This could probably be due to two reasons. First, the effect of rural electrification might have been captured by IRRI and CI due to the endogenity problem. Second, rural electrification is basically used as a proxy variable for energization of pump sets but the vague definition of rural electrification followed in India may not have captured the complete effect of it. Instead of rural electrification, if one uses electricity availability for agricultural purpose in terms of hours as well as the intensity of pump sets in each district, the relationship might turn out to be significant in impacting VAO. Unfortunately, we could not use these variables in the analysis because of data constraints.

Table 11.4 Infrastructure and Other Factors' Contribution to Agricultural Output: Multivariate Regression Results

Independent Variables	Without Lagged Infrastructure Variables			With Lagged Infrastructure Variables	
	1970–1	1980–1	1990–1	1980–1	1990–1
CI	5.24 (0.42)	4.13 (0.56)	8.71 (1.13)	9.53 (1.35)	7.26 (0.96)
FERT	2.73 (0.17)	11.91 (4.48)[a]	9.43 (3.80)[a]	11.78 (4.63)[a]	9.10 (3.64)[a]
ELEC	–34.87 (–2.83)[a]	–4.79 (–0.76)	–11.42 (1.42)	—	—
IRRI	58.15 (3.94)[a]	43.29 (5.86)[a]	61.95 (7.55)[a]	—	—
LITE	61.67 (2.26)[b]	45.63 (4.67)[a]	43.56 (3.45)[a]	—	—
ROAD	81.01 (3.70)[a]	32.65 (4.06)[a]	37.36 (4.38)[a]	—	—
$ELEC_{t-10}$	—	—	—	–9.53 (–1.52)	–9.00 (–1.05)
$IRRI_{t-10}$	—	—	—	46.02 (6.66)[a]	61.82 (7.68)[a]
$ROAD_{t-10}$	—	—	—	51.99 (4.68)[a]	45.72 (4.21)[a]
$LITE_{t-10}$	—	—	—	84.30 (6.09)[a]	42.51 (3.16)[a]
Constant	–868.17 (–0.59)	709.61 (0.80)	203.38 (0.80)	–875.53 (1.01)	627.93 (0.67)
R^2	0.27	0.65	0.63	0.68	0.64
Adjusted R^2	0.25	0.64	0.62	0.67	0.63
F value	15.47[a]	77.33[a]	71.58[a]	86.69[a]	74.43[a]
D–W stat	1.99	1.78	1.95	1.98	1.85
N	256	256	256	256	256

Source: Bhalla and Singh (2001); *Census of India*, *Primary Census Abstract*, India (various years); and GoI (various years).

Note: Figures in brackets are 't' values; a and b are significant at 1 and 5 per cent levels.

the regression analysis. The regression coefficients of infrastructure variables do not show any clear picture on this. Though the coefficients of IRRI improved over time from 58.15 in 1970–1 to 61.95 in 1990–1, the same trend is not seen with the other infrastructure variables LITE and ROAD. In fact, the magnitude of regression coefficients of LITE and ROAD variables have reduced considerably over time. For example, the coefficients of ROAD declined from 81.01 to 37.36 between 1970–1 and 1990–1, while the coefficient of LITE declined from 61.67 to 43.56 during the same period. This could be due to two reasons. First, since VOP is also determined by seasonal variation (supply and demand factors) and other associated factors, the contribution of ROAD and LITE may have been affected by them. Second, the agricultural sector has been changing at a rapid pace since 1970–1 owing to the adoption of Green Revolution technologies and, therefore, one may not be able to see the same level of contribution by infrastructure factors to agricultural output at different time points. The impact could have been mediated by technology factors such as irrigation and modern varieties over time.

As mentioned earlier, the impact of each infrastructure variable on agricultural output is expected to be different. Therefore, it is interesting to identify the most crucial variable that determines agricultural output. The regression results reveal that the role played by each infrastructure variable considerably changes over time. During 1970–1, ROAD impacted the output more significantly followed by LITE and IRRI, but the trend changed during 1990–1, where IRRI became the most dominant factor followed by LITE and ROAD. This means that ROAD played a dominant role in determining VOP at the initial stage of the Green Revolution (during 1970–1), whereas IRRI started playing a dominant role during the second phase of the Green Revolution (during 1990–1). Similarly, rural literacy must have played a greater role during the initial phase of the GRP because of relatively less development of extension services, but its role might have changed in recent years because of significant development in the extension network of Indian agriculture. Another explanation could be that during the first phase of the GRP, a larger subset of schoolgoers were from farm households, whereas during the second phase, the landless households subset became larger, which may not have made any impact on VAO. This suggests that the role played by the infrastructure factors tend to vary over time because of simultaneous changes that are taking place in other factors determining agricultural output. The role of infrastructure factors also changes between different time points even when they are treated as lagged variables in the regression model, which further reinforces the point that the contribution of each infrastructure variable to agricultural output tends to change over time.

Conclusion and Policy Implications

It is widely believed that rural infrastructure remains under-provided in most parts of India and this hinders agricultural output growth. However, precise linkages between infrastructure and output growth remain debated. Against this backdrop, this chapter attempted to better understand the linkages between rural infrastructure development and agricultural output using cross-sectional data for 256 Indian districts drawn from 13 states at three time points: 1970–1, 1980–1, and 1990–1. Both descriptive and regression analyses were used to study the relationship. Descriptive analysis shows that the districts having VAO above the average are better placed in terms of rural infrastructure development (irrigation, road, literacy, school facility, rural electrification, fertilizer use) than other districts. The univariate regression analysis carried out to investigate the independent relationship between each infrastructure variable and the VAO shows that except rural electrification, the remaining three infrastructure factors (irrigation, roads, and literacy) appear to significantly explain the variation in output for all three time points; and, the impact of irrigation infrastructure on VOP appears to have increased over time. Multivariate regression analysis suggests that rural roads play a dominant role in increasing VOP, followed by literacy and irrigation during 1970–1, whereas irrigation played a dominant role in 1990–1. That is, while the regression coefficient of irrigation increased from 58.15 in 1970–1 to 61.95 in 1990–1, the coefficients of road and literacy declined considerably between the two time points. This also suggests that the role played by each infrastructure type changes over time. The impact of infrastructure variables on VOP turns out to be stronger when they are used as lagged variables in the regression analysis.

The study thus establishes strong linkages between rural infrastructure development and VAO. It also notes that large inequities in rural infrastructure exist among the districts studied. This implies significant scope for increasing agricultural output by improving rural infrastructure such as irrigation, roads, education, and electrification. While a mega-scale step-up in India's rural infrastructure remains warranted for almost all districts, 'one size fits all' solutions are unlikely to be optimal; rather a targeted approach might be more promising for enhancing agricultural output and growth. However, the right infrastructure mix for the backward districts remains unknown. Though this study does reveal the close nexus between different rural infrastructure and the VAO, the level of aggregation used (district-level data) enabled the determination of only broad infrastructural priorities for various areas. While irrigation emerges as a critical infrastructural priority, due to its key role in agricultural output growth in all areas, some areas may not be simply reachable or suitable for large-scale irrigation in future. Without irrigation, other infrastructure may perform poorly; watershed development and land and water conservation interventions, rainwater harvesting, no tillage method, mulching, and others may offer a promising alternative to irrigation development for such settings. To that end, studies using more disaggregated or micro-level data might be useful. Further research is needed for identifying water conservation alternatives and for selecting the right mix of complementary rural infrastructure suited to areas with limited scope for traditional irrigation.

Bibliography

Ahmed, R., and C. Donovan. 1992. *Issues of Infrastructural Development: A Synthesis of the Literature.* International Food Policy Research Institute, Washington, D. C., U. S. A.

Ahmed, R., and M. Hossain. 1990. *Development Impact of Rural Infrastructure in Bangladesh*, Research Report No. 83. International Food Policy Research Institute, Washington, D. C., U. S. A.

Ali, I., and E. M. Pernia. 2003. *Infrastructure and Poverty Reduction. What Is the Connection?* ERD Policy Brief Series No. 13. Asian Development Bank, Manila.

Antle, J. M. 1983. 'Infrastructure and Aggregate Agricultural Productivity: International Evidence'. *Economic Development and Cultural Change*, vol. 31, no. 3, pp. 609–19.

———. 1984. 'Human Capital, Infrastructure and Productivity of Indian Rice Farmers'. *Journal of Development Economics*, vol. 14, pp. 163–81.

Aschauer, D. A. 1989. 'Is Public Expenditure Productive?'. *Journal of Monetary Economics*, vol. 23, 177–200.

Asian Development Bank, Japan Bank for International Cooperation, and World Bank. 2005. *Connecting East Asia: A New Framework for Infrastructure*. Asian Development Bank, Manila.

Ballabh, V., and S. Pandey. 1999. 'Transition in Rice Production Systems in Eastern India: Evidence from Two Villages in Uttar Pradesh'. *Economic and Political Weekly*, vol. 34, no. 13 (27 March), pp. A11–16.

Barnes, D. F., and H. P. Binswanger. 1986. 'Impact of Rural Electrification and Infrastructure on Agricultural Changes'. *Economic and Political Weekly*, vol. 21, no. 1, pp. 26–34.

Bhalla, G. S., and G. Singh. 2001. *Indian Agriculture: Four Decades of Development*. Sage Publications Private Ltd, New Delhi.

Bhatia, M. S. 1999. 'Rural Infrastructure and Growth in Agriculture'. *Economic and Political Weekly*, vol. 34, no. 13 (27 March), pp. A43–8.

Bhattarai, M., and A. Narayanamoorthy. 2003. 'Impact of Irrigation on Rural Poverty: An Aggregate Panel-Data Analysis for India'. *Water Policy*, vol. 5, nos 5–6, pp. 443–58.

Binswanger, H. P., M. C. Vang, A. Bower, and Y. Mundlak. 1987. 'On Determinants of Cross-Country Aggregate Agriculture Supply'. *Journal of Econometrics*, vol. 36, no. 1, pp. 111–13.

Binswanger, H. P., S. R. Khandker, and M. R. Rosenzweig. 1993. 'How Infrastructure and Financial Institutions Affect Agricultural Output and Investment in India'. *Journal of Development Economics*, vol. 41, no. 2, pp. 337–66.

Calderon, C., and A. Chong. 2004. 'Volume and Quality of Infrastructure and the Distribution of Income: An Empirical Investigation'. *Review of Income and Wealth*, vol. 50, no. 1, pp. 87–106.

Canning, D. 1998. 'A Database of World Stocks of Infrastructure, 1950–95'. *World Bank Economic Review*, vol. 12, no. 3, pp. 529–47.

Datt, G., and M. Ravallion. 1998. 'Farm Productivity and Rural Poverty in India'. *The Journal of Development Studies*, vol. 34, no. 4, pp. 62–85.

Dhawan, B. D. 1988. *Irrigation in India's Agricultural Development: Productivity, Stability, Equity*. Sage Publications, New Delhi.

ESCAP (Economic and Social Commission for Asia and the Pacific). 2000. *Evaluation of Infrastructural Interventions for Rural Poverty Alleviation.* The United Nations Economic and Social Commission for Asia and the Pacific, Bangkok, Thailand.

Estache, A., S. Perelman, and I. Trujillo. 2005. *Infrastructure Performance and Reform in Developing and Transition Economies: Evidence from a Survey of Productivity Measures.* World Bank Policy Research Working Paper No. 3514. Washington, D. C., U. S. A.

Evenson, R. E. 1986. 'Infrastructure, Output Supply and Input Demand in Philippine Agriculture: Provisional Estimates'. *Journal of Philippine Development*, vol. 13, no. 23, pp. 62–76.

Evenson, R. E., and D. Gollin. 2003. 'Assessing the Impact of the Green Revolution: 1960 to 2000'. *Science*, vol. 300 (2 May), pp. 758–62.

Fan, S., P. Hazell, and T. Haque. 2000. 'Targeting Public Investments by Agro-ecological Zone to Achieve Growth and Poverty Alleviation Goals in Rural India'. *Food Policy*, vol. 25, no. 4, pp. 411–28.

Fan, S., P. Hazell, and S. K. Thorat. 1999. *Linkages between Government Spending, Growth, and Poverty in Rural India*, Research Report no. 110. International Food Policy Research Institute, Washington, D. C., U. S. A.

———. 2000. 'Government Spending, Growth and Poverty in Rural India'. *American Journal of Agricultural Economics*, vol. 82, no. 4, pp. 1038–51.

Ghosh, N. 2002. 'Infrastructure, Cost and Labour Income in Agriculture'. *Indian Journal of Agricultural Economics*, vol. 57, no. 2, pp. 153–68

Gidwani, V. 2002. 'The Unbearable Modernity of "Development"? Canal Irrigation and Development Planning in Western India'. *Progress in Planning*, vol. 58, no. 1, pp. 1–80.

GoI. Various years. *Indian Agricultural Statistics*. Ministry of Agriculture, New Delhi.

Hussain, I., and M. A. Hanjra. 2003. 'Does Irrigation Water Matter for Rural Poverty Alleviation? Evidence from South and South-East Asia'. *Water Policy*, vol. 5, nos 5–6, pp. 429–42.

———. 2004. 'Irrigation and Poverty Alleviation: Review of the Empirical Evidence'. *Irrigation and Drainage*, vol. 53, no. 1, pp. 1–15.

Mundlak, Y., D. Larson, and R. Butzer. 2004. 'Agricultural Dynamics in Thailand, Indonesia and the Philippines'. *The Australian Journal of Agricultural and Resource Economics*, vol. 48, no. 1, pp. 95–126.

Murgai, R., M. Ali, and D. Byerlee. 2001. 'Productivity Growth and Sustainability in Post Green-Revolution Agriculture: The Case of Indian and Pakistani Punjabs'. *World Bank Research Observer*, vol. 16, no. 2, pp. 199–218.

Narayanamoorthy, A. 2000. 'Farmers' Education and Productivity of Crops: A New Approach'. *Indian Journal of Agricultural Economics*, vol. 55, no. 3, pp. 511–20.

Narayanamoorthy, A., and R. S. Deshpande. 2005. *Where Water Seeps! Towards a New Phase in India's Irrigation Reforms*. Academic Foundation, New Delhi.

Nayyer, R. 2002. *The Contribution of Public Works and Other Labour-Based Infrastructure to Poverty Alleviation: The Indian Experience*. Issues in Employment and Poverty, Discussion Paper 3. ILO, Geneva.

Palmer-Jones, R. 2003. 'Agricultural Growth, Poverty Reduction and Agro-ecological Zones in India: An Ecological Fallacy?'. *Food Policy*, vol. 28, nos 5–6, pp. 423–31.

Pinstrup-Andersen, P., and S. Shimokawa. 2006. *Rural Infrastructure and Agricultural Development*. Paper for presentation at the Annual Bank Conference on Development Economics, Tokyo, Japan, May 29–30.

Ramachandran, V. K., and M. Swaminathan. 2002. 'Rural Banking and Landless Labour Households: Institutional Reform and Rural Credit Markets in India'. *Journal of Agrarian Change*, vol. 2, no. 4, pp. 502–44.

Rosenzweig, M. R., and K. I. Wolpin. 1993. 'Credit Market Constraints, Consumption Smoothing, and the Accumulation of Durable Production Assets in Low-Income Countries: Investments in Bullocks in India'. *Journal of Political Economy*, vol. 101, no. 2, pp. 223–44.

Ruttan, V. W. 2002. 'Productivity Growth in World Agriculture: Sources and Constraints'. *The Journal of Economic Perspectives*, vol. 16, no. 4, pp. 161–84.

Saleth, M. R., M. Samad, D. Molden, and I. Hussain. 2003. 'Water, Poverty and Gender: A Review of Issues and Policies'. *Water Policy*, vol. 5, nos 5–6, pp. 385–98.

Sawada, Y. 2000. 'Dynamic Poverty Problem and the Role of Infrastructure'. *JBIC Review*, vol. 3, no. 1, pp. 20–40.

Shah, T. 1993. *Groundwater Markets and Irrigation Development: Political Economy and Practical Policy*. Oxford University Press, New Delhi.

Shah, T., and O. P. Singh. 2004. 'Irrigation Development and Rural Poverty in Gujarat, India: A Disaggregated Analysis'. *Water International*, vol. 29, no. 2, pp. 167–77.

Shah, T., O. P. Singh, and A. Mukherji. 2006. 'Some Aspects of South Asia's Groundwater Irrigation Economy: Analyses from a Survey in India, Pakistan, Nepal Terai and Bangladesh'. *Hydrogeology Journal*, vol. 14, no. 3, pp. 286–309.

Vaidyanathan, A. 1993. *Fertilisers in Indian Agriculture.* LSV Memorial Lecture, Institute for Social and Economic Change, Bangalore.

———. 1999. *Water Resource Management: Institutions and Irrigation Development in India.* Oxford University Press, New Delhi.

Vaidyanathan, A., A. Krishanakumar, A. Rajagopal, and D. Varatharajan. 1994. 'Impact of Irrigation on Productivity of Land'. *Journal of Indian School of Political Economy*, vol. 6, no. 4, pp. 60–145.

van de Walle, D. 2002. 'Choosing Rural Road Investments to Help Reduce Poverty'. *World Development*, vol. 30, no. 4, pp. 575–89.

12

Are Inputs Used Efficiently in Crop Cultivation?

The introduction of Green Revolution technology during the mid-1960s has brought about dramatic changes in Indian agriculture. Not only has the adoption of technological inputs such as HYV seeds, fertilizers, and pesticides increased substantially, but the use of tube well irrigation and machineries in crop cultivation has also become widespread. This has completely changed the scenario of food production in the country, which was branded as living from ship to mouth during the 1950s and 1960s. Today, with about 265 mt of production, India stands as one of the largest producers of foodgrains in the world (GoI, 2016). While increasing the production of foodgrains and other agricultural commodities, the Green Revolution has also generated debates on its benefits. The debate on farm size versus productivity relationship which started immediately after the introduction of Green Revolution technology is continuing even today (Sen, 1964; Athreya, Djurfeldt, and Lindberg, 1990; Haque, 1996; Tadesse and Krishnamoorthy, 1997). The issue of the impact of Green Revolution on cropping pattern, favouring high-value water-intensive crops and replacing low-value crops, has also attracted researchers (Rao, 1975; Chand and Haque, 1997; Bhalla and Singh, 2012).

The issue of how efficiently farmers are using various farm inputs in crop cultivation has been an important topic of research over the years (Channareddy, 1967; Sampath, 1979; Shapiro, 1983; Rao et al., 2003; Shanmugam and Venkataramani, 2006). It is theoretically expected that an efficient farmer tends to use all the resources required for crop cultivation in an optimal way so as to reduce cost and maximize income (Haque, 2006). But, in practice, achieving high-level efficiency in resource use is very difficult as it is determined by various factors. Access to farm technology, cost of farm inputs, availability of credit, market facility, roads and its related infrastructures, level of support prices announced by the government, procurement infrastructure, and others play a pivotal role in determining the efficiency of input use. The efficiency of input use is measured in terms of returns from farming, where market condition plays a crucial role that is often not under the control of farmers. This means that even if the farmer uses inputs efficiently in crop cultivation at farm level, there is no guarantee that the farmer can achieve optimal level of economic efficiency in terms of returns.

Since efficiency of input use is determined by the returns from farming, quite a few studies have analysed the efficiency of farm inputs using micro- and macro-level data over the years. Fertilizer is one of the important inputs of modern agriculture and, therefore, many scholars have studied its efficiency in different crops. Though most studies on fertilizers seem to suggest a continuing decline in fertilizer response through the 1980s, Sagar (1995) showed a contrary result using field data. While analysing the productivity of agricultural credit in India, Narayanan (2015) concluded that 'input use is sensitive to credit flow, whereas GDP of agriculture is not. Credit seems therefore to be an enabling input, but one whose effectiveness is undermined by low technical efficiency and productivity' (p. 1). Utilizing panel data from India, Foster and Rosenzweig (2011) studied the mechanization, agency costs, and farm efficiency of Indian farmers. They concluded that although small farmers have lower unit labour costs, large farms use substantially less labour per acre but are more mechanized and also more efficient.

As irrigation is crucial to crop production, quite a few scholars have estimated the efficiency of water use in relation to productivity (Saleth, 2009; Sharma, Molden, and Cook, 2015). After making detailed estimates using state-wise data, Vaidyanathan and Sivasubramanian (2004) found a weak correlation between consumptive use rate of water and yield per millimetre (mm) of water use, meaning that water use efficiency in terms of crop productivity is poor. With the use of farm-level data from Gujarat, Kumar (2005) analysed water use efficiency in terms of money value (INR/m^3) among water sellers, water buyers, and sharecroppers and found that water buyers are more efficient as compared to water sellers. Using farm-level data, some studies have shown that drip method of irrigation helps to increase the efficiency of input use in different crop cultivations as compared to the conventional flood method of irrigation (Narayanamoorthy, 1997; 2003; 2004; Saleth, 2009; Narayanamoorthy, Devika, and Bhattarai, 2016).

Although a large number of studies have analysed the input use efficiency in crop cultivation, most of them are specific to an individual input (either for fertilizer or water or credit, and others). Some studies have also used data from only one time point to study the resource efficiency. The input use efficiency is not static but is instead dynamic in nature, which may undergo changes due to various factors. For instance, fertilizer may turn out to be an inefficient input in paddy cultivation in a particular year, say t1, but it may turn out to be the most efficient input in year t2 because the efficiency of farm input is controlled by many exogenous factors (Tadesse and Krishnamoorthy, 1997). As Gulati and Sharma (1997) rightly mentioned, 'Resource use efficiency is a dynamic concept which may undergo a change because of changes in factors such as technology, prices' (p. 1). Similarly, the efficiency of input use is also expected to vary from crop to crop, region to region, and also between low and high productivity of crop. Not many studies are available on input use efficiency covering these aspects in India using temporal data. In this chapter, therefore, an attempt is made to determine the efficiency of different farm inputs used in six crop cultivations in different states covering data from 1985–6 to 2013–14.

Data and Method

The major objective of the study is to find the dynamics of input use efficiency in six different crops over time, where time series data are essential for the analysis. In India, the time series data on input use (both in quantity and value terms) as well as on VOP for different crops and states are available only from the CCS data published by the CACP. This study has used CCS data for its entire analysis covering the period from 1985–6 to 2013–14. Apart from studying the changing nature of input use efficiency, the study also attempts to find the nexus between input use efficiency and productivity of crops, as it is generally believed that efficiency in input use is better in the states where productivity of crops is higher. In order to study this issue, two states have been considered for each selected crop, one from HAHP states and another one from HALP states. The states and crops selected for the analysis are presented in Table 12.1.

In order to ascertain the dynamics of input use efficiency in different crops (after converting all the cost- and income-related data at 1986–7 prices using CPIAL deflator), two types of analysis

Table 12.1 Crops and States Selected for the Study on Input Use Efficiency

Crop	State Selected	Category of State	Cropped Area (mha) (Average of TE2013–14)	Productivity (kg/ha) (Average of TE2013–14)
Paddy	Andhra Pradesh	HAHP	4.03	3,081
	Odisha	HALP	4.07	1,695
Wheat	Punjab	HAHP	3.52	4,880
	Madhya Pradesh	HALP	5.19	2,414
Gram	Madhya Pradesh	HAHP	3.11	1,115
	Rajasthan	HALP	1.54	871
Groundnut	Gujarat	HAHP	1.60	1,623
	Andhra Pradesh	HALP	1.42	789
Cotton	Gujarat	HAHP	2.66	659
	Maharashtra	HALP	4.15	323
Sugarcane	Maharashtra	HAHP	0.96	80,529
	Uttar Pradesh	HALP	2.20	59,968

Sources: Computed utilizing data from MoA (2015) and www.dacenet.nic.in.

Notes: HAHP: high area with high productivity; HALP: high area with low productivity; mha: million hectares; TE: triennium ending.

have been carried out in this study. First, the efficiency of all the major inputs have been worked out by dividing the value of crop output (VCO) by the cost of each major input for four time points, namely 1985–6, 1995–6, 2005–6, and 2013–14. This is expected to explain the average output per unit of input generated in terms of INR in different time points. The major inputs considered for this analysis are human labour cost (HLC), machine labour cost (MLC), fertilizer and manure cost (FMC), irrigation cost (IRC) as well as all operational cost (A2+FL). Further, to strengthen the analysis and also to determine the efficiency of different inputs over time, multiple regression model (OLS method) has been estimated for all the selected crops and states for the period 1995–6 to 2013–14. The specification of the regression model used in the analysis is as follows:

$$VCO = \beta_0 + \beta_1 HLC + \beta_2 BLC + \beta_3 MLC + \beta_4 SDC + \beta_5 FMC + \beta_6 PIC + \beta_7 IRC + t \quad (1)$$

Where,

VCO = Value of crop output (INR/ha at 1986–7 prices)
$\beta_0, \ldots, \beta_1$ = Parameters to be estimated
HLC = Human labour cost (INR/ha at 1986–7 prices)
BLC = Bullock labour cost (INR/ha at 1986–7 prices)
MLC = Machine labour cost (INR/ha at 1986–7 prices)
SDC = Seed cost (INR/ha at 1986–7 prices)
FMC = Fertilizer and manure cost (INR/ha at 1986–7 prices)
PIC = Pesticide and insecticide cost (INR/ha at 1986–7 prices)
IRC = Irrigation cost (INR/ha at 1986–7 prices)
t = Time variable (1985–6 to 2013–14)

The above specified regression is estimated separately for each crop and for each state. By this estimation, we would obtain the regression coefficient that would reveal the efficiency of each input in determining the VCO in terms of money value. The regression coefficient would also allow us to compare the efficiency of the same input used among HPS and LPS.

Results and Discussion

Due to fast increase in the price of farm inputs, it is essential to attain a high level of efficiency in its use to harvest increased yield and profit. Attaining optimum level of efficiency in every input use is also very much needed to double farm income, which is the focus of policymakers today. The recently published policy paper by NITI Aayog (2015), *Raising Agricultural Productivity and Making Farming Remunerative to Farmers*, has given a lot of thrust to improve the efficiency of various farm inputs to translate farming into a remunerative job. But most studies have shown that farmers often use resources suboptimally due to various reasons. For instance, NITI Aayog's (2015) report mentions that India uses two to three times the water used to produce one tonne of grain in countries such as China, Brazil, and the USA. Let us now analyse the results of the present study generated from CCS data.

Input Use Efficiency in Selected Foodgrain Crops

As mentioned in the methodology section, one of the aims of the study is to find the varying nature of input use efficiency in different crops over time. To study this, we have computed the VCO generated from every INR of cost in different inputs by dividing the VOP (INR/ha) by the cost of each input. Input use efficiency generally varies from crop to crop because of varied use of irrigation and productivity of crops. The objective of the study is not only to analyse input use efficiency over time but also to study the variations in it among different crops, namely foodgrain and non-foodgrain crops. Table 12.2 presents the input use efficiency for three foodgrain crops—paddy, wheat, and gram—for four time points: 1985–6, 1995–6, 2005–6, and 2013–14. It is evident from the results that input use efficiency is not static but quite dynamic in all the crops and in both HAHP and HALP states. It is generally believed that the resources are used more efficiently in high productivity regions than in low productivity regions. But, the results of the study do not completely support this assertion. Even in LPS, the inputs seem to have been used more efficiently than in those states that have relatively less crop productivity in certain crops.

Table 12.2 Input Use Efficiency (crop output per INR of cost) for Selected Foodgrain Crops (INR at 1986–7 prices)

Crop	States	Cost	1985–6	1995–6	2005–6	2013–14
Paddy	Andhra Pradesh (HAHP)	HLC	3.43	2.89	3.21	3.21
		MLC	20.55	18.89	12.94	9.36
		FMC	6.56	7.61	10.07	10.64
		IRC	36.52	30.57	44.88	80.10
		All Cost (A2+FL)	1.52	1.76	1.83	1.92
	Odisha (HALP)	HLC	2.68	2.50	2.04	1.41
		MLC	1,692.05	155.88	27.68	19.09
		FMC	7.57	9.12	7.98	8.02
		IRC	180.05	358.41	129.84	472.52
		All Cost (A2+FL)	1.56	1.71	1.48	1.42
Wheat	Punjab (HAHP)	HLC	6.55	5.52	10.10	12.52
		MLC	8.67	9.90	7.13	8.58
		FMC	7.08	6.33	10.22	13.44
		IRC	27.58	40.08	51.11	200.67
		All Cost (A2+FL)	1.80	1.62	2.18	2.56
	Madhya Pradesh (HALP)	HLC	6.04	5.64	6.76	2.30
		MLC	30.79	13.46	9.20	5.23
		FMC	13.61	11.02	14.80	7.98
		IRC	14.20	12.60	11.10	7.91
		All Cost (A2+FL)	1.96	2.08	2.18	1.87
Gram	Madhya Pradesh (HAHP)	HLC	8.23	5.28	8.97	4.40
		MLC	118.61	11.96	13.26	6.93
		FMC	52.68	14.32	38.35	17.27
		IRC	128.80	14.69	17.26	16.59
		All Cost (A2+FL)	2.76	1.79	2.60	1.71
	Rajasthan (HALP)	HLC	8.10	4.88	6.42	3.44
		MLC	45.52	18.43	13.55	10.08
		FMC	175.14	109.34	99.18	50.11
		IRC	83.74	101.09	13.16	25.40
		All Cost (A2+FL)	3.24	3.09	3.40	3.06

Source: Computed using data from CACP (various years).

Paddy is one of the foodgrain crops where two states, Andhra Pradesh (HAHP state) and Odisha (HALP state), are considered to study input use efficiency across different time points. The results show that overall resource use efficiency seems to be relatively better in HAHP states as compared to HALP states. The output generated from every INR 1 of cost has increased from INR 1.52 in 1985–6 to INR 1.92 in 2013–14 for farmers belonging to the HAHP state, while the same has declined from INR 1.56 to INR 1.42 for the HALP state during the same period. However, the same trend is not observed among the different inputs considered for the analysis in paddy crop. Although the effect of HLC and MLC on generating the crop output has declined in both the HAHP and HALP state, FFC and IRC have showed improvement in generating crop output in both the states, albeit with variations in different time points. Interestingly, the efficiency of IRC in the HALP state appears to be far better than in the HAHP state. On the whole, what is clear from the analysis of paddy is that although the overall cost efficiency is better in the HAHP state, the HALP state has equally achieved improved efficiency in certain farm inputs.

Punjab and Madhya Pradesh are considered as HAHP and HALP states respectively for studying input use efficiency for wheat. Unlike paddy, wheat shows somewhat different results in input use efficiency. Of the four time points, the overall (total cost) input use efficiency of HALP state is relatively higher than that of the HAHP state in two time points, namely 1995–6 and 2005–6. This suggests that input use efficiency need not always be higher in case of a HAHP state. Among the important inputs used for the cultivation of wheat crop, except for IRC in Punjab, the efficiency of other inputs has not consistently increased in either the HAHP or the HALP states. Contrary to the expectations of many, the efficiency of some of the inputs is much better in a low productivity state than its high productivity counterpart.

The efficiency of different inputs used for gram cultivation is totally different from what is observed for paddy and wheat crops. In all the four time points, the total resource use efficiency is substantially lower in the HAHP state (Madhya Pradesh) as compared to the HALP state of Rajasthan. For instance, the VCO generated from every INR of cost is varying from INR 1.71 to INR 2.76 during the four time points for the farmers belonging to the HAHP state, whereas the same is varying from INR 3.06 to INR 3.40 for the farmers belonging to the HALP state during the same period. Of the four major inputs, the efficiency of FFC and IRC during certain time points seems to be substantially higher than other two major inputs in both the HALP and the HAHP state. However, we do not observe any consistent increase in the output generated from every 1 INR of cost in any of the inputs over time in either state considered for the analysis. On the whole, the analysis on foodgrain crops shows that the efficiency of different inputs used for cultivation varies from crop to crop and there is no evidence to show that the inputs are used more efficiently by HPS than LPS.

Input Use Efficiency in Selected Non-foodgrain Crops

Input use efficiency is expected to vary from crop to crop and, therefore, after studying foodgrain crops, we have studied three non-foodgrain commercial crops, namely groundnut, cotton, and sugarcane. This is done specifically to determine whether or not the pattern of input use efficiency of non-foodgrain crops is different from that of foodgrain crops. Generally, non-foodgrain crops are cultivated for commercial purpose and, therefore, not only the use of inputs would be higher for these crops but the expected income from these crops would also be higher. As a result of increased expected income, the resource use efficiency is also expected to be better among commercial crops.

Table 12.3 presents the amount of income generated from per unit of cost for different inputs and crops for four time points. Groundnut is one of the commercial crops considered for the analysis, which shows that the overall resource use efficiency of the HAHP state (Gujarat) is relatively better in three out of four time points as compared to the HALP state (Andhra Pradesh). However, the overall resource use efficiency has not increased consistently over time in either state, which was also observed in foodgrain crops. Among the various inputs, IRC and MLC seem to have been used more efficiently than other inputs in groundnut cultivation in both the states. But, none of the inputs considered for the analysis has shown consistency in its efficiency over time in both the states. On the whole, the results of groundnut crop are not much different from that of foodgrain crops.

Table 12.3 Input Use Efficiency (crop output per INR of cost) for Selected Non-foodgrain Crops (INR at 1986–7 prices)

Crop	States	Cost	1985–6	1995–6	2005–6	2013–14
Groundnut	Gujarat (HAHP)	HLC	6.60	3.11	5.33	4.12
		MLC	41.50	29.03	16.76	13.49
		FMC	9.62	8.19	14.32	13.39
		IRC	16.32	26.25	94.17	66.06
		All Cost (A2+FL)	1.72	1.33	2.02	1.84
	Andhra Pradesh (HALP)	HLC	3.96	3.82	2.48	2.27
		MLC	50.63	30.85	19.10	16.03
		FMC	10.06	11.31	8.17	10.25
		IRC	43.97	97.07	73.30	41.60
		All Cost (A2+FL)	1.34	1.76	1.22	1.36
Cotton	Gujarat (HAHP)	HLC	3.44	4.37	4.20	2.65
		MLC	37.85	21.72	22.31	25.26
		FMC	6.23	12.48	14.30	9.78
		IRC	9.56	22.85	27.92	36.18
		All Cost (A2+FL)	1.19	2.04	2.15	2.08
	Maharashtra (HALP)	HLC	3.29	4.04	3.77	3.37
		MLC	65.64	59.02	38.01	23.51
		FMC	4.58	8.68	10.07	7.69
		IRC	75.09	125.32	70.50	63.27
		All Cost (A2+FL)	1.14	1.86	1.23	1.75
Sugarcane	Maharashtra (HAHP)	HLC	4.64	3.45	4.05	4.85
		MLC	285.02	73.07	11.80	11.72
		FMC	9.10	8.42	6.98	10.51
		IRC	9.59	15.04	7.97	21.52
		All Cost (A2+FL)	1.84	1.71	1.39	2.17
	Uttar Pradesh (HALP)	HLC	7.44	4.55	6.36	5.13
		MLC	143.19	82.13	56.46	124.46
		FMC	22.66	16.58	23.40	33.27
		IRC	25.17	32.02	25.82	27.76
		All Cost (A2+FL)	4.32	3.43	4.00	3.98

Source: Computed using data from CACP (various years).

Cotton is one of the important commercial crops cultivated predominantly under rainfed condition by farmers in India. The introduction of Bt cotton seed in 2004 has brought substantial changes in its area and productivity (Narayanamoorthy and Kalamkar, 2006; Choudhary and Gaur, 2015). Therefore, we might expect interesting results on input use efficiency by studying cotton crop. As the introduction of Bt seed increased the productivity of cotton considerably, there is a possibility that this might have helped to increase the overall resource use efficiency. But, against our expectation, the overall resource efficiency has not increased uniformly over time in either the HAHP (Gujarat) or the HALP (Maharashtra) state. In fact, the overall resource use efficiency was much better during 1995–6 as compared to 2013–14 in both the states. It appears from these results that the farmers were able to generate more income from every INR of cost that they had spent in growing cotton before the introduction of Bt seed. This apart, the efficiency in any of the major inputs used for cultivation has not increased consistently in either state. Irrigation and machine labour seem to have generated more income for farmers cultivating cotton in both the HALP and HAHP state. Again, the results from cotton too show enormous inconsistency in input use efficiency over time in both HPS and LPS.

Sugarcane is another commercial crop selected for the analysis, where Maharashtra and Uttar Pradesh are considered as the HAHP and HALP state respectively. Unlike the other two commercial crops, the results of sugarcane crop show some definite pattern in input use efficiency. The overall resource use efficiency of the HALP state is distinctly better than the HAHP state. For every INR of cost, farmers belonging to the HALP state were to able generate an income of INR 3.43 to INR 4.32 during four time points considered for the analysis, whereas it varied only from INR 1.39 to INR 2.17 for the HAHP state. It is also observed that farmers belonging to the HALP state seem to have achieved much better efficiency in almost all the inputs considered for the analysis than their counterparts in the HAHP state of Maharashtra. On the whole, the analysis of six foodgrain and non-foodgrain crops suggests two important points. First, there is no clear pattern emerging in the overall resource use efficiency between HPS and LPS. Second, none of the major inputs considered for analysis showed consistent increase in its efficiency over time in both LPS and HPS.

Input Use Efficiency Over Time—an Analysis of Regression Results

After studying the input use efficiency at different time points by computing average output (in terms of INR) generated from every INR of investment (cost) for different inputs, an attempt is made to study the input use efficiency over time by employing multiple regression analysis, as specified in the methodology section. In this analysis, the costs of all the major inputs—HLC, bullock labour (BLC), MLC, seed (SDC), FMC, pesticides and insecticides (PIC), IRC—and time factor are treated as independent variables and VCO as dependent variable. Regression analysis is carried out for each crop and state separately covering data from 1995–6 to 2013–14. As the analysis focuses on efficiency of different inputs over time, all the values (in INR) have been converted into constant terms at 1986–7 prices using CPIAL deflator.

The objectives of this analysis are to find the following: (*a*) Are inputs used efficiently in different crops over time? (*b*) Which is the farm input used more efficiently? (*c*) Are there variations in input use efficiency between HAHP and HALP states? (*d*) Is there any input which has shown consistency in positively influencing VOP in all the crops selected for analysis? The results of the regression model estimated for the three foodgrain crops of paddy, wheat, and gram are presented in Table 12.4. It is evident from the regression results that the efficiency of different inputs is not the same in all the three crops and also between HAHP and HALP states. Also only a few inputs appear to have been used efficiently in the cultivation of all the three foodgrain crops. In paddy crop, seed cost, followed by HLC, seems to have been used efficiently in the HAHP state, but the same is not true with the HALP state. In the case of wheat crop, only MLC seems to have been used efficiently in the HAHP state (Punjab), whereas in case of the HALP state of Madhya Pradesh, both MLC and SDC have been used efficiently in cultivating the crop. Seed is the only input that seems to have been used efficiently in gram cultivation by both the HAHP and

Table 12.4 Multiple Regression Results: Efficiency of Different Inputs Used for Foodgrain Crop Cultivation during 1995–6 to 2013–14

Variables	Dependent Variable: Value of Crop Output INR/ha at 1986–7 prices					
	Paddy		Wheat		Gram	
	Andhra Pradesh (HAHP state)	Odisha (HALP state)	Punjab (HAHP state)	Madhya Pradesh (HALP state)	Madhya Pradesh (HAHP state)	Rajasthan (HALP state)
HLC	3.22 (1.94)[c]	−1.77 (−1.35)[ns]	2.14 (0.65)[ns]	−2.30 (−1.16)[ns]	−0.11 (−0.03)[ns]	0.07 (0.03)[ns]
BLC	3.63 (0.89)[ns]	−1.44 (−0.43)[ns]	6.47 (0.199)[ns]	−0.48 (−0.13)[ns]	3.178 (0.534)[ns]	−3.39 (−0.56)[ns]
MLC	−6.98 (−1.36)[d]	1.57 (0.13)[ns]	7.91 (2.92)[b]	9.21 (2.61)[b]	4.46 (0.567)[ns]	4.32 (0.42)[ns]
SDC	6.45 (2.15)[b]	26.21 (0.958)[ns]	−0.59 (−0.05)[ns]	7.36 (2.06)[b]	7.521 (3.17)[c]	6.01 (1.33)[ns]
FMC	3.17 (1.07)[ns]	2.82 (0.45)[ns]	1.56 (0.32)[ns]	0.015 (0.004)[ns]	0.18 (0.02)[ns]	3.59 (0.179)[ns]
PIC	0.09 (0.06)[ns]	15.93 (0.549)[ns]	−3.96 (−0.52)[ns]	−36.51 (−0.72)[ns]	−5.04 (−0.55)[ns]	−0.77 (−0.03)[ns]
IRC	−5.16 (−1.19)[ns]	−45.69 (−1.41)[d]	−12.93 (−1.28)[ns]	0.51 (0.23)[ns]	−0.90 (−0.22)[ns]	2.31 (0.56)[ns]
Time	328.03 (2.17)[b]	225.37 (1.46)[d]	−61.08 (−0.55)[ns]	−48.03 (−0.39)[ns]	−12.14 (−0.09)[ns]	−45.69 (−0.50)[ns]
Constant	−2,634.86 (−0.53)	1,604.46 (0.35)	812.91 (0.11)	314.17 (0.16)	−773.04 (−0.29)	563.17 (0.32)
R^2	0.79	0.61	0.72	0.94	0.701	0.68
Adjusted R^2	0.63	0.32	0.48	0.89	0.47	0.43
F Value	4.83	1.55	3.15	18.64	3.02	2.68
D–W	1.91	1.96	2.56	1.86	1.89	1.77
N	19	17	19	19	19	19

Source: Computed using data from CACP (various years).

Notes: a, b, c, and d are significant at 1 per cent, 5 per cent, 10 per cent, and 20 per cent levels respectively; ns: not significant; figures in parentheses are 't' values.

HALP state. Not unexpectedly, in all the foodgrain crops considered for the analysis, not even a single input seems to have been used efficiently and consistently over time from 1995–6 to 2013–14. Yield-increasing inputs such as FMC and IRC too seem to have not been used efficiently in all the foodgrain crops. While the regression coefficients of FMC turned out to be positive in all the three crops and in both HAHP and HALP states, IRC turned out to be negative in most cases, suggesting that the yield-increasing inputs are used suboptimally in foodgrain crops over time.

The pattern of input use efficiency of non-foodgrain crops is somewhat different from that of foodgrain crops. Human labour appears to have been used efficiently in all the three crops by both HAHP and HALP states (see Table 12.5). But this kind of consistency is not observed for any other input. For groundnut, besides HLC, seed cost appears to have been used efficiently by both HAHP and HALP states. Expectedly, pesticides and insecticides have been used efficiently by both categories of states in cotton cultivation. For instance, 1 INR increase in PIC in cotton cultivation seems to have increased the VCO by INR 14.94 in the HAHP state and by INR 20.72 in the HALP state. This could be due to the introduction of Bt seed in cotton crop, which has substantially reduced the consumption of pesticides (for details, see Choudhary and Gaur, 2015). Since fertilizers are costly inputs that are also used heavily in sugarcane cultivation, we expected that yield-increasing inputs such as FMC would have been used efficiently in sugarcane cultivation. But, contrary to our expectation, except HLC, none of the other inputs including fertilizers have been used efficiently. It is also surprising to observe that the regression coefficients of fertilizers estimated for non-foodgrain crops are totally different from the one estimated for foodgrain crops. While the coefficients of fertilizers turned out to be uniformly positive (though not significant) for all the three foodgrain crops and for both HAHP and HALP states, the same turned out to be negative for all the three non-foodgrain crops considered for the analysis. However, as in the case of foodgrain crops, irrigation seems to have been used suboptimally in non-foodgrain crops as well, which is an unexpected result.

It is clear from the preceding analysis that the efficiency level of different inputs used over time is either very low or insignificant

Table 12.5 Multiple Regression Results: Efficiency of Different Inputs Used for Non-foodgrain Crop Cultivation during 1995–6 to 2013–14

Variables	Dependent Variable: Value of Crop Output in INR/ha at 1986–7 Prices					
	Groundnut		Cotton		Sugarcane	
	Gujarat (HAHP state)	Andhra Pradesh (HALP state)	Gujarat (HAHP state)	Maharashtra (HALP state)	Maharashtra (HAHP state)	Uttar Pradesh (HALP state)
HLC	6.08 (2.07)[c]	1.45 (0.61)[ns]	3.69 (1.89)[c]	1.97 (2.72)[b]	4.18 (1.62)[d]	10.38 (2.42)[b]
BLC	6.16 (1.98)[c]	8.44 (1.24)[ns]	−11.74 (−1.77)[d]	0.67 (0.54)[ns]	−5.66 (−0.61)[ns]	−2.95 (−0.24)[ns]
MLC	−0.94 (−0.10)[ns]	8.12 (0.69)[ns]	10.32 (1.05)[ns]	−9.36 (−1.10)[ns]	−2.38 (−0.69)[ns]	26.19 (1.09)[ns]
SDC	5.46 (1.64)[d]	12.71 (2.14)[c]	0.27 (0.08)[ns]	−2.47 (−0.80)[ns]	4.46 (0.85)[ns]	−1.89 (−0.32)[ns]
FMC	−11.19 (−1.38)[d]	−8.03 (−1.32)[ns]	−12.60 (−3.32)[a]	−4.04 (−1.81)[c]	−2.87 (−0.65)[ns]	−28.11 (−2.07)[c]
PIC	−6.26 (−1.27)[ns]	−1.49 (−0.07)[ns]	14.94 (2.40)[b]	20.72 (2.01)[c]	−41.96 (−0.60)[ns]	−97.55 (−1.68)[d]
IRC	−11.40 (−1.42)[d]	3.53 (0.43)[ns]	3.44 (1.00)[ns]	−1.08 (−0.23)[ns]	−1.17 (−0.28)[ns]	5.72 (0.93)[ns]
Time	−41.74 (−0.20)[ns]	−347.51 (−1.69)[c]	305.62 (1.39)[d]	353.18 (2.44)[b]	1258.79 (2.46)[b]	−266.26 (−0.79)[ns]
Constant	−2,650.53 (−1.034)	−7,501.41 (−2.10)	−264.36 (−0.07)	827.59 (0.34)	1,608.09 (0.17)	3,754.29 (0.38)
R^2	0.77	0.89	0.89	0.95	0.73	0.79
Adjusted R^2	0.59	0.80	0.79	0.89	0.52	0.64
F Value	4.19	10.04	9.33	18.18	3.39	4.94
D–W	1.97	1.82	2.41	1.75	1.95	2.59
N	19	19	18	18	19	19

Source: Computed using data from CACP (various years).

Notes: a, b, c, and d are significant at 1 per cent, 5 per cent, 10 per cent, and 20 per cent levels respectively; ns: not significant; figures in parentheses are 't' values.

or negative in almost all the selected crops, and also in both HPS and LPS. Does it mean that the inputs are not used efficiently for crop cultivation in India? One may not be able to make a firm conclusion that the inputs are not used efficiently in crop cultivation using the results arrived at in this study. More than exogenous factors, endogenous factors play a paramount role in deciding the level of efficiency of different inputs. Market condition (factor and product) is one which plays a paramount role in deciding input use efficiency (see Deshpande, 1996). Because of the prevalence of imperfect agricultural market condition and poor procurement arrangements, most of the time farmers do not receive sufficient price for their produce, which ultimately reduces their gross income from crop cultivation. As a result of suboptimal price received by farmers in the market, the efficiency of most of the inputs used for different crop cultivation turns out to be suboptimal in most cases. Another important reason for the suboptimal efficiency could be the enormous increase in cost of inputs needed for farming, especially after the late 1990s. Studies carried out using CCS data emphatically show that COC for different crops has increased at a faster rate than the rate of increase in income from farming (see Deshpande and Arora, 2010; Narayanamoorthy and Suresh, 2012; 2013; Narayanamoorthy, Alli, and Suresh, 2015; Narayanamoorthy, 2007; 2013; and 2017). Since the efficiency of the inputs is measured by using its cost, the fast increase in input costs may have also dampened their efficiency. Therefore, given the excessive role of endogenous factors in deciding the efficiency of each input, it is possible that the efficiency level of farm inputs would be suboptimal even if farmers use the inputs efficiently at the farm level.

Conclusion and Suggestions

Achieving optimal level of efficiency in the use of various farm inputs for crop cultivation is essential to increase farm profitability. Many studies from India seem to suggest that farm inputs are mostly used suboptimally or are not used efficiently. However, not many studies are available on input use efficiency covering different crops and states using recent temporal and spatial data. In this chapter, therefore, an attempt has been made to study the efficiency of different inputs used for cultivating the six crops paddy, wheat, gram, groundnut, cotton, and sugarcane by utilizing CCS data from 1985–6 to 2013–14. After converting the data on input costs and VCO into constant prices, the efficiency of different inputs has been worked out by two methods: (*a*) average output per unit of input has been calculated by dividing the VCO by the cost of each major input used for crop cultivation, and (*b*) multiple regression has been estimated separately for each crop by treating value crop output as dependent variable and all the major inputs costs as independent variables.

The study shows that the average crop output per unit of input cost has not increased consistently over different time periods in either foodgrain or non-foodgrain crops. The efficiency of yield augmenting inputs such as fertilizers and irrigation has either declined or fluctuated in most crops and states. There is no conclusive evidence to show that the inputs are used more efficiently in HPS than in LPS for all the six crops considered for the analysis. In fact, in crops such as gram and sugarcane, LPS have outperformed HPS not only in the overall resource use efficiency (computed taking into account the total A2+FL cost) but even at the individual-level input use efficiency. The regression analysis carried out to determine the efficiency of different inputs over time seems to suggest that none of the inputs have been used efficiently and consistently for any of the six crops. For paddy crop, human labour and seed seem to have been used efficiently, whereas machine labour seems to have been used efficiently for wheat crop. Similarly, pesticides and insecticides appear to have been used efficiently for cotton crop, but seed seems to have been used efficiently for groundnut crop. Even the yield-augmenting cost-intensive inputs such as fertilizers, irrigation, and seed seem to have not been used efficiently in any of the crops from 1995–6 to 2013–14. This kind of pattern is observed not only with HPS but also with LPS for all the six crops.

From these results, it is difficult to conclude that the inputs are not used efficiently in crop cultivation over time. This inefficiency may have occurred due to suboptimal price received by farmers from the market, which is imperfect and dominated by middlemen in India. There is a possibility that farmers may have used the inputs efficiently at the farm level and harvested increased productivity (kg/ha), but did not achieve desired efficiency in terms of resource use. Markets (factor and product) are possibly eroding the extra income generated through increased productivity. Therefore, in order to ascertain the real efficiency of different inputs used for crop cultivation, one must consider the optimal price of crop produce (potential price) that the farmer is supposed to get in a perfectly governed market and then estimate the input use efficiency.

Bibliography

Athreya, V. B., G. Djurfeldt, and S. Lindberg. 1990. *Barriers Broken: Production Relations and Agrarian Change in Tamil Nadu*. Sage Publications India, New Delhi.

Bhalla G. S., and G. Singh. 2012. *Economic Liberalisation and Indian Agriculture: A District-Level Study*. Sage Publications India, New Delhi.

CACP (Commission for Agricultural Costs and Prices). Various years. *Report of the Commission for Agricultural Costs and Prices*. Ministry of Agriculture, Government of India, New Delhi.

Chand, R., and T. Haque. 1997. 'Sustainability of Rice and Wheat Crop System in Indo Gangetic Region'. *Economic and Political Weekly*, vol. 32, no. 13 (29 March), pp. A108–12.

Channareddy, V. 1967. 'Production Efficiency in South Indian Agriculture'. *American Journal of Agricultural Economics*, vol. 49, no. 4, pp. 816–20.

Choudhary, B., and K. Gaur. 2015. *Biotech Cotton in India 2002 to 2014: Adoption, Impact, Progress and Future*. ISAAA Series of Biotech Crop Profiles. International Service for the Acquisition of Agri-biotech Applications (ISAAA), Ithaca, New York, U. S. A.

Deshpande, R. S. 1996. 'Demand and Supply of Agricultural Commodities: A Review'. *Indian Journal of Agricultural Economics*, vol. 51, nos 1–2, pp. 270–87.

Deshpande, R. S., and S. Arora (eds). 2010. *Agrarian Crisis and Farmer Suicides*. Sage Publications, New Delhi.

Foster, A. D., and M. R. Rosenzweig. 2011. *Are Indian Farms Too Small? Mechanization, Agency Costs and Farm Efficiency*. Economic Growth Centre, Yale University, New Haven, CT.

GoI (Government of India). 2016. *Agricultural Statistics at a Glance*. Directorate of Economics and Statistics, Ministry of Agriculture, Government of India, New Delhi.

Gulati, A., and A. Sharma. 1997. 'Freeing Trade in Agriculture: Implications for Resource Use Efficiency and Cropping Pattern Changes'. *Economic and Political Weekly*, vol. 32, no. 52 (27 December), pp. A155–64.

Haque, T. 1996. *Sustainability of Small Holder Agriculture.* Concept Publishing Company, New Delhi.

———. 2006. 'Resource Use Efficiency in Indian Agriculture'. *Indian Journal of Agricultural Economics,* vol. 61, no. l, p. 37.

Kumar, M. D. 2005. 'Impact of Electricity Prices and Volumetric Water Allocation on Energy and Groundwater Demand Management: Analysis from Western India'. *Energy Policy,* vol. 33, no. 1, pp. 39–51.

MoA (Ministry of Agriculture). 2015. *Agricultural Statistics at a Glance: 2013–14.* Government of India, New Delhi.

Narayanamoorthy, A. 1997. 'Economic Viability of Drip Irrigation: An Empirical Analysis from Maharashtra'. *Indian Journal of Agricultural Economics,* vol. 52, no. 4, pp. 728–39.

———. 2003. 'Averting Water Crisis by Drip Method of Irrigation: A Study of Two Water-Intensive Crops'. *Indian Journal of Agricultural Economics,* vol. 58, no. 3, pp. 427–37.

———. 2004. 'Impact Assessment of Drip Irrigation in India: The Case of Sugarcane'. *Development Policy Review,* vol. 22, no. 4, pp. 443–62.

———. 2007. 'Deceleration in Agricultural Growth: Technology Fatigue or Policy Fatigue?'. *Economic and Political Weekly,* vol. 42, no. 25, pp. 2375–9.

———. 2013. 'Profitability in Crops Cultivation in India: Some Evidence from Cost of Cultivation Survey Data'. *Indian Journal of Agricultural Economics,* vol. 68, no. 1, pp. 104–21.

———. 2017. 'Farm Income in India: Myths and Realities'. *Indian Journal of Agricultural Economics,* vol. 72, no. 1 (January–March), pp. 49–75.

Narayanamoorthy, A., P. Alli, and R. Suresh. 2015. 'How Profitable Is Cultivation of Rainfed Crops? Some Insights from Cost of Cultivation Studies'. *Agricultural Economics Research Review,* vol. 27, no. 2, 233–41.

Narayanamoorthy, A., N. Devika, and M. Bhattarai. 2016. 'More Crop and Profit per Drop of Water: Drip Irrigation for Empowering Distressed Small Farmers'. *IIM Kozhikode Society and Management Review,* vol. 5, no.1, pp. 83–90.

Narayanamoorthy, A., and S. S. Kalamkar. 2006. 'Is Bt Cotton Cultivation Economically Viable for Indian Farmers? An Empirical Analysis'. *Economic and Political Weakly,* vol. 46, no. 26, pp. 2716–24.

Narayanamoorthy, A., and R. Suresh. 2012. 'Agricultural Price Policy in India: Has It Benefitted Paddy Farmers?'. *Indian Journal of Agricultural Marketing,* vol. 26, no. 3 (September–December), pp. 87–106.

———. 2013. 'An Uncovered Truth in Fixation of MSP for Crops in India'. *Review of Development and Change,* vol. 18, no. 1 (January–June), pp. 53–62.

Narayanan, S. 2015. *The Productivity of Agricultural Credit in India.* Working Paper No. 2015–01. Indira Gandhi Institute for Development Research, Mumbai.

NITI Aayog. 2015. *Raising Agricultural Productivity and Making Farming Remunerative to Farmers.* Government of India, New Delhi.

Rao, C. H. Hanumantha. 1975. *Technological Change and Distribution of Gains in Indian Agriculture.* The Macmillan Company of India Ltd, New Delhi.

Rao, C. A. Rama, K. R. Chowdry, Y. V. R. Reddy, and G. V. Krishna Rao. 2003. 'Measuring and Explaining Technical Efficiency in Crop Production in Andhra Pradesh'. *Indian Journal of Agricultural Economics*, vol. 58, no. 4, pp. 768–80.

Sagar, Vidya. 1995. 'Fertiliser Use Efficiency in Indian Agriculture'. *Economic and Political Weekly*, vol. 30, no. 52 (30 December), pp. A160–80.

Saleth, R. M., ed. 2009. *Promoting Irrigation Demand Management in India: Potentials, Problems and Prospects.* International Water Management Institute, Colombo, Sri Lanka.

Sampath, R. K. 1979. *Economic Efficiency in Indian Agriculture: Theory and Measurement.* MacMillan Publication, New Delhi.

Sen, A. K. 1964. 'Size of Holding and Productivity'. *The Economic Weekly*, vol. 16, nos 17–18, pp. 777–8.

Shanmugam, K. R., and A. Venkataramani. 2006. 'Technical Efficiency in Agricultural Production and Its Determinants: An Exploratory Study at the District Level'. *Indian Journal of Agricultural Economics*, vol. 61, no. 2, pp. 169–84.

Shapiro, K. H. 1983. 'Efficiency Differentials in Peasant Agriculture and their Implications for Development Policies'. *Journal of Development Studies*, vol. 19, no. 2, pp. 179–90.

Sharma, B. R., D. Molden, and S. Cook. 2015. 'Water Use Efficiency in Agriculture: Measurement, Current Situation and Trends'. In P. Drechsel, P. Heffer, H. Magan, R. Mikkelsen, and D. Wichlens (eds.), *Managing Water and Fertiliser for Sustainable Intensification.* International Fertiliser Association, Paris, France, pp. 39–64.

Tadesse, B., and S. Krishnamoorthy. 1997. 'Technical Efficiency in Paddy Farms of Tamil Nadu: An Analysis based on Farm Size and Ecological Zone'. *Agricultural Economics*, vol. 16, no. 3, pp. 185–92.

Vaidyanathan, A., and K. Sivasubramanian. 2004. 'Efficiency of Water Use in Agriculture'. *Economic and Political Weekly*, vol. 39, no. 27 (3 July), pp. 2989–96.

Index

About the Author

A. Narayanamoorthy, former member (official), Commission for Agricultural Costs and Prices, Government of India, New Delhi, is presently senior professor and head of the Department of Economics and Rural Development, Alagappa University, Tamil Nadu, India. He has previously taught at the Gokhale Institute of Politics and Economics, Pune. Professor Narayanamoorthy has published widely and some of his works include *Where Water Seeps!: Towards A New Phase in India's Irrigation Reforms* (2005); *The Water, Energy and Food Security Nexus: Lessons from India for Development* (2014); *Indian Water Policy at the Crossroads: Resources, Technology and Reforms* (2016); *Micro Irrigation Systems in India: Emergence, Status and Impact* (2016); and *Whither Rural India? Political Economy of Agrarian Transformation in Contemporary India* (2019).